D0429848

Shattering
Silences

Shattering Silences

Strategies to Prevent Sexual Assault, Heal Survivors, and Bring Assailants to Justice

Christopher Johnston

Skyhorse Publishing

For Patrice, my favorite feminist

Skyhorse Publishing books may be purchased in bulk at special discounts for sales promotion, corporate gifts, fund-raising, or educational purposes. Special editions can also be created to specifications. For details, contact the Special Sales Department, Skyhorse Publishing, 307 West 36th Street, 11th Floor, New York, NY 10018 or info@skyhorsepublishing.com.

Skyhorse® and Skyhorse Publishing® are registered trademarks of Skyhorse Publishing, Inc.®, a Delaware corporation.

Visit our website at www.skyhorsepublishing.com.

10 9 8 7 6 5 4 3 2 1

Library of Congress Cataloging-in-Publication Data is available on file.

Cover design by Brian Peterson

Print ISBN: 978-1-5107-2757-1
Ebook ISBN: 978-1-5107-2758-8

Printed in the United States of America

Table of Contents

Introduction

An End to the Dark Ages:
Giving Voice to Survivors

C OMPASSIONATE PROFESSIONALS IN a variety of fields have been promoting rape reform for decades. They were often working on their own as individuals or groups of advocates and activists, social workers or counselors, or staff at bellwether organizations such as the rape crisis centers in Cleveland, Boston, the District of Columbia, Oakland, Pittsburgh, and San Francisco.

Fortunately, we are now in the midst of a growing movement that began to coalesce through a synergy of events: the advent of DNA testing in the early 1990s and the subsequent launching of the FBI's Combined DNA Index System (CODIS) database in 1999 that greatly facilitated suspect identification; the revelatory research of people like Rebecca Campbell, PhD, who brought training on the neurobiology of trauma studies that lucidly explain the sometimes erratic behavior and memory of victims of rape and sexual assault in a way not previously known to many of the professionals in the field; the discovery in the first decade of the twenty-first century of backlogs of an estimated 400,000 untested sexual assault kits (SAKs) in police property rooms and warehouses throughout the United States and the ensuing decisions by an enlightened cadre of attorneys general, county prosecutors, district attorneys, and law enforcement leadership to test and investigate the cases. Much credit goes to the investigative reporters who wrote about the neglected evidence and brought it to the public's attention.

However, the federal Sexual Assault Kit Initiative (SAKI) in 2014 represents the culmination and true turning point in the rape kit testing and processing and rape culture reform movement that's crossing the country now. It provides financial, technical, and training support crucial to furnishing jurisdictions with the resources and knowledge to identify and disseminate best practices for this endeavor.

In fact, Kevin Strom, program director in the Research Triangle Institute's Center for Justice, Safety, and Resilience—this nonprofit organization oversees the SAKI project—labels this era "The Golden Age of Sexual Assault Reform."

"We're still on the front end of this, but there is a lot of optimism that things are changing and improving," Strom says. "We did things incorrectly for a long period of time, but there are a lot of good people out there improving the way we treat sexual assault, so it's very inspirational."

I first learned of these significant changes and improvements when, in November of 2009, I got involved in the case of serial rapist and murderer Anthony Sowell, who had been arrested in Cleveland on Halloween after murdering eleven women and burying them in his backyard and house. A good friend and fellow journalist, Robert Sberna, asked if I would be interested in coauthoring a book about the case. I wasn't sure. Mainly, I wanted to see whether my hometown swept it under the rug or stepped up and said, "No more." So, I did some preliminary interviews with people in Sowell's neighborhood—police, urban affairs professors, and so on—and then later covered the trial with Robert. He writes a lot more about the crime beat than I do, so he went on to pen the definitive study of the case: *House of Horrors: The Shocking True Story of Anthony Sowell, the Cleveland Strangler* (The Kent State University Press, 2012).

Along the way, though, I began to meet people who were responding to this terrifying, soulless criminal by improving the way sexual violence victims and cases were handled in Cleveland. They were the solution providers to this ancient problem of cruel victim-blaming, ignoring and disregarding rape and sexual assault victims, and allowing many of the predators committing these crimes to roam freely.

Professionals such as Elizabeth Booth, RN, a Sexual Assault Nurse Examiner (SANE) at the MetroHealth System, or Megan O'Bryan at the Cleveland Rape Crisis Center (CRCC) or then Lieutenant Jim McPike, supervisor of the Cleveland Police Department's Sex Crimes and Child Abuse Unit, became my initial guides into this world. Ever since then, they and many others I have met along the way—anyone included in this book—have continued to help me understand the challenges their organizations were facing, the tribulations of survivors trying to recover, and the radical new approaches and initiatives that were starting to be implemented not just in Cleveland, but also in Detroit, Houston, Memphis, and now many other cities.

In 2016, I wrote a cover story for the *Christian Science Monitor* on what Cleveland had learned in responding to the "Cleveland Strangler" and how that had blossomed into a set of innovative and effective approaches. Just as important, the key players had all come out of their silos to work together on this insidious phenomenon, and their camaraderie was apparent at press conferences or meetings and in the friendly way they related to each other as colleagues. Because I knew it was happening elsewhere, and that Cleveland, Detroit, and Memphis have partnered their Sexual Assault Kit Task Forces (SAKTFs), I felt there was need for a compelling book that would explore the successes and challenges of this movement, as well as the professionals who were committed to doing the right thing and spreading the good word.

The history of how SAKI originated is an interesting one, with some roots in 2009. Two years prior, the National Institute of Justice (NIJ)—the research, development, and evaluation agency of the US Department of Justice—funded a study by Research Triangle Institute of why law enforcement agencies did not take sexual assault cases seriously or send evidence forward to initiate prosecution of offenders. The study found that often they didn't understand the complex dynamics around sexual assault cases, nor did they understand the victims; law enforcement thought they were lying or partially to blame for the assault. Some didn't fully understand the value of DNA evidence yet or believed it would cost too much to test the evidence in sexual assault kits.

That set the stage for a distinctive federal response in 2009, when Human Rights Watch published its report on the backlog of 12,669 untested SAKs found in Los Angeles that were the property of the Los Angeles Police and Sheriff's Departments, which shared a criminal evidence laboratory.

The report quoted Marta Miyakawa, a detective for the Los Angeles Police Department Cold Case Robbery and Homicide Division: "If people in Los Angeles hear about this rape kit backlog, and it makes them not want to work with the police in reporting their rape, then this backlog of ours would be tragic."

The report triggered an avalanche of public, private, and journalistic responses. According to a source I spoke to who was working there at the time but who asked not to be named, NIJ reached out to the LAPD and Sheriff's Department and the crime lab directors they had existing relationships with to offer any help or guide them to any resources they might need to resolve the untested kits issue. The law enforcement departments were both open to disclosing what the situation was, and NIJ used it as an opportunity to research the problem in what they call a "natural experiment," where something is already happening so they take advantage and study it. LA allowed NIJ to perform random sampling on 370 backlogged kits to see what evidence they could reap from the testing. Subsequently, NIJ published the "Sexual Assault Kit Backlog Study" in June 2012.

Concurrently, other jurisdictions started reporting enormous collections of untested kits in their property storage, and everyone began to realize it was a more widespread problem than initially thought. In 2011, NIJ decided to solicit one of their "Action-Research Projects" to get to the root of why jurisdictions were experiencing these massive numbers of untested kits. Detroit and Houston were selected as the test sites. The objective was to have researchers and practitioners in those jurisdictions work together to understand and solve the problem. If they couldn't solve the problem with their current methods, they could make "midcourse corrections," providing an evolutionary type of research project to uncover solutions and generate protocols for other jurisdictions to follow.

Both cities developed safe, effective means of handling victim notification. Houston devised what they called a "whole-time justice advocate," embedding advocates in their police department to work directly with victims and investigators. Both cities began to deploy funds to hire victim advocates, investigators, and prosecutors specifically to address the backlogged rape kits. NIJ credits that project with creating the groundswell of best practices and protocols, many of which other cities, counties, states, and jurisdictions continue to implement. Additionally, according to my source, the former NIJ staff member, the number one lesson learned was the importance of having a multidisciplinary approach to take on the untested kits and resulting criminal cases.

At roughly that same time, NIJ had another opportunity to perform a "natural experiment" in post–Hurricane Katrina New Orleans, when the police there revealed—along with other serious criminal justice issues—a backlog of more than seven hundred untested kits. Mayor C. Ray Nagin, the sixtieth mayor of New Orleans, requested assistance from NIJ, which provided financial support for testing the kits and launched a pilot project known as CHOP, or CODIS Hit Outcome Project. The NIJ earned about the backlog of untested kits through involvement with DOJ working group and responded with a solution. The goal was to test a new system that notified police departments when there was a hit in the national DNA database, so that they could follow up on investigating those cases to prevent them from falling through the cracks.

In 2009, upon entering office, Vice President Joe Biden appointed the first White House Advisor on Violence Against Women, Lynn Rosenthal. (Nearly two decades earlier, Senator Biden had introduced the Violence Against Women Act in the US Congress in June 1990, and it passed in 1994.) When Rosenthal left to become Vice President of Strategic Partnerships at the National Domestic Violence Hotline,

Biden replaced her with Caroline "Carrie" Bettinger-López in May 2015. Biden had also decided untested SAKs would be one of his signature issues, along with campus sexual assaults. He became the first vice president to publicly address the issue of sexual violence.

Under Biden's leadership, Lynn Rosenthall and the Office on Violence Against Women worked closely with NIJ and other organizations such as the Department of Justice's Bureau of Justice Assistance (BJA) and its Office for Victims of Crime to obtain a Congressional appropriation for SAKI to consolidate all the lessons learned from Los Angeles, the Detroit and Houston action research projects, New Orleans, and other research to create the Sexual Assault Kit Initiative. Angela Williamson, PhD, was named by BJA to administer the SAKI program, after she was hired in 2014 as Senior Policy Advisor (Forensics) at the Bureau of Justice Assistance, Office of Justice Programs.

In September 2014, Vice President Biden and Attorney General Loretta Lynch announced the $41 million FY2015 SAKI program. (Cy Vance, the Manhattan District Attorney, was also part of this announcement, as he released $35 million in New York City asset forfeiture funds as additional support for kit testing nationwide.) The initial awards went to twenty jurisdictions across the United States to fund kit testing, enhance investigations and prosecutions, and develop victim-centered protocols for notifying and interviewing victims.

Thus far, Congress has approved $131 million for the thirty-two jurisdictions that have now received SAKI grants, including $40 million that was expected to be disbursed in fall of 2017 that would bring the total of SAKI sites to forty. The FY2018 budget Congress is considering has not been passed as of this writing, but the proposal includes another $45 million to help eliminate rape kit backlogs nationwide. SAKI's mission is to ensure that kits get tested and to provide the sites the resources they need to fully investigate and solve these violent crimes while always keeping victims as the focus of the cases and making sure their voices are heard and they are treated with the respect and understanding that they deserve.

SAKI grants stipulate that only 50 percent of the funding may be used for testing. The rest must be applied to investigation and tracking down offenders for prosecution. Research Triangle Institute (RTI) received $11 million to serve as the training and technical assistance (TTA) partner. They assembled a team of experts who travel to any of the sites requesting assistance or any of the District Attorney of New York (DANY)–funded sites to help them implement a tracking system, investigate a cold case, understand the victim's response through the neurobiology of trauma research, train Sexual Assault Nurse Examiners, and so on. Key members of the TTA team include Dr. Rebecca Campbell and James Markey, who are both featured in this book.

"We meet with a site and create their TTA development plan," explains Patricia Melton, PhD, codirector of the BJA National Training and Technical Assistance Program. "We outline and identify all of their training and technical assistance needs at that time, but it's a living document that keeps getting evaluated and modified. Then we build the subject matter expert team they need to provide their TTA, and that continues throughout the period of their grant." The SAKI TTA website provides virtual training and support resources, too, she adds. That site is public, so the training resources are available to any law enforcement agency in the United States.

In August 2017, the NIJ published the "National Best Practices for Sexual Assault Kits: A Multidisciplinary Approach," which includes thirty-five recommendations that provide a guide to victim-centered approaches for responding to sexual assault cases and better supporting victims throughout the criminal justice process.

In the end, there are two primary missions of this national effort to combat sexual violence. "We want to send a message to the perpetrators that they're not going to get away with this," Williamson informs me. "But the SAKI project also sends an even more important message to the victims that they do matter, and that's who we're doing this for. My hope is that it changes the way everyone addresses the crime of sexual assault."

Strom and Melton concur. "This is just the tip of the iceberg," Strom says of this Golden Age of Sexual Assault Reform. "We need to look back twenty years from now and say, 'This was just the start.'"

Of course, there are numerous advocates, SANEs, Sexual Assault Forensic Examiners (SAFEs), police, participating prosecutors, and organizations such as Rape, Abuse, and Incest National Network (RAINN), the nation's largest anti–sexual violence organization, that I was not able to fit in the book but are doing important and far-reaching work. That was a good problem for me to have, as more and more professionals and volunteers step up to help these victims who for millennia have been left alone in their suffering and silence. There are also specific populations where the prevalence of rape and sexual assault is at such epidemic proportions that I couldn't fairly or adequately cover them: college students, human sex trafficking victims, military personnel, and prison inmates. Perhaps in the future.

One final note on the terminology I used for people who have been raped or assaulted. At one of the breakout sessions I attended at the Sexual Assault Kit Task Force Summit in Detroit in September 2016, one of the presenters—I believe it was Kim Hurst, SAFE and director of the Wayne County SAFE program in Detroit—explained in an inside-baseball way that law enforcement agents, prosecutors, and our criminal justice system refer to these individuals as "victims"; rape crisis advocates refer to them as "survivors" or "clients," if they have a relationship with a rape crisis center, and nurses call them "patients."

Essentially, on the law enforcement and legal side, those professionals have to refer to them as victims, because that's what they are in the eyes of the law. However, rape crisis advocates refer to them as survivors, whether they were assaulted two hours ago or twenty years ago. I was chided a couple times for referring to someone as a victim, even though I was talking about it in a legal context, so advocates are vehement proponents of always using the word "survivor."

What I also found, however, is that some people in the field refer to someone as a victim if they have been assaulted recently or if they are involved in the prosecution of their assailant. Once they are on the other side of that, especially if they have made strides in taking their lives back through counseling, therapy, moving, getting a new job, exercise and fitness, etc., then they are more likely to be considered survivors.

There is no exact definition or timeline, so I have tried to use the word that best fits their status at the time I was writing about someone.

Each one of the survivors I met and spoke with, and numerous others I have read about or learned about from the professionals I interviewed—stands as a model of courage and heroism, even if they were still struggling with their recovery. Similar to veterans suffering from PTSD, whom I've also gotten to know in writing about Vietnam veterans or meeting veterans of the Middle East conflicts, there is no cure to the trauma they have suffered. They must find ways to recover their lives and move ahead for as long as they live. Some fare better than others.

After eight years of researching, reporting, and interviewing about rape and sexual assault, I am more convinced than ever that it is our absolute responsibility as human beings to offer any survivors the support, compassion, respect, and dignity they deserve and do everything in our power to ensure that we hold their assailants accountable and put them where they belong: prison.

PART 1

What Cleveland Has Learned

Chapter 1

Abandoned Evidence:
Shondreka Lloyd's Case, Part 1

SHONDREKA LLOYD REMEMBERS standing on the front porch of her friend Vincent's house. She could barely walk. Her head hurt and her brain buzzed. Then she started vomiting purple.

Earlier that afternoon, she had fallen asleep after braiding Darlell's hair. She didn't really know him well, but he was Vincent's friend. They had been hanging out together, waiting for Vincent to return from Saturday school. She was fourteen and a "skinny-minnie." Darlell seemed a lot older, so when he started hitting on her, she took him to McDonald's and treated him to lunch to change to a more comfortable situation before they returned to the house.

"He just sat there, and he was just cool, like everything was cool," she recalls. "So, I'm thinking everything was cool, and he's off it."

When Vincent came home, she woke up and told them she was thirsty. The two boys gave her a large glass of a dark liquid to quench her thirst; she thought it was Kool-Aid, because it tasted so sweet. Soon, the room started spinning, until she felt herself stumbling outside. She realized later it was Cisco, a fortified wine known on the street as "liquid crack," mixed with she's not sure exactly what else.

She made it to the front yard before she vomited more purple stuff. A lot more purple stuff.

"Get that girl in the house," said an old man sitting on the porch who she later learned was Vincent's grandfather. "She need to go lie down somewhere!"

She couldn't walk up the steps. She remembers hearing laughter as she crawled up the stairs on her hands and knees. Painstakingly, she crawled into the house. More laughter exploded above and behind her. She stood and fell forward onto a bed. Just layin' down. Chillin'. Trying to get her swirling brain to come to a stop.

The next thing she knew, she was fighting somebody off of her body. The slender, athletic tomboy had on her trademark T-shirt and silken shorts that fell past her knees. She never dressed flashy. She didn't even know she was pretty until she got into her twenties. People would tell her, "You're pretty," but she would just think, "Whatever."

Now, Darlell yanked at her dark blue and gold basketball shorts. He picked her legs up over her head. She felt like a baby getting its Pampers changed. She tried to fight, but every time she could force her legs down, he punched or choked her.

At one point, Shondreka realized there was a window above and behind her head. She moved to scream for help.

"If you holler out that window, I'm gonna kill you," Darlell scowled.

He jerked her away from the window and punched her in the face. Harder, more viciously this time. Throwing her whole body backward so forcefully that her head got stuck between the bed and the wall. He shoved his forearm across her throat, holding her down.

She realized there's only so much you can do when you're drunk and you can't breathe . . . and you're fourteen. She thought, do I fight or do I just let him do it? She fought.

"Oh my gosh. I've never had sex before," Shondreka recalls thinking. "You're not just going to take something from me. I've been a fighter all my life. You're not just going to take my virginity from me like that."

But he did. He raped her. All alone. On a small bed. In someone else's house. While she was sick, scared, and confused. And fourteen.

After it was over, Darlell gave her a funny look. "I'm sorry."

"You're sorry?"

Shondreka curled up in a ball and began perseverating, rocking on the bed. She couldn't believe it had happened. She didn't know what to do.

Vincent entered the room. Where had he been this whole time? Was he in cahoots?

"Are you okay?"

At first, she was too stunned to utter a sound. When he began to exit the room, she moved to say something. Darlell kicked her in the face. The thought that she was being held hostage and it was going to happen all over again overwhelmed her. She'd lost all track of time and any sense of what was happening to her.

She couldn't breathe. She began hyperventilating. She kept rocking.

"Oh my gosh. What am I going to do?" she thought, sucking in air. "I done fucked up. How did I end up here?"

Vincent and Darlell entered with a pot of boiling water. Vincent told her if she inhaled the steam, it could help her breath more easily and deeply. She was unfamiliar with the remedy.

The handles on the pot were loose. The two knuckleheads let it slip and dumped the boiling water on her left foot. Driven by the intense flash of pain, Shondreka jumped up and ran out of the room. She ran out of the house, past the old man on the porch. She ran down the street to her friend Charles's house.

How she ran anywhere, she still can't tell you. By the time she showed Charles and his mother, all of the skin on her foot, from her ankle to her toes, was slimy and hanging loose. When she saw how it moved, it made her nauseous again.

"I have scars to this day, so I have an every-day memory of what that motherfucker—I'm sorry—did to me," Shondreka, now thirty-eight, steams.

Just before the ambulance arrived, she had started to tell Charles and his mom that this dude down the street had raped her.

First the ambulance paramedics, then the ER nurses at St. Luke's Hospital on Shaker Boulevard, not far from Charles's house, bombarded her with questions.

"What's wrong? What happened to you? Where is your mother? We have to call your mom right now!"

Her mother came to the hospital. It was a bit of an uneasy reunion, because they hadn't seen much of each other since, earlier that year [1993], she had told Shondreka she was no longer welcome to live at her house. Because Shondreka was a minor, the nurses wanted her mother's consent to perform the sexual assault kit examination to collect evidence of the rape.

"I don't believe she was raped," her mother said. "She shouldn't have had her ass in the streets in the first place."

"That's besides the point," the teen responded. "I want it done. Fuck y'all. I know what happened to me. Y'all not goin' to play me like I'm some fool or something. I want you to focus on what happened to me now!"

A nurse performed the sexual assault examination. It was thorough. Took almost two hours. It was invasive. For many years afterward, Shondreka would cry quietly whenever she endured a pelvic exam or a Pap smear.

After the rape kit was complete, Shondreka lay on the exam table. Her mother had made a quick exit. Shondreka wanted to pursue her rapist, but her mother didn't believe her and told the police she wouldn't allow her daughter to participate in the case. Shondreka spoke to the police officers that the nurses had had to call by law to report her rape. They interviewed her. She told them his name was Darnell instead of Darlell, because that's what he had told her when they first met. They took her report. They took the rape kit. They left.

She overheard the medical staff discussing what to do next with "the patient." Her mother had reported her as "unruly" to the police, so she thought the juvenile detention facility was coming to take her. "I got raped, and you're going to lock me up?" she thought.

She looked around the exam room and started grabbing every bit of sterile gauze and wrapping she could hold and stuff into her clothes. She snuck through the curtains and out of the emergency room. Despite the excruciating pain shooting up her leg, she limped the several miles to the Garden Valley Projects, where Paula, the sister of her extended cousin's baby daddy, lived. She knew she couldn't stay long, but she just needed a safe place to "heal and medicate," to get herself together.

Her stay turned out to be shorter than she thought. Nor was it as safe a haven as she had hoped. A number of cousins, baby mommas, baby daddies, and babies populated the two-bedroom apartment. At night, some of the young men would touch her inappropriately.

"Like you'd be sleeping, and they would try to put their penis in you," she shudders. "Like what the fuck?! You know what I mean?"

Shondreka stayed just long enough for her foot to heal. Then she returned to her perilous life on the streets.

"In my mind, it was me against the world, because I had nobody," she says. "When I say nobody, I mean nobody."

Returning to her mother's was not an option. It had never been great, especially since her mom preferred her younger brother to her and her sister. Home life had gotten so bad before her exile—the neglect, the yelling, the arguments—that she became obsessed with finding any way to gain attention. Her mother's. A teacher's. Any potentially caring adult, really. Then she started a wrestling match with God. What is my purpose? Why am I here? Why am I going through this? Do you not love me? No answers.

Shondreka struggled with the teen's plague: acne. She talked her mother into taking her to a doctor so she could get some acne medicine. Hoping to kill herself, she swallowed the entire bottle of pills. It didn't do anything except give her a stomach ache and make her throw up.

"I know it was a messed up way to get her attention," Shondreka admits. "But I wanted her to feel for me. Like, what if I wasn't here? What if I killed myself? Would you love me then?"

When her mother remained unmoved, then told her to leave, living on the streets became preferable. Shondreka sold drugs—crack and cocaine mostly—but she never did drugs herself, never drank after her rape, because when you're drunk, you can't fight. She watched people all around her abuse chemical substances. When "water" hit the streets, a deadly combination of PCP and embalming fluid, she saw a number of friends die while testing out their substance-induced superpowers by jumping off high buildings or driving faster than sharp curves allowed.

Shondreka sold guns. TEC-9s, AR-15s, Glocks, .38s, .22s. Easy access to guns today doesn't surprise her, because back then she could acquire them fresh out of the manufacturer's box. Her weapon of choice? The TEC-9 with an extended clip. She dropped fifty dollars on a double shoulder holster, with the goal of carrying as many guns as possible. She packed others into her baggy tomboy clothes. "I used to be a lil gangsta!" she claims. At night, in a field behind nearby Glenville High School, she and her crew would fire guns at bats, completely oblivious to the fact that bullets can carry for a mile or more and hit an innocent bystander.

She sold drugs out of the Town House Motel in East Cleveland, an area rife with cheap motels and low-rent apartment buildings filled with tenants popularly referred to as "crackheads." A savvy street businesswoman at fourteen, fifteen, she was there to supply a great demand.

She made her headquarters in room 110. One fond memory: it was the only room with a waterbed (that's how long ago this was). Here is how her drugstore in room 110 worked: the room had a window that opened onto a narrow, paved walkway behind the building. Her trusted salesman, Bubba, would solicit crack fiends and bring them up to the window, where Shondreka would complete the transaction.

"When I say I counted stacks of money the length of that bookshelf right there," indicating a shelving unit about fifty feet long at the public library where we met, "I counted money the length of that bookshelf."

People working the front desk of the Town House served as her security guards. They enjoyed an occasional snort now and again, so she would keep them in coke as compensation. In return, they would notify her when the police arrived. She would retreat to a second room that she kept on another floor until they left.

She always wore her double shoulder holster and other guns, because she never knew when she would get into a shootout with the Hastings Boys. Their territory was directly across the street from her pharmaceutical headquarters in the Town House. One day, the Hastings Boys crossed the main drag, Euclid Avenue, to jump her ex-boyfriend, Mongo. (He survived that day but is now dead. She's not sure what killed him.) Started with a fist fight. As usual, she was the only girl fighting. Then it turned into a shootout in the hallway of the Town House.

Seeing it play out in her head today, she says: "The streets is crazy. Crazy. I've seen people get their head blown off next to me. You see some very cruel people. Some mean, mean people out there."

"I could have been dead so many times," she adds after a pause. "When I say God has been with me, God has been with me."

She got older. Old enough to stop being bounced in and out of juvenile detention facilities. She went through a series of abusive boyfriends. She finally left the streets and got a job at Popeyes Louisiana Chicken, where one of her boyfriends was the manager. He also turned out to be abusive. Hitting her. Holding a gun on her. Chasing her naked from the house. She left him, too. She had no adult to give consent for counseling, none to give consent for even playing high school sports. She was a pretty good athlete, but competing in track events and seeing the other girls' mothers there to support them became too overwhelming, so she quit. Despite the lack of parental support, despite the random madness of street life, she found a way to earn her GED from the Job Corps so she could go to Wright State University. She wasn't perfect. Who was? Spent almost a year in the Ohio Reformatory for Women in Marysville for taking money from a joint account with a former boyfriend and he accused her of forgery. Married and divorced a guy who cheated on her.

No one ever talked about her rape. Shondreka didn't talk about her rape. Her mother still didn't believe her, and no one else seemed to care about that assault or her general wellbeing in any way. So she stayed silent. The silence served as a wall, a defense mechanism against thinking or feeling anything about her rape. It toughened her. Helped her survive in the jungle, where someone wanting to take your money, beat or kill you lurked around every corner. In fact, she didn't talk much at all about anything. There were no adults in her life to advocate for her, to seek counseling, to press the police to investigate.

She didn't know where her assailant lived or if he was even still in Cleveland, but Shondreka saw her rapist everywhere. Like that one time at a party. In the blaring, throbbing music and flashing strobe lights, she zeroed in on his face. There. Deep in the pulsing, vivid maelstrom of partiers in this suddenly psycho disco, there he was. The dude who raped her. It looked like his face. Maybe. She couldn't take her eyes off that face. Her heart plummeted. She couldn't find her way out of the house fast enough. She ran. She cried. She looked back to make sure he wasn't chasing her.

For many years, he had chased her in her dreams. That face. Nightmares tortured her sleep. She would fight in her dark unconsciousness, twisting, turning, punching, kicking. If someone lay next to her, she would hit him or her. She slapped at them wildly. She saw that face, both faces actually, all the time, because she didn't know where the two men lived now.

Her rape kit sat on a shelf gathering dust and time. Thanks to her mother's decision not to cooperate, the police and the prosecutor's office let the case die. And there was that one detective who told her that if she ever returned to East Cleveland, he'd make sure she served a life sentence for drug sales.

But she had been raped. What about that? She thought the police, the prosecutors were there to protect her, too. Seriously. They needed a parent or guardian's permission to move forward with the case? So, no call. Silence all around. A child brutally beaten and raped. No case.

No one touched her kit. No one investigated her case. No one thought about her case. No one cared about her case.

For twenty years.

Chapter 2

The Rock:
Kirsti Mouncey and the Cleveland
Rape Crisis Center

"I WOULD ALSO be remiss if I didn't thank Attorney General Mike DeWine and his team," gently intones Sondra Miller, president and CEO, of the Cleveland Rape Crisis Center (CRCC), after thanking the staff, board members, volunteers, public officials, and "our friends in law enforcement," most of whom are wearing mirrored sunglasses. It's the grand opening of the center's new facility in Westlake, Ohio, a western suburb of Cleveland, on a June Thursday afternoon that could not be more perfect: breezy, 80 degrees, and resplendently awash in sunshine.

"It was a grant awarded through the Victims of Crime program that allowed us to open the doors," she continues as fifty or sixty people encircle her as she stands on the red-carpeted sidewalk leading up to the entrance and a symbolic red ribbon.

In October 2016, the center announced that it had received two grants from the Ohio Attorney General's Office totaling $3,113, 868, one from the Victims of Crime Act (VOCA) program and a State Victim Assistance Act (SVAA) grant that would fund their new Westlake location.

The location is about as ideal as possible to promote peace, quiet, and serenity for survivors of rape or sexual assault in need of a place to come for counseling, therapy, or restorative respite and asylum.

Surrounded by a deeply wooded lot at the far end of a light industrial and office parkway, the new center makes visitors feel like they're in a forest garden, with regular appearances by a range of birds, rabbits, deer, and wild turkeys. It's also slightly more than a stone's throw south of the shores of Lake Erie.

"I'm telling you, when we drove up here the first time to tour it, I said, 'This is the space. I want to be here,'" recalls Kirsti Mouncey, chief program officer for the CRCC, who led the search committee to iden- tify a site and worked closely with the development department to raise the funding necessary. To take advantage of the woodland splendor, she's been seriously ruminating about types of outdoor group activities they could schedule, such as hikes, tai chi, or yoga.

During her ribbon-cutting speech, Miller discloses that the goal of opening this "beautiful, welcoming, warm facility" is to serve more sur- vivors throughout western Cuyahoga County and be closer to where they live. She then enumerates the three reasons her organization is opening a facility in Westlake.

"First is rape and sexual abuse do not know any geographic bounda- ries, and when we look at the data of the number of people calling the Cleveland Rape Crisis Center and asking for help, those survivors live in every single municipality and represent every single city in Cuyahoga County and even quite a bit in Akron," she says. "We have been answer- ing a number of phone calls that go something like this: 'I need help.' 'Our office is downtown.' And then we hear 'click.'

"Even though we know survivors are in every corner of Cuyahoga County, and we need to be centrally located at a place where as many survivors as possible can get to us, we know that some people can't get downtown, and we can do even greater good if we can take our services outside of downtown, closer to them."

As expected, she continues, they've already received calls from nearby suburbs such as Strongsville and Olmsted Falls from clients who are planning to come to the new facility. Additionally, there are already enormous barriers that keeps survivors of sexual violence from moving forward with their healing, so they did not want location to act as yet another barrier. The fact that one in five women and one in seventy-one men in Ohio will be raped in their lifetime and about two-thirds of those assaults will never be reported to law enforcement—sexual assault is the most underreported crime in the United States—or see their way through prosecution underscores the need for augmenting the availability of the CRCC's services.

Miller then enumerated some of the reasons they've heard over the years why people are not willing to come forward, starting with fear of retaliation from the perpetrator or perhaps the perpetrator's family or friends. Others are ashamed of what happened to them, believe it's their fault, or think they can merely move on and forget about it. The ability to call, request help, and then actually visit the center requires a great deal of courage. Thus, she says, they consider it a great honor that survivors would entrust their personal care to the CRCC.

"My amazing colleagues and our mighty volunteers, we are working twenty-four hours a day, seven days a week, three hundred sixty-five days a year to reduce all of those barriers," Miller continues. "We put everything we have into breaking down the stigma that is often associated with rape. We train many of our partners and our first responders on trauma-informed techniques."

The third reason for opening this suburban center that Miller cites is, quite simply, the survivors deserve it. No matter how long ago or where it happened, all survivors deserve access to comprehensive services to help them recover and once again be happy, healthy, and enjoying their lives. That will always be the CRCC's guiding mission. In closing, they want survivors to hear a very simple message from the CRCC:

"You are not alone, and you can recover, and not just recover, but you can feel and thrive," she says. "Survivors of rape and sexual abuse, you are welcome here. And I want to thank each and every person who took the time to show up today to back up that message to survivors and to help the Cleveland Rape Crisis Center in our fight to eliminate sexual violence from this world."

With that, Miller stepped forward with an immense, industrial pair of ceremonial scissors furnished by the Westlake Chamber of Commerce and snipped the red ribbon to officially open the CRCC's Westside Office.

A few minutes later, I chat with Mouncey near the party tent in the corner of the parking lot that provides refreshments or shade for those who want to limit their consumption of early summer vitamin D. We've spent a lot of time together for the past year, as she's very generously let me shadow her at various training events, but this is the culmination of one of her priority strategic initiatives: provide rape crisis services closer to their constituency in all parts of Northeast Ohio.

"A lot of thought went into: Will clients come to a freestanding building? Will clients feel comfortable parking and walking in? What should the signage be?" she explains, as they want people to be able to find the facility but maintain privacy and comfort levels, too. "So, this is the culmination of years of thinking about how can we do this business differently."

The Cleveland Rape Crisis Center also recently moved into a new downtown headquarters in the Halle Building, a historic Cleveland department store converted to an office building, its third location since opening in 1974. You can only get to their floor via a private, secure elevator. From its humble beginnings, the center has grown into one of the finest, most comprehensive such organizations in the US.

"Nationally, we need a lot of work to make all of our rape crisis centers the beacon of hope in their communities that Cleveland has accomplished," said Monika Johnson Hostler, president of the National Alliance to End Sexual Violence, based in Washington, DC, when I spoke to her in 2015 for an article I was writing. She considers Cleveland one of the five cornerstone rape crisis centers in the country, along with Boston, Washington, Pittsburgh, and San Francisco.

The CRCC offers a diverse range of services for its clients, including a twenty-four-hour crisis and support hotline, with chat and text capabilities; individual counseling; support groups; art therapy; hospital support; offices on the major college campuses; Project STAR for sex trafficking advocacy and recovery; Hogar Consuelo (Comfort Place), counseling and victim services for Spanish-speaking survivors; and a full range of services for children survivors. In 2017, during April, which is Sexual Assault Awareness Month, the center offered forty-seven events throughout the region to raise public awareness, from film screenings and panel discussions to resource fairs and consent workshops.

Throughout the past several years, as Cleveland has committed to the growing movement to take a completely different, more compassionate, victim-centered approach to rape and sexual assault cases, and as more and more disciplines and organizations have come out of their silos to partner in this effort, the Cleveland Rape Crisis Center has provided the foundation and center of gravity for everyone involved.

Early in May 2017, Mouncey led the first in a series of three new training sessions for the Cuyahoga County Sexual Assault Kit Task Force. Roughly twenty-five or thirty investigators and prosecutors are assembled at the long tables, some with bottles of water and snacks in front of them for the afternoon program. Each has a copy of the PowerPoint screen captures and note-taking pages Mouncey handed out as a guide to her presentation. The group includes Special Investigations Division Chief Rick Bell and SAKTF Supervisor Brett Kyker. It's a pretty tight-knit group, so they joke and tease each other about projects they're working on, what they're wearing, and so on; several others trickle in during the next hour. Some low-level construction noise seeps into the lower level conference room of the Halle Building as workers finish building a new Planet Fitness center across the way, but that doesn't stop Mouncey from launching into part one of her presentation: Understanding Trauma and Its Impact.

For the next forty-five minutes, Mouncey reviews the key principles of trauma-informed care, which recognizes that the horrific shock and distress of being raped physically, mentally, and emotionally impairs a victim's ability to remember and relate the details of her or his attack when interviewed by law enforcement agents, nurses, prosecutors, family, and friends. She also discusses how in the past there was little to no training specific to this complex condition experienced by victims for police, prosecutors, or judges handling sexual assault cases. That led to misinterpretations of victim's reactions that discouraged them from cooperating with the criminal justice system. Due to the minimal knowledge of the psychological and physical affects of trauma, offenders often ended up not being held accountable for their crimes.

Next, she reviews the latest research and thinking regarding the optimum ways to work with victims and take a more respectful, compassionate approach to understanding what they've experienced and working with them appropriately. She cites the important studies of Rebecca Campbell, PhD, a professor of psychology at Michigan State University, who has heightened awareness of "the neurobiology of trauma" among professionals dealing with sexual violence. In her work, Campbell focuses on summarizing the expansive research on NBT and conveys the implications for practitioners. Her trainings have changed and advanced the best practices of these professionals by revealing the impact of the hormones released in response to trauma that affect a victim's brain (particularly the amygdala, the almond-sized gland that functions as the emotional control center), emotional response, and memory.

Many of the audience members are jotting notes as Mouncey explains further. One of the hormones released as part of the body's defense mechanism is an opiate to dull the pain but which also creates a flat affect and diminished response to questioning about the attack, behavior police and others have long misinterpreted as lack of concern or being uncooperative. Campbell's trainings also clearly explain that at the time of an attack, instead of the believed two reactions of fight or flight, there are actually three: fight, flight, or freeze/submit. The latter condition is known as "tonic immobility," an uncontrollable mammalian reaction of the body's autonomic system in extremely fearful situations that causes increased breathing, eye closure, and paralysis. TI occurs in 12 percent to 50 percent of rape victims, Mouncey relates, and it is more common in victims who have been previously assaulted.

In fact, multiple hormones become dysregulated during trauma, which affects how victims feel and how they behave. It is all part of what Mouncey and Campbell label "Hormone Soup" that is likely to be present for up to ninety-six hours.

Prosecutor Bell raises his hand. When Mouncey calls on him, he informs her that, because of this last fact, some states are exploring extending the testing time for rape kits from ninety-six to one hundred twenty hours.

However, she continues, one substance they do not find is catecholamine, a hormone released by the adrenal gland to fuel a fight or flight response. She also discusses how victim blaming or indelicate interviewing can trigger victims into another round of hormone output that will negatively affect their behavior and emotional responses, further impairing their ability to convey helpful information. She offers significantly more details about trauma and its effects on victims. Mouncey then closes the first part of her presentation by showing one of Dr. Campbell's YouTube videos in which she discusses how victims assemble memories randomly as they return to them, not in the exact order of what transpired during their assault.

During the break, one of the assistant prosecutors from the task force asks Mouncey if they could use some of the training information or enlist the CRCC to help them work with their victim witnesses. She says, "Certainly," and the two exchange contact information. To start the second portion, Mouncey presents a case of a rape victim at a college fraternity house party who suffered a terrifying tonic immobility experience.

"From what we now know of the impact of trauma, we must be patient with a victim who cannot give a cogent, linear account of the story from beginning to end," she says. She then has two advocates, Marya Simmons from the SAKTF and Shelley Hunt from the CRCC, present two detailed case studies for everyone to consider and discuss. Simmons uses her case study to review the preferred ways to build rapport with a client who has been sexually assaulted, while Hunt discusses dealing with survivor trauma within the criminal justice system.

Victims often don't remember the most egregious things that happened to them, possibly as a defense mechanism, for example, so it can be confusing or upsetting when an investigator or prosecutor presses them for exact details.

Mouncey shifts to a focus on vicarious trauma and self-care for professionals who work closely with victims on a regular basis and experience increasing symptoms and fallout from the stress of absorbing their emotional suffering vicariously. "We learn to help everyone but ourselves," her first slide says, followed by a photograph of two police officers carrying a baby alligator that is captioned: Our Jobs Can Be Killers, Even If No One Is Shooting at Us!

Mouncey explains that vicarious trauma is a cumulative process that can overwhelm someone eventually as a result of listening to the stories of one inhumane act of cruelty after another. The metaphor she uses is the frog put into a pot of water that is gradually brought to a boil. Instead of jumping out, the frog adjusts to the hot water until it dies. She breaks down what can happen to a person and defines the various names for vicarious trauma, such as secondary trauma, compassion fatigue, and burnout. Stress isn't necessarily good or bad, she says. It's how you react to it that matters.

After talking about a slide that defines burnout as "when health is suffering or outlook on life turns negative because of the impact or overload of their work," she then reveals that she had a rather severe experience with stress/burnout just a couple of years ago. She started getting hit with dizzy spells that lasted a few weeks. Finally, a doctor confirmed there was nothing wrong with her physically. She asked Mouncey if she thought it was stress-related. That little red light went off and she said, "Oh yeah. That's right."

"These unexpected symptoms—not slowing down, not taking breaks, not looking at what this work is doing—will take a heavy toll," she says. In addition to being self-aware, she prescribes a hearty regimen of self-care and stress relief through exercise, meditation, yoga, hobbies, a balanced and healthy diet, lots of laughter, family time, and time off whenever possible. She also suggests, when a particular issue becomes an obsession, setting a timer for fifteen minutes of "obsession time" or "worry time," and when the timer stops, stop obsessing about it.

Part of ongoing training for the SAKTF, Mouncey programmed this session to be an introduction for new members and a refresher course for veteran members. "The training is definitely beneficial for the newer investigators that are coming in to understand trauma and how trauma affects victims of sexual assault," Simmons concludes later. "The second and third training will be a little more in-depth about trauma and vicarious trauma and how to identify the neurobiology of victims in sexual assault, which should broaden the training of the task force."

When I catch up to the hardworking Mouncey a few weeks later, I ask about her dizzy spell burnout incident. She promises she learned her lesson and now tries to "stay in a rhythm" of meditating and doing yoga and therapy sessions as needed to balance her hectic and emotionally draining job. She had conducted a similar series of training events primarily with investigators at the prosecutor's office last year, she explains, that are mandated by the SAKI project funding requirements. This year, the sessions are also open to Cleveland Police Department (CPD)'s Sex Crimes and Child Abuse Unit detectives, and there were more prosecutors there as well.

"It's important for them to understand how trauma manifests itself in behaviors," she says. "People react in all kinds of different ways. If you don't understand it in the context of trauma, you can really misinterpret that behavior. So, to be a trauma-informed system, people need to understand how trauma impacts the brain and then enhances what the behaviors look like."

―――――――――――

Growing up in Saxony, in a small town on the border of the Czech Republic in communist East Germany, Mouncey says no one talked about addictions or alcoholism or gays and lesbians, and there were no social services available to anyone. When the Berlin Wall was torn down in 1989, she became fascinated with reading about depression and addiction and how people could get help. She earned her degree in social work at a college in the small university town of Jena. "There was really never a question that I would become a helper and a social worker," she recalls.

After college, she traveled a bit, then relocated to Boston in 1998 and worked with developmentally disabled individuals for several years before moving to Cleveland. She earned her master's degree in social work at Cleveland State University, then took a job with Mental Health Services (now Frontline Services) that sent her to work as a crisis intervention worker/case manager at the Community Women's Shelter. In doing extensive mental health assessments with the women, she remembers that *every single woman* had a history of being a victim of sexual violence. She launched a group at the shelter for the women to talk about their experiences, create art, and have a space to talk with each other. She tried to connect them with supportive services in the community and made "lots and lots" of referrals to the Cleveland Rape Crisis Center. Then her employer enrolled her in a group facilitator training program at the CRCC, so she came to know a number of people there.

In 2006, knowing Mouncey had also earned her chemical dependency counselor credentials along the way, the CRCC recruited her to serve as their trauma and addiction therapist. She focused on clients who suffered from core, recurring addictions. Of course, their recurring addictions were driven by a need to self-medicate because of their sexual trauma. At that time, that realization, she says, was fairly new in the field, to realize how many people who had been sexually assaulted develop addictions throughout their lives and how many of the people they treat struggle with addiction.

In her eleven years at the CRCC, Mouncey has worked in every department, from the hotline through training and outreach, and estimates she has treated thousands of survivors.

"I don't have time to do a lot of counseling anymore, unfortunately," she says. "Now my role has grown more of a teacher and mentor to the clinicians on the staff, so certainly that expertise is within everybody and continues to be nurtured so our clients still get that benefit, but now I am responsible for supervising and bringing up the next generation of leaders for the organization."

When Mouncey started, the CRCC was still a small, grassroots organization, and she was one of four therapists. The twenty-four-hour hotline was up and running, but each of the fifteen full-time staff performed multiple roles, and the counseling department had a six-month waiting list, which indicated the center was lacking the funding and support that it has today. The director at the time, Megan O'Bryan, continued to develop their funding sources and built the CRCC into a larger, healthier organization before turning over the reigns to Miller, who was a vice president at the time, in 2013. Today, the CRCC has fifty-three employees with locations in four counties.

In June 2016, the Ohio Alliance to End Sexual Violence, Ohio's statewide sexual assault coalition, recognized Mouncey's decade of helping grow the organization by presenting her with a Visionary Voice Award.

"Kirsti is a phenomenal leader who has positively impacted the lives of countless survivors and the sexual violence field, both in Northeast Ohio and nationally," stated Katie Hanna, executive director of the OAESV. "Kirsti's expertise in trauma-informed responses, as a clinician and advocate, is visible in any interaction you have with her. She embodies a supportive, trauma-informed individual and system response."

In 1974, when Mouncey was still a child, the Cleveland Rape Crisis Center was founded by four intrepid women. Lynn Hammond and Carrie Zander started the CRCC hotline; Jeanne Van Atta and Lorraine Schalamon soon joined them. Each had personal experience with sexual violence or knew someone close who had. Each could no longer tolerate how victims had to suffer their guilt, humiliation, and shame in silence.

"I just felt so frustrated, because the silence has been going on so long," recalls Jeanne Van Atta of her inner fire to take a stand against rape. "Having a voice for anyone who has been sexually assaulted, taking shame away and the blame: 'Why did you let him do that to you? How could you have done that or why were you dressed that way?' All of the blame going on because people didn't understand what rape was about. They thought it was a sexual relationship. Far from it."

While her cohorts have moved on to other things in their lives after burning out from the countless hours and years invested in launching what is now considered a model rape crisis center, Van Atta, seventy-two, stays involved when it seems right. One morning, as she was preparing for a trip to Thailand with her husband to visit old friends and old haunts, she took time out to tell me about the birth of the CRCC.

It was the early 1970s, a time of turmoil, with the Civil Rights and Anti–Vietnam War movements raging in high dudgeon. Seeing that both groups were despised and abused by the police, the four women recognized that they needed a different approach to make a dent in the world of sexual violence.

"We had a lot to learn, but instead of looking at police as adversaries, we knew we had to become partners with them and they had to become partners with us," she says. "We had to bridge that gap."

Hammond, who had a more positive view of the police than the others, spent a lot of time working with the police, teaching them that victims needed compassion, not contempt, if they were to have any chance to heal and to help in prosecuting their assailants. Initially, because hotlines were sparse at the time, Hammond and Zander, who had been raped, took calls from people in any kind of trouble, but they soon decided to specialize in rape and sexual assault.

As a reporter for the *Call & Post* newspaper, Van Atta decided to do a story about their benevolent efforts and then never left. "I realized that's where I wanted to be, working on that issue," she says. "I had been assaulted twice, so I knew it was a problem, and I knew there wasn't anyone to turn to for help." She told her friend Schalamon, who had also been assaulted, and she wanted to be involved for the same reasons.

They recruited about twenty-five volunteers to operate the hotline, and got the YWCA (Young Women's Christian Alliance) to donate a telephone line and a small office with one desk, one telephone, and two people. From 6 p.m. to 10 p.m., it was the dedicated hotline. Two years later, a $50,000 grant from the Cleveland and George Gund foundations enabled them to make it a twenty-four-hour hotline with call forwarding so that should they receive a call from a hospital emergency room that someone had been raped, they could drop everything and go serve as an advocate for them and connect them to support services. They would also work with the doctors and nurses to try to collect evidence, should the victim want to pursue prosecution.

One of the first cases Van Atta became deeply involved in was the abduction and rape of a young woman who was held hostage by a group of Hells Angels for three days. They even carved a crude tattoo into her arm. When she finally ran away, she called the CRCC hotline. In most cases, the brutal rapists were tried and found not guilty, which still horrifies Van Atta. But the good news, she says, was it connected Van Atta with a couple of prosecutors who appreciated her help. So, she became the CRCC's liaison with the prosecutor's office. Meanwhile, Schalamon had begun to focus on medical training and working with emergency rooms, while Hammond concentrated on recruiting volunteers. With her newspaper background, Van Atta started to generate more public relations and continuing education efforts with police and prosecutors, and all four of them did public speaking events.

As they grew, they connected with other rape crisis centers in Boston, Santa Cruz, and Washington, DC. Some were focused on prosecution, others on feminist philosophies. They began to deal with more sexual assaults of children, within families, within the Catholic Church. They began to learn just how vulnerable women living on the streets were, since many were also mentally ill, addicted, impoverished, and disenfranchised. The founders understood rape was an issue of power and anger for women, but they also knew that men were raped, so they had men involved as volunteers and on their board from the start.

The four came away from an important meeting with the United Way very discouraged about their possibilities of receiving any funding, because they had met with a room full of white men. But the men stepped up, and their support enabled the CRCC to diversify its funding from foundations' one-time donations to other ongoing, stable sources.

After ten years, even though the organization was strong and the camaraderie among staff and volunteers was exceptional, handling all of the major tasks and seeing the worst of human behavior day after day started to wear the founders down. Burnout was inevitable. Van Atta had even taken a month-long vacation to Mexico, which refreshed her temporarily, but her renewed vigor soon faded after she returned. In the early 1980s, Schalamon and Van Atta left first, followed by Zander and Hammond a couple years later. But they had left the Cleveland Rape Crisis Center in a position to go nowhere but up.

Looking back, Van Atta wistfully sighs, "Of course, we were naïve, and we thought that we could accomplish more than we did. Though seeing the success of the Cleveland Rape Crisis Center now, we accomplished quite a bit."

———————

One of the hallmarks of that success is the thriving alumni group that meets once a month. The group is open to survivors who have graduated from their individual and group therapy programs at the center.

The therapist-facilitated gatherings range in size from four or five people to fifteen or so and run for an hour and a half. Each person gets ten minutes to talk about how they're doing, whether they're in a good or stressful and anxious place. They can share a poem or sing a song or tell a story. They can discuss something they're struggling with in their lives.

"We support each other," relates Jacqueline Pfadt. "You find validation, and you find understanding, and you find compassion and a connection, which is important because as a survivor in the outside world, you often feel very disconnected or isolated."

Pfadt wishes they had the group when she first came to the CRCC at seventeen in 1997, when they were still in the original building. She had been sexually abused and assaulted by an older boy as a child. She tried to suppress it and kept silent about it, but by high school she was constantly wrestling with her memories and began drinking heavily to tamp them down. Her mother found a letter she had written to her brother living in Washington, DC, that talked about her drinking. "I hid a bottle of liquor in my closet, because I just couldn't sleep and was melting down and self-destructing," Pfadt remembers. Fearing she would be grounded for the rest of her life, she decided to reveal everything to her mother, who then brought her to the Cleveland Rape Crisis Center.

She went to a therapist that she liked, and after turning eighteen and enrolling in Ashland University in western Ohio, she continued to visit her therapist secretly when she'd come home. When her therapist left in 2000, however, afraid to start all over with a new therapist, she didn't return. Although she was a 4.0 student in college, Pfadt admits that when she wasn't studying, she was "partying her ass off and getting really drunk." Still, she graduated with a degree in mathematics and computer science in 2002 and got married a year later. She worked for the US DoD Defense Finance and Accounting Service in software development and then project management. She earned her MBA at Lake Erie College in 2009 and now telecommutes for Homeland Security.

But not everything was smooth. Her memories of her sexual abuse continued to rumble underneath the surface. In 2011, her mother was diagnosed with ALS. Then her father-in-law was diagnosed with the same fatal disease. She dove into her work, became a workaholic. But every couple of months, she'd fall into a weekend drinking stupor to self-medicate her way through this dark period. Somehow, she was struggling her way through, even to the point of asking God to take her from this life. Until May 2013, when the final trigger was pulled. The three Cleveland women who had been abducted and held for ten years of physical and emotional torment—Amanda Berry, Gina DeJesus, and Michelle Knight—were discovered and freed. She suffered a total breakdown that led her to a return to the CRCC in June 2013.

She started seeing Annette Kent, a trauma therapist there, for six months, and then asked for recommendations to find a psychologist for long-term therapy, which she started in February 2014. "A lot of the center's approach is working on mindfulness, being present, and learning how to cope with your symptoms," Pfadt explains. "That was really important. That stabilized me where I could continue to function, but I knew I needed to dig deeper into the details."

Pfadt leveraged the CRCC's services, including the alumni group, to "make space for what happened to me and build courage to use my own voice." Last year, she was comfortable enough with her voice to join the CRCC's speakers bureau, make a video about her experiences with the organization, and write her own book, *PTSD Raw and Real: A Reason for Hope and Motivation to Fight On* (Christian Faith Publishing, 2016). The book chronicles the aftermath of her sexual abuse and the steps she took to fight it and not only get healthy but also find a way to once again thrive, enjoy her life, and be successful.

"I read my book every two to four weeks, because it's my guide," Pfadt says. "It's who I am and it calms me. I describe it as a miracle of repairing my soul." She hopes others who read it will gain from her willingness to break the silence and pursue the healing services she desperately needed, no matter how difficult or whatever other obstacles life threw at her. Her father, in fact, also reads it regularly to help him understand what his daughter had to endure as a result of her sexual abuse to become a survivor and thriver.

After taking an evening to share her harrowing story with me, Pfadt sums it up quite easily: "The Cleveland Rape Crisis Center saved my life."

In late April 2017, I observed a training session Mouncey conducted on the far eastern side of the Cleveland metro area in Lake County at Lake Health Hospital. Yet another component of the CRCC's strategic commitment to provide services to the outer edges of their territory, the program is another three-part series, like the one for the SAKTF. However, the attendees represent multiple disciplines, from police and prosecutors to nurses and other medical personnel, mental health specialists, and even some higher education professionals. Some attendees had previous experience with the CRCC; some were new to the entire realm of compassionate, victim-centered, trauma-informed care.

The CRCC had begun providing services to adjoining Geauga County six years before. Recognizing a similar need for special training, Kim Frazier, executive director of the Lake County Alcohol, Drug Addiction, and Mental Health Services (ADAMHS) Board, and Peggy Grant, MS, LPT, who heads the Victim Assistance Program for the Lake County Prosecutor's Office, proposed hiring the CRCC to raise awareness through their training programs.

When Mouncey and I debrief in the hospital cafeteria afterward, she talks about how having those key multidisciplinary players in the room speaks to a community's commitment to offering a diverse range of services for victims and survivors of sexual violence. Taking that step means change and improvements can happen.

"We can't just close our eyes anymore, and they can't close their eyes anymore," she says. "We have so much research and evidence for all of this now."

Reflecting on her decade-plus of experience with survivors of sexual violence and the substantial progression she's seen in the field, she concludes: "I started this work at the perfect time. There has been just so much learning for me and other researchers and writers who've caught on, and it's been just incredible how quickly the field has moved forward and how much we've learned in the last ten years. It's really good."

I leave. She stays to grab a little lunch before journeying back to her office downtown in the Halle Building at the Cleveland Rape Crisis Center.

Chapter 3

The Healers:
Elizabeth Booth, RN, SANE-A,
and Sexual Assault Nurse
Examiners

I T's 7:50 A.M. on a blustery January Sunday at the MetroHealth Parma Medical Center. Nestled within an expansive plain of low-rise industrial buildings in the suburb of Parma, this satellite facility stands roughly ten miles east of the main hospital, MetroHealth Medical Center, on Cleveland's Near West Side.

A few cars and ambulances loiter around the emergency department side of the building. The rest of the couple acres of parking lots, however, are barren, with snow devils swirling through as the grounds crew spreads salt on every inch of pavement and sidewalk, a preemptive measure to counter an impending afternoon snowstorm. Except for a security guard or two patrolling the halls, the pediatrics side of the building is empty.

Elizabeth Booth, RN, SANE-A, and Sexual Assault Nurse Examiner Coordinator for MetroHealth, has been hustling since 6:30 a.m., setting everything up in the simulation center at the back of the building. (The A in the SANE-A credential means she is certified to examine adolescents in addition to adults.) Several of her SANE nurses from the main hospital who will assist in this day-long session are helping her. Nine other nurses training to become SANEs are relaxing or reviewing their manuals, preparing to perform simulated forensic exams given to patients who have been raped or sexually assaulted.

Booth and her crew each wear black pants, a blue T-shirt, comfortable shoes, and a green warm-up pullover with "Forensic Nurse" embroidered on the left upper front and emblazoned in big white letters across the back.

Due to HIPAA regulations and just plain common sense, I can't observe an actual sexual assault nurse examination, so Booth suggested this training as the best way to see what they do when a rape or sexual assault patient comes to the hospital. The trainees are here because they have completed the forty hours of classroom training and three hundred clinical hours before they can do this practicum and then sit to take the certification exam. "Most candidates have never done a speculum exam or the head-to-toe exam," Booth says. "So what we always see in the morning is they stumble a little bit, trying to figure out the order of things, but by the afternoon, they've got their system down and put it all together."

Today, rather than using dummies, they will work with live standardized patients, what they refer to for this exercise as GTAs, short for gynecological training aides.

In a dark control room flanked by two examination rooms on the other side of one-way mirrors, Booth wrangles with the video monitoring audio communications equipment. The cameras are working fine, but the speakers for one of the exam rooms are not.

"We have headsets so we can hear everything that's going on in the room," she explains. "We use the little walkie-talkies to talk with them, because we want to make everything as real as possible so we don't want to have to keep going in the room to answer questions. We don't want to throw the GTAs off, either, because some of them really get into it."

Previously all of the simulation sessions have been held during the week, when the tech staff is available to help. Booth scheduled this one for the weekend to accommodate the work schedules of the GTAs. A third monitoring system is set up in the adjoining lunch/conference/ storage room connected to a GoPro camera in an examination room in the adjacent urology department that they've borrowed for today.

At 8:10 a.m.: Colleen Coyne-Hall, RN, enters the exam room with the working speakers, carrying her sealed Sexual Assault Kit (SAK), more popularly referred to as a rape kit. She sets it on top of the cart of drawers that contains all of the medical equipment she will need to complete the comprehensive, full-body examination. The primary intention of the Sexual Assault Nurse Examiner is to ensure that the victim is okay physically; the secondary purpose is to acquire as much DNA and physical evidence of their assault as possible to aid in the arrest and prosecution of their assailant. The SAK contains the swabs, bags, and microscope slides to collect and store the individual test evidence.

In the control room, Kady West, RN, SANE, who is overseeing the exam, can view the computer monitor with one camera angle focused on the patient and one on the nurse. However, for the next hour and a half, she will watch mostly through the one-way mirror.

Coyne-Hall begins by explaining to the patient that if she would like an advocate present, she can connect to the Cleveland Rape Crisis Center to get her one. The patient, who says her name is Sally Gates, asks whether the police will be notified so they can catch her rapist.

"Yes, but right now, we want to make sure you are physically healthy, mentally healthy, and then get and process the evidence so that he can be prosecuted," Coyne-Hall assures. "Our first priority is to take care of you. An advocate from the Rape Crisis Center is on their way now."

Coyne-Hall discusses the patient consent form with the patient, and Gates asks to be tested for sexually transmitted diseases. Assured that she will be, she signs the form.

The petite, short-haired blonde wears wire-frame glasses, a blue PITT sweatshirt over a brown T-shirt and red pants. Her real name is Amy Harmon. Prepped by Booth beforehand that the first exams of the day should be low-key, the veteran GTA has thought through the rest of her character for this morning's exercise and has the green light to improvise as necessary. Right now, she's sitting quietly on the side of the hospital bed, gently crying.

Coyne-Hall explains the photography consent form, saying that she does not have to agree to any photography, but if her case goes to court, photos can help the prosecutor obtain a conviction. Gates vacillates for a few moments and decides not to have any pictures taken.

Before moving on to documenting details about what happened to her patient, Coyne-Hall asks if she would like any water or coffee, and Gates rejects that request, too. She seems more confused and upset than angry or intractable.

"Were you assaulted by a complete stranger?" Coyne-Hall inquires.

"Yeah," Gates responds quietly.

"Adult male?"

"Yeah."

"By himself?"

"Yeah."

"Was he bleeding at all?"

"I punched him in the face. I swear he was a little chicken shit. He got off me as soon as I hit him."

"He did get vaginal penetration with his penis?"

"Yeah."

"Vaginal penetration with his fingers?" Coyne-Hall asks, continuing through the checklist and jotting notes.

"I don't know," Gates says after a slight pause.

"Anal penetration?"

"No."

"Not with his fingers or penis?"

"No."

"Did he ejaculate that you know of?"

"I don't think he did."

"Did he have any lubricant?"

"He spit on himself. He spit on his fingers."

"And then he put it on his penis?"

"Yeah."

"You said you have not showered."

"No.

"Changed your clothes?"

"No."

"Had a bowel movement?"

"No."

"Peed?"

"No."

"Thrown up?"

"No."

"Have you eaten any food?"

"No."

"Don't have a tampon in?"

"No. I have an IUD."

"Suspect did not use a condom?"

In the dark control room, West jots a note on a sheet of paper.

"No. That's why I wanted to get tested."

"We'll give you a complete exam."

"Boyfriend or husband?"

"I have a husband."

"Had consensual sex in the last ninety-six hours?"

Acting a little confused, Gates says, "Ninety-six hours?"

"This is Sunday at 8:23 a.m., so that would be Friday," Coyne-Hall states, though her math is a little off.

"Friday? Yeah."

"Time?"

"Maybe 10 p.m."

"Okay, good. Thank you. Now, I'm going to take down your assault story," Coyne-Hall says. "You can just relax and tell me your story. Would you like some water now?" Gates declines.

"I was doing my morning jog," Gates hesitantly begins. "I don't even know where he came from. . . . He had a gun."

"He had a gun?" Coyne-Hall interrupts. Gates nods her head and continues.

"Thought I was going to get robbed. I didn't know what else was going to happen."

"You're doing good. It's very brave of you to come forward," Coyne-Hall calmly says, trying her best to comfort Gates at every opportunity.

"He took me to an alley by a store. Pushed me down."

"On your face?"

"No, on my back. Yeah. Said, 'If you scream, I'll kill you.' I don't know. He pushed me down and was kissing my face and grabbing my breasts and then he started to unzip my pants. I tried to fight him off, but it's like he sat on my legs. He opened up his pants. He spat on his hand and was moving . . ." She motions up and down with her hand.

"He was moving it up and down on his penis?"

"Yes."

"Do you remember which hand?"

"No. Then he put himself inside of me. I started hitting him. Then he got off me and ran."

"Did you come right here from that?"

"No. I went home first. My husband doesn't know, though. I can't tell him."

"That's okay. That's completely fine," Coyne-Hall assures. "Do you remember anything else?"

"That's all I can tell you."

"I'm going to examine your shoulders first, since you said he pushed you down," Coyne-Hall informs Gates. "Then we'll get to the more invasive exam." Pushing her exam cart closer to the bed, she continues: "It's a horrible, trying event that you had to suffer through, but it's brave that you came in here."

Booth returns to the control room around 8:40 a.m. and asks West how it's going. She says fine, jotting another note on her comments form. Booth puts the headphones on to listen for a few minutes. Because the speakers weren't working in the other exam room next to the control room, Jennifer Beigie, RN, SANE (pronounced "Biggie"), sits in the corner, so she can answer any questions the nurse in training may have.

After checking Gates's back, neck, and head for injuries, Coyne-Hall wheels her cart closer to the head of the bed, places a Dry-Fast Swab Dryer on top of the cart, and plugs it into a wall socket. As she places the swab holder on top of the dryer, Gates asks what it is. "This big piece of equipment? It's just a dryer," her SANE-in-training explains. "We're going to put the swabs that we get from your mouth, fingernails, and skin in here to dry so that the police can collect it as evidence."

"I'm going to rub this between your teeth and your outer gum," says Coyne-Hall, who has put on latex-free gloves and picked up a Q-tip swab. She changes gloves after each test to prevent evidence contamination. She gently inserts the tip into Gates's mouth. "It's just a swab. I'm not hurting you, am I?"

"Nuhweh," Gates manages to respond. She's quiet and cooperative, but holds her jacket in her lap like a security blanket.

"Okay, we're going to do two more sets, between the left cheek and the lower gums, and then the right. You're doing good."

After completing a swabbing, she rubs the tip on a microscope slide, puts the slide into one of the plastic evidence bags she has preset on the cart, and then places each Q-tip in the swab holder and occasionally checks her watch to mark the time. The SANE swabs the evidence onto a slide for later testing, but the swab is kept and dried as a redundancy or in case the prosecutor needs to share evidence with the defendant's legal team. After real exams, to maintain the chain of evidence, a SAK is immediately placed into a locked storage vault until law enforcement officers can collect it.

Next are the fingernails. Coyne-Hall moistens the swab tips with sterile water. She rubs the first swab under one of Gates's fingernails so that she sees how to do it, and then she lets her swab the other fingernails on her right hand.

Later, Beigie, thirty-three, tells me that little exchange is a key part of a SANE's job: "You're the first person they see after they've just lost all control, and you're the one who starts the healing process by giving them back control. We teach our SANE nurses to focus on what the patient is going through and let them lead the exam. That's why you explain everything you are doing to the patient, why you are doing it, and that they have the right to decline any and all parts of the exam."

When Gates finishes the fingernails on her right hand, she tells Coyne-Hall that she was wearing gloves so her hands are probably not worth swabbing anyway.

"You never had them off?"

"No. It was cold."

"That's okay. I'm sure other little details will emerge," Coyne-Hall assures, as West jots a note on her sheet. "Now, we're going to swab the outside of your cheek to see if we can get some DNA from him kissing you there."

A few minutes later, at 8:55 a.m., having completed all of the swab tests, Coyne-Hall asks Gates to change into a hospital gown. To give her some privacy, she leaves and tells her to let her know when she's changed. She exits into the lunchroom. West jots a note. Two minutes later, West, who can see Gates is gowned, tells Coyne-Hall she can return. She knocks, asks permission to enter, and when Gates says yes, enters.

Eyeing the pile of clothing on a chair, Coyne-Hall asks, "Can I have your panties, please?" Gates nods. Coyne-Hall picks them up. "Do you want me to tie your gown?"

"I don't know. I don't know," Gates mumbles, as Coyne-Hall drops the panties into a large evidence envelope.

"May I take your pants?"

"No."

The point is to collect as much potential physical evidence as possible. Sometimes, however, even though most SANE programs today provide replacement clothing instead of making victims go home in gowns like they used to, patients don't want to part with a particular item because it possesses personal or monetary value. Later in the day, for example, one of the GTAs tells the nurse she can't give up her brassiere because her larger size is difficult to find, expensive, and that piece fits quite comfortably.

"Did he pull your hair at all?" Coyne-Hall asks, while searching through the cart.

"No."

West lifts the walkie-talkie to her mouth. "What are you looking for, if I can help you at all?"

"The speculum?"

"It's in the third or fourth drawer," West says.

"Thanks," says Coyne-Hall, who removes the speculum from the bottom drawer and places it on top of the cart. She then pulls out a special light used to test for a rapist's bodily fluids on a victim's skin. "Now, I'm going to check for any signs of injury. You doing okay? Do you need anything?"

"No."

"Can you help me pull up the gown? You have no signs of bruising on your belly. May I check your chest? You have no signs of bruising or injury." Coyne-Hall also checks Gates's legs. Then it's time for the pelvic exam. The hospital bed in this room has no stirrups or foot rests, as most hospital beds don't.

"Just have her slide down and put her legs on the end of the bed," West says. Knowing the drill, Gates has already started to position herself.

"Okay. Thank you." Once Gates is comfortably settled—as comfortable as lying spread-eagled on a hospital bed can be—Coyne-Hall says, "Right now, I'm going to comb your pubic hair for evidentiary value. You're okay?"

"Yeah."

"I'm going to put the comb on you now. This doesn't hurt, correct?"

"No. It just feels weird," Gates sighs.

"Now, I'm going to cut just a couple of the pubic hairs to check for dried semen for DNA analysis." Coyne-Hall pretends to cut the hairs and place them in a small evidence bag. She removes her gloves and puts on a new pair, as SANE nurses do for each part of the exam to prevent contamination of evidence.

"Sally, the next step is we're going to do an anal swab," Coyne-Hall gently cautions. "It will not go into your anus, just around it to see if any semen he may or may not have ejaculated drained down, again, for DNA testing. Could you please turn on your left side?"

Gates does as instructed. "I'm just going to lift the sheet." Coyne-Hall continues to explain her every move before she does it, especially when her prone patient can't see her. "I'm going to put my hand on your right butt cheek, so don't be alarmed. Sorry. Okay. You can put this back down."

Gates pulls the sheet back down. She's grown quiet. Coyne-Hall places swabs into the evidence bags, removes her gloves, jots some notes, looks at the next evidence envelope. At 9:15 a.m., she says: "This is the final step of the exam, okay?"

"Okay."

"We're going to swab the interior of the vagina. Okay?"

"Okay."

"Then we're going to discuss prophylactic treatment."

Coyne-Hall opens the sealed plastic bag and removes a plastic speculum for the vaginal inspection. "This is called a speculum."

"Okay."

"I use it to do the exam."

"Okay."

"I'll tell you everything I'm going to do as we go through the exam. If you feel any pain, we can readjust, okay?"

"Okay."

As she pulls her cart closer to the foot of the bed, Coyne-Hall says, "I'm going to raise the sheet." SANEs keep patients as completely covered as possible, except when they need to look at a particular part of their body. They want them to remain warm, as comfortable as possible, and with their dignity intact. "Can I have you scoot down, with your bottom towards the end of the bed."

"This is really not comfortable," Gates mutters.

Coyne-Hall spreads out her arms to indicate with her elbows where she would like Gates's suspended feet to be at the end of the bed. "Can I have you put your legs out so that they touch my arms? Okay. First, you're going to feel my hand touching your vagina. Let me know if I am hurting you. I'm just looking for any areas of injury or trauma." She examines the exterior of Gates's vagina.

"Now, I'm going to insert the speculum. I've lubricated it. I'm going to open the speculum now, so that I can look at your cervix for any injury. You're not in pain?"

"No."

"You're doing okay?"

"Yes."

"We're almost done, honey. You're doing great." After a few more moments: "You can scooch back now. We're done."

Gates's exhale is audible on the headphones and speakers in the control room. As she slides back, she grabs a tissue from a Kleenex box on the bed. Coyne-Hall swabs the speculum and then throws it into the wastebasket. She jots a few notes before saying, "We're going to discuss prophylaxis now. Would you rather be dressed?"

"Yes." Coyne-Hall leaves the room. West jots a note, and then a few minutes later, tells Coyne-Hall Gates is dressed so she can return. She proceeds to inform Gates about a variety of options she has for counseling, including calling the Cleveland Rape Crisis Center any time of day or night, what drugs are available in the event of STDs, and so on.

"We will notify you of your test results," Coyne-Hall says.

"Can you tell me more about my tests?" Gates inquires.

"That's all I can tell you for today. But you've taken a big step, and you are very brave for coming here," Coyne-Hall concludes, knowing full well Gates is not a real patient. She is still brave, however, for serving as a live person upon whom these SANEs-in-training can perfect their full examination techniques so they are better prepared when the time comes to grab a rape kit and enter an exam room where a real patient who's been raped or assaulted nervously waits.

At 9:29 a.m., West lifts her little neon-green walkie-talkie to her mouth, pushes the button, and says, "We're all done. I'll come in and talk to you." She picks up her notes and goes through the lunchroom into the examination room.

"Colleen, you did a great job. I have a couple of things."

"Just a couple?" Coyne-Hall says.

Inside the exam room, she's very serious and compassionate. Outside, though, she's more inclined to flash her quick wit. It was her first time through the exam with a live patient, and though she's well prepared, she was a little bit nervous trying to find where everything is located, how best to lay it out, and how to get through the entire head-to-toe and pelvic exams efficiently. She does the exam several more times, and each time it goes a little smoother, even though the patient scenarios change throughout the day.

"You have to give the patient more options regarding whether or not to do each test and that they can tell you to get the hell out of the room," West instructs. "Ask again for photo consent, because if you don't have all that in court, you will get denied.

"Try to get exact times when the rape happened, get a tighter window on the timeline on when they were attacked, when they got home, and so on.

"You don't want to offer them anything to eat or drink right away because you'll wash down the DNA. After the oral swabs, they can get something to drink or eat. If they have to pee, don't let them until after the speculum exam.

"You did great in getting the oral history. Very comforting throughout. A lot of note taking, though. Don't worry about documentation too much, because the patient is lying there waiting to finish.

"Take fingernail swabs and head hair, even if the patient says he didn't touch them there. We want every bit of evidence off you. Never leave the room when you have open evidence on your cart. At Metro, you can close the curtain and have the cart with you so the evidence is protected. You have great compassion, but we want the pants. He pulled them down. We want as much evidence as possible.

"Just have that all laid out before you need to use it. Take a minute and have everything ready for the speculum exam and the anal exam. You were great talking about the resources, but you didn't really talk about the STD treatments. The Cleveland Rape Crisis Center advocate and social worker will tell them more, but you can inform them more about the STD treatment options."

At the end of a SANE exam, the nurse is supposed to ask if the patient would like to be prophylactically medicated to prevent STDs, HIV, and pregnancy. The medication options include: ceftriaxone 250 mg IM (shot) to prevent gonorrhea; azithromycin 1 g PO (oral) to prevent chlamydia; Flagyl (metronidazole) 2 g PO to prevent trichomoniasis; hepatitis B vaccine, if needed; Plan B One-Step (levonorgestrel) 1.5 mg PO to prevent pregnancy; Raltegravir 400 mg PO twice a day; and Truvada (emtricitabine/tenofovir disoproxil fumarate) 300 mg/200 mg PO once a day to prevent HIV. The patient also needs a negative pregnancy urine test and blood work (HIV, CBC, BMP) before HIV prophylaxis meds can be given.

Upon completing her review of Coyne-Hall's exam, West turns to Gates, who's been a standardized patient in various capacities since 2007, for her thoughts: "I wanted a little more communication, because there was a lot of dead silence."

"How are your kids? Do you run 5Ks?" West suggests. "It's tough here. You'll be a lot more comfortable once someone is not sitting behind the glass. You did great for your first time. The first time I did it, I dropped the speculum! I know you'll be great this afternoon."

"So, I'm not getting sent home?" Coyne-Hall deadpans.

"No, you can still be a SANE," West says with a laugh. "Now give Amy her underwear back."

Putting her notes back in the control room, West, twenty-six, says she's been a certified SANE for about a year and a half. She's from Southern Ohio, but her ultimate goal was to work at MetroHealth. She started as a nurse at several smaller hospitals and then came to Cleveland to work at another major medical center, University Hospitals, to gain ER experience before applying to Metro. She likes the hectic activity of the level 1 trauma center emergency department, but prefers the one-on-one SANE exam. "When you get called in for a SANE case, it doesn't matter how long you take," she says. "You're focused on that one patient, so it's kind of a nice change from the fast pace of the ER."

She got involved with the training because she also enjoys teaching. West continues to learn a lot from her mentor Booth, whom she just called at 4 a.m. a few days earlier with a question about a sexual assault case as she was doing a post-assault examination. As for what she emphasizes with trainees, she says: "I just want to make sure that, if they get called in to testify in court, they're covering their butts! That they are documenting everything they need to, while making sure they're taking care of the victim well while getting that report, and that they're maintaining communication and explaining everything they're doing after the traumatic events that happened to the patient."

A few minutes later in the control room, after West leaves for the lunch break, the fully clothed Harmon, thirty-nine, tells me how she got into this gig. In 2007, she started as a standardized patient at the Free Medical Clinic of Greater Cleveland, now known as Circle Health Services, where medical and nursing students learn how to give pelvic and breast exams. Since then, she's carved out a full-time career as a "fake patient," working at a variety of universities and medical schools. She began working for Booth in 2011 and enjoys the camaraderie with the other GTAs.

The experience of the multiple exams in one day can be draining, but she's committed to helping advance the SANE training. "It's rewarding because I'm ensuring that women who have been sexually assaulted have a better experience," she informs, adding, "Self-care is important, though, so later tonight or even tomorrow, I'll be just kind of relaxing and not really overdoing it."

As for the invasive aspect of the pelvic exam, she says, "I don't mean to sound blasé about it, but there's lubricant, so it's not as bad, and that's just a natural part of the training." However, Harmon also reveals that she's been sexually assaulted twice, once during her freshman year at Case Western Reserve University in 1996 and once in 2002, a year after she graduated.

Her first assailant was never charged. "At the time, I thought I deserved it," Harmon reveals. "I was drunk and believed that it was my fault. I didn't report it because I wasn't even sure it was rape. I was nineteen."

In 2006, she went through Prolonged Exposure Therapy (PET), which is used to treat combat veterans with PTSD; it helped her make the breakthrough that she didn't deserve to be attacked and that it was, in fact, rape.

Her second attacker received probation. "Too many people do not report their sexual assaults because they are aware of how the system fails survivors or they don't think people will believe them, fight for them, care about them," she speculates. "There can be doubt that what happened really was rape. You have people with drug charges that are in prison longer than even rapists, so . . . ."

She went through the SANE exam herself in 2012, so she can draw on that personal experience. However, she tries to dissociate herself from that time. "In here, it's safe, and I can say to myself, it really didn't happen to me," she says. "This is what I'm doing now, so I'm being more in the present moment instead of looking backward. There are times when I use that background to help make me cry, and it makes it a little more cathartic, too."

I catch up with Coyne-Hall in the adjoining lunch/storage room as she's finishing her midday meal. She explains why one of the notes she received from West was about not using legal terms such as "suspect." In her previous career, she worked as a state trooper in the Chardon, Ohio, post. (Chardon is a far eastern suburb of Cleveland.) At the end of December 2016, she retired from the not-quite-as-far-east suburb of Willoughby Hills Police Department, where she handled undercover narcotics and prostitution cases and welfare fraud investigation. She also earned her EMT credentials more than twenty years ago.

After she retired from the state police, her husband, also a retired state trooper and a Baptist pastor for the Chardon jail, told her God wanted her to be a nurse. Raised Catholic, she joked, "Can't we just whip out a few Hail Marys?"

"No, no! You don't do that!" he chided.

"So, I said, 'Okay. We'll see.'" She studied at Lakeland Community College, where she earned straight As and added a BSN diploma to her psychology and advertising degrees. Currently, she's considering a master's degree in forensic nursing at Cleveland State University, but she works full time at Metro in the post-procedural care department and part-time at Cleveland's VA hospital, where she worked full time before starting at Metro.

Before she goes into the urology department exam room for her next exam, Coyne-Hall, forty-eight, reveals that she was raped at eighteen while attending Kent State University. She never told anyone or pursued law enforcement. Because of her police background, I press her on that decision not to tell anyone.

"Oh, no! I was Catholic. I was wrong. I was born guilty. So fifteen Hail Marys. It must have been my fault. I wasn't even drinking. I always dress like a dweeb, so I wasn't wearing anything provocative, and I got nothing in this department [indicating her chest] to show!"

She comments on her earlier examination, where she incorrectly used the special flashlight to identify bodily fluids. As a police officer, she was used to relying on the toluidine blue dye at crime scenes. "I was just nervous because I was being watched, and the patients, the GTAs, know way more about the exam procedure than I could ever know. But

I definitely appreciate any feedback. In all my years of law enforcement and nursing, we've never had live patients. These women are amazing. Amy was really excellent, too. I mean, she cried," she says, waiting a beat before quipping: "I don't know if she was crying because I suck and going, 'Damn, who did I get now?'"

In her next session, Coyne-Hall appears more relaxed and fluid. One minor challenge: adjusting to a completely different room configuration and determining the best location to put her equipment cart in the tight confines. She covers all the information she needs to convey to the patient, who is less cooperative, but all goes well. Afterward, Booth gives her a few notes.

Why is the GTA less cooperative? Booth explains in the control room that they up the ante in the afternoon, asking them to give the SANEs more pushback. They also enact different, more challenging scenarios, such as a patient who was on or has been given drugs or has been strangled to the point of passing out, which requires immediate medical attention before the SANE exam can continue. As she is saying this, out of the corner of my eye, I see Harmon up against the window. At first it appears that she's trying to look through the mirror. But I realize she's just using it to apply heavy makeup, brushing blue onto her face as if it were a Lautrec oil painting, and settling a thick wig. She's wearing a short floral summer dress. Her next scenario? An angry street prostitute who's been strangled. Quite a transformation.

Liz Booth grew up about an hour south of Cleveland in Rittman, Ohio, before her family moved east and north to Madison. By the time she got to high school, she aspired to be a veterinarian. She enrolled in Lakeland Community College, just east of Cleveland. When she learned how expensive vet school was and how little she'd earn as a vet, she followed in the footsteps of her father, Dale, and joined the US Air Force in September of 1997 to let them pay for it. She asked to become

either an air traffic controller or an EMT; eyeing her previous experience working in a vet's office and as a home health aide, the air force
sent her to EMT school. "That's when I fell in love with medicine and,
specifically, nursing," Booth recalls.

Honorably discharged as a senior airman in 2001, she returned full
time to Lakeland Community College's nursing school. To help pay her
way, Booth worked as a medical assistant at Akron Children's Hospital.
Her mentor there, Natalie Jedacek, MD, told her MetroHealth Medical Center, where Dr. Jedacek's mother worked, was looking for clinical
assistants and would be lucky to have her. She also told her that she
should avoid the step-down or medical floor positions, because her skills
would be better served in a more difficult environment. Encouraged,
the soft-spoken young nurse applied. There were also positions available in the neonatal intensive care unit or emergency department. A
self-confessed "adrenaline junkie" from her air force days, Booth chose
the ED.

Shortly after she was hired, Booth began to notice a stark deficiency
in the way rape and sexual assault victims were treated in Metro's ED.
Because it is Cleveland's only level 1 trauma center, emergency triage
was handled one way, she says: Life threatening first. Then everything
else. Unless a rape victim had sustained injuries requiring emergency
care, they had to be, well, patient.

One rape victim haunts her to this day. What happened that afternoon crystallized Booth's indefatigable motivation to do everything she
has done since. Petite, late twenties, clad in jeans and a sweatshirt, the
girl sat alone, crying, nose running, with a hollow look on her face as she
twirled the long blonde hair coursing down her back. Slumped forward
in a chair, knees bouncing nervously, she waited in Metro's perpetually
frenetic emergency room.

Booth watched from behind the nurses' station as the young woman
returned, asking to be examined again and again. Each time, the charge
nurse explained she would have to wait. More severely injured patients
were ahead of her. Growing increasingly agitated, the young woman

began pacing the hallway, cursing under her breath. Finally, after five or six hours of stomping and fuming, she screamed, "Give me a break!" and stormed out of the ER. That was in 2008, and it wasn't the last time Booth would become upset by the look of hopelessness in the eyes of a rape victim forced to endure the humiliating experience of feeling as if no one cared.

Booth still shudders at how victims who chose to wait were treated. Since none of the hospital staff were trained in how to provide a thorough medical and forensic rape examination, someone would crack open a manual and read the directions for the procedure.

"There was no other area of medicine where that would be acceptable," she says. "It just got me, so I thought, 'All right, I'll do the training myself and see where it goes.'"

Under her guidance, Metro signed a memorandum of understanding with Cuyahoga County to become a certified SANE program in 2010. She has trained more than thirty other nurses at Metro to become certified SANEs who can be on call. Metro is now a national training center for this growing specialty area of forensic nursing.

Ten years ago, approximately 200 such examination programs existed throughout the US, and now there are more than 772. Currently, the International Association of Forensic Nurses (IAFN) counts more than 3,700 members who are SANEs and other types of forensic nurses. In 2000, there were 1,966 members.

"We do see it as a growing field," says Sally Laskey, then-CEO of the International Association of Forensic Nurses in Elkridge, Maryland. "We see that the need is ever-increasing. The shortage of qualified nurses is a challenge, but we see communities looking at ways that they can provide these services, and with the support of hospital administrators and other community-based programs, we will see an increase.

"The dialogue that is happening at the national level in the US has put more attention on forensic nursing programs and specifically around Sexual Assault Nurse Examiner programs. The Violence Against

Women Act of 1994 has provided funding for some of those programs, so we have seen an increase as there's been more dialogue and federal legislation supporting SANE practice as a response to violence."

A recent IAFN poll revealed that some states have only one certified program, whereas Ohio has the most, with eighty.

"We are fortunate in Northeast Ohio to have four hospitals with established programs, but a lot of our rural areas still don't have easy access," Booth says.

"The issue of access is critical," Laskey comments. "We're working on ways to assist communities with building access to care in the way that makes the most sense for that community. Making sure no one is ever turned away from services is a key issue for us."

While more SANEs are needed, as well as an increased awareness that they even exist to help patients, a deeper cultural change has already taken hold. Booth and her SANE nurses interact with the police almost daily. Forced to hold one of our first meetings in the hospital café because her office is stacked floor to ceiling with boxes of new clothes and toiletries donated for victims through a recent campaign, Booth tells me of the important change she has seen: "If the frontline person didn't believe the survivor of a sexual assault, the patient would just take off before we could do our exam. Now that they're being believed and treated well, they stay and complete the entire extensive and exhausting examination."

Cooperative patients are more inclined to participate in the prosecution and testify in court, something Booth and her nurses do regularly themselves. Also, the victims' healing process is improved, since they are more willing to seek counseling and discuss the assault with family members and friends who can support them.

The police interviews she hears today no longer lead with questions like: What were you wearing? How much did you drink? Were you doing drugs? Instead, they focus immediately on the assault. Often officers will stay until the person's SANE examination is finished so that they can take the person home or to a safe location.

At Metro, Booth still handles many of the cases herself. But Beigie, who was one of two other nurses that Booth convinced to become certified in the specialty roughly a year after she started at Metro, remembers the early days when the three handled more than twelve hundred on-call hours before they added other SANEs.

"We're a trauma center, so the doctors didn't want to do the rape exams, because they take a long time," Beigie recalls during her lunch break. "Once you open a kit, you can't leave it, so they didn't understand the chain of custody process. They didn't want to go to court, either. So, we would watch those poor sexual assault patients languish for hours."

She's seen a tremendous change, however, in the past decade. "Now that we have the SANE program, it's awesome. The doctors love us because they know we're there to help them out. They trust our assessment skills, and they trust our knowledge base of how we treat patients, and they're willing to help us out. It's been a long time coming, and we still have kinks like everybody does, but people know now that we're here at Metro, and SANE nurses even get called into the ICU to help there."

By late afternoon of the training, I've given up asking what anyone thinks of Booth, because the uniform response is, "Oh, I love Liz." "Liz is very easygoing, but she knows what she's doing," Beigie offers. "She's a great resource. She never makes me feel stupid for asking a question. She's always able to answer any questions, because she's very knowledgeable. She's made great contacts throughout Cuyahoga County, and she gets it out there that we have a great program, so we learn from all of that."

The SANE exam has changed over the past few years, too, starting with the elimination of blood collection that required a finger poke and placement of three drops of the patient's blood on a special tissue. Nurses are no longer required to collect head and pubic hair.

Significantly more emphasis has been placed on ensuring the emotional health of the patient, Booth says, as well as allowing them to have complete control of the exam and participation in the legal system. More emphasis on debunking the rape myths and ensuring that the patient understands that it was not her or his fault.

"Collaboration amongst the various agencies is a must now, ensuring that we work together as a team in the best interest of each individual sexual assault patient," Booth adds. "Every patient will have different needs that need to be addressed."

In addition to the MetroHealth System, the Cleveland Clinic has SANE programs at three of its hospital facilities, and University Hospitals has a pediatric SANE at Rainbow Babies and Children's Hospital and an adult program, both on its main campus. The Clinic and UH arc the city's two major medical institutions.

"We work together constantly, ignoring the fact that we work for separate health care institutions," Booth says. "All we are interested in is providing the best care for our patients that are affected by sexual violence. I can go to any one of the coordinators for advice and consider them a part of my family. I would not have been able to develop the SANE program at Metro without the help from the other coordinators, who already had established SANE programs in their hospitals and years of experience."

Booth and her staff have ensured that when a sexual assault victim arrives, the hospital's ED nurses or social workers immediately contact the Cleveland Rape Crisis Center to send an advocate for the victim. The person assists and comforts the victim until the person can be treated in a private, separate area of the ED. Typical wait time: thirty minutes. No one waits more than an hour. No one.

Almost ten years after stepping up to help victims of sexual violence, Booth ensures that the improvements continue. In 2015, she participated in a *Shark Tank*–style competition held by the hospital to fund innovative projects. The quiet, self-deprecating Booth had to stand before a panel of five judges to present her idea for a new, freestanding SANE unit.

"When she was talking about herself, she was anxious, clearly jittery, and didn't want to be up there," says Akram Boutros, MD, FACHE, president and CEO of MetroHealth. Metro's Think Tank competition was his brainchild. "As soon as she transitioned to speaking about the women and men that she's helped, all that went away, and she became incredibly confident."

For her presentation, Booth had applied makeup used by the GTAs during simulations and cried to depict a battered rape victim's experience in the ER and underscore the critical need for a separate SANE unit.

"It was very powerful," Dr. Boutros recalls. "We were all palpably uncomfortable watching her."

Out of 105 submissions, Booth was one of six approved for funding. She was awarded $100,000. Several days before the simulation training, Dr. Boutros called Booth in for a private meeting to assure her they had identified the best space to accommodate all of her space and equipment needs, including a sizable closet to hold new clothing for adults and children who leave theirs as evidence. Construction of the new SANE unit was scheduled to begin in 2017 but was delayed as Metro continues to design the complete reconstruction and layout of its campus.

Several times over the past year, Booth climbed into her gray 2012 Honda Odyssey minivan and drove several miles west of Metro to a Sears Outlet Store in the suburb of Fairview Park. Tonight, she's there to meet a friend and supporter, Mike Pistorino. Since learning of Metro's need for clothing for patients, Pistorino has teased, chided, and cajoled the store into donating several thousand items of children's clothing.

Himself a victim of childhood rape, Pistorino is now a staunch advocate for preventing child abuse and a popular local and national speaker about healthy recovery for survivors. While waiting for Booth to meet him in the parking lot, he goofs around with his "minions," three young daughters, at one point taking selfies with them around several large boxes and bags containing 1,600 pieces in a back storage room. The last batch a couple of months earlier included racks and hangers.

Two other off-duty nurses arrive in their cars to help load and transport the clothing back to the hospital. Booth will use the clothes whenever they are needed, but she has also begun to stockpile for the walk-in closet designed specifically for her new SANE unit. Thanks to Pistorino's deal with Sears, she can also disburse some of the growing stockpile to the other SANE programs in Cleveland.

"Giving a sexual assault patient new clothes may seem trivial to many people, but to us, it is our way of reassuring them that they have value and are not 'dirty and used up,' like many of our patients describe," Booth says. "The fact that so many people donated these clothes further provides proof to our patients that they have support, not just from us, but from the entire community."

Currently, Booth is pursuing her family nurse practitioner credentials through Chamberlain College of Nursing and expects to finish in June 2018. Watching her mom struggle and eventually lose her battle with common variable immune deficiency when physicians took too long to diagnose her condition, she was inspired to pursue the FNP credentials.

In her increasingly precious free time, Booth is a fervid equestrian. Lately she has been giving more time to raising foster children, including a three-year-old boy, Colin, whom she later adopted in June 2017. Her parents participated in the foster care program for several years, and her two sisters have been foster parents. Her youngest sister, Brianne, ended up adopting a boy, and her middle sister, Andria, adopted three foster children.

Whenever Booth is on call, she knows she can drop Colin off at Andria's house, no matter the time, if she needs to treat and test a rape or sexual assault victim at Metro.

To that end, the new SANE unit, Booth believes, will create a safer and quieter setting to care for patients that will feel more like a home, not a hospital. "Even as adults, when we are hurt and traumatized, we long for the comforts of home," she says. "I hope that sexual assault patients will start their healing process within the new SANE center. I will be able to take my time caring for my patients, instead of feeling pressure to get them discharged to open a room for a new ED patient."**

** Author's Note: In September 2017, Booth left MetroHealth to pursue her family nurse practitioner credentials, which require twenty to thirty unpaid clinical hours per week in addition to classwork. She should graduate in June 2018. Beigie passed her SANE-A exam in November 2017 and in January 2018 accepted the SANE coordinator position to replace Booth. "I have a lot to do, but I am motivated and ready to put in the work," she told me.

Chapter 4

The Enlightened Leader: Commander James McPike and the CPD Sex Crimes and Child Abuse Unit

ONE OF THE first policies Sergeant James McPike implemented when he became head of the Sex Crimes and Child Abuse Unit at the Cleveland Police Department in 2011 may appear small on the surface—a change of one word on police reports—but represents a radical departure and improvement in police practices for sex crimes.

"I'm a little bit different," he allows. "When I first took over, I requested a DN, a divisional notice, go out that we no longer use the title 'alleged' in our police reports. I did not like that, particularly in sexual assault reports. In essence, what we were telling a victim right up front was, 'I don't believe you.'"

The policy was immediately approved and executed. Should an officer submit a report using that title, McPike would fax it back to their supervisor who signed off on it with a copy of the divisional notice and a request to change the wording.

"So, I haven't seen an alleged sexual assault report in a long time now," he says, almost ten years later.

Also not long after he assumed the small, private, central office overlooking the cubicles in Sex Crimes, McPike initiated a program to have his detectives work directly with advocates from the Cleveland Rape Crisis Center who were assigned to victims from Day 1 of a case. In an unprecedented move for the Cleveland constabulary, the CPD funded an advocate to work with the unit full time and later added a second. The advocates are embedded in the unit, with a directly adjacent office. They advise victims on counseling, health care advocacy, and other services available through the CRCC. They also guide victims through the police interview and investigation and the typically convoluted justice system process.

In an interview with Sondra Miller, president and CEO of the Cleveland Rape Crisis Center, she told me, "Our partnership with the Cleveland Police Department has never been as strong as it is now. The Sowell case moved us in that direction."

McPike took over the Sex Crimes Unit a couple of years after the notorious Anthony Sowell case, which led to several changes in the department. The CPD refurbished the unit's offices to make them less imposing to victims. The department was painted with softer, warmer colors, and two private rooms were added so that detectives would no longer have to interview victims in an open bullpen.

For McPike and his detectives, the Sowell case reinforced two lessons: First, sexual predators often attack people who live on the margins of society, because they are easier prey and are less likely to report their crimes or be believed if they do report. Since then, CPD's attitude toward victims has changed due to better understanding of the importance of believing all victims and because of a second lesson.

"I tell police officers, 'Please do not judge what you are hearing, because sometimes the craziest story could be the truth,'" says McPike. "If the first-responding officers judge the victims, it causes them to have doubts, and then they become less likely to cooperate with the detectives' investigation."

It's well known now that McPike has a zero-tolerance policy for any officer under his command who does not treat a victim with kindness. Booth told me she remembered one time many years ago when a detective was rude to a nurse and a victim, and McPike chastised him and made him apologize to both. She hasn't seen that since, and she considers the police valuable partners in their efforts to help victims. She also knows McPike is only a phone call away if she has a question or concern. He's also famous for making himself readily available to all of the community partners involved in fighting sexual violence.

"Every new employee I get, particularly as a commander now, I sit down and set expectations," McPike says. "One of my key expectations is we are going to deal with people with compassion and empathy. They come to us at the worst moments in their lives. They deserve a little respect. There are a lot more expectations of us, but that's part of it. So my message has always been, 'We need to treat people well.'"

While he says that is more the rule than the exception now, he's experienced enough to understand that police can have bad days, too. "That happens, because the workload is horrible," he explains, with Sex Crimes and Child Abuse detectives typically juggling twenty-five to thirty cases at a time, and often up to around one hundred cases a year. "The caseload drove me nuts when I was a detective. I cared about my cases, and I had difficulty explaining to a victim why I hadn't touched her case in a month. She didn't know that I was just getting slammed with investigations and fresh arrests. But our victims deserve better than that."

That's why one of McPike's priorities these days as a commander is solving staffing deficiencies. Sex Crimes, for example, is meant to have sixteen detectives, which has rarely happened, either because of retirements or transfers. A new staffing plan he has recently put into place will bring the standard total for the unit up to twenty detectives. "I believe a manageable caseload in Sex Crimes is under twenty cases at a time," he states.

I first meet McPike in April 2014 when he was the lieutenant in charge of the unit. Since then, his jaunt along the fast track to leadership elevated him to captain in July 2015, and he was then assigned to be his commander's executive officer, and then commander, one of twelve in the CPD. The at-will promotion to commander at the end of April 2016 came as "a complete surprise and a shock," after his commander resigned unexpectedly. "I really wanted to be an executive officer for a while, because I have ideas in my head to bring to the department," he says. "That's very difficult when you don't have enough personnel around to do those things."

Today, as a commander he is responsible for ten units, including Sex Crimes and Child Abuse, Domestic Violence, Homicide, and Financial Crimes. He oversees one hundred employees and at that time had thirty personnel openings. By the end of 2017, the perpetual innovator was pushing to implement an upgrade to an electronic document format for the Statement Unit he also manages. The unit is responsible for handling paper documents for all grand jury packages for the entire police department. "Right now, it's an absolute waste of trees," McPike sighs.

After catching up for fifteen minutes, we're on our way to a meeting I'm sitting in on. McPike will discuss how CPD is about to completely change its organizational structure with the commander of SWAT, Narcotics, and the Gang Impact Unit.

As he grabs the files he needs for the meeting, I check out the personal appointments in his spacious corner office with panoramic views of downtown Cleveland that feature framed photos of his family on his book shelves, including some snaps at the beach (his self-proclaimed "happy place"). A colorful, baked-glass palm tree decoration he made sits atop a file cabinet near his desk. Born in Cleveland, he lived in Florida twice as a youth, and attended Brandon High School just east of Tampa. His parents and his brother's family still live in the Tampa Bay area, so those are the beaches he tends to visit. "Just not often enough," he says.

The first police officer in his family, McPike claims it was almost accidental. In his "trying to find myself" stage, he flirted briefly with college and considered becoming a history teacher. But at twenty-six, he took the exam on a whim and was accepted into the Cleveland Police Department in June 1995. Shortly after, he transferred his credits to Cleveland State University, attending part-time until he earned his BA in sociology.

He served as a patrolman until 2002, when he was detailed to the Sex Crimes and Child Abuse Unit as a detective. In 2008, he was promoted to the rank of sergeant and assigned to supervise officers in the 4th District before returning to the Sex Crimes Unit four years later.

After the half-hour meeting, McPike takes me down to the Sex Crimes Unit on the sixth floor. A couple days earlier, I spent a day interviewing a few of the detectives, hanging out primarily with Charlie McNeely. We were supposed to go on a ride-along, but the unit shares four cars, and all of them were out in the field. It is yet another occasional resource challenge for the unit should a detective need a car, though they always have plenty of paperwork, phone calls, and computer searching to do while waiting. So, we've rescheduled for today, after my meeting with Commander McPike.

When we walk in, Detective McNeely is ready to roll. He's been trying to connect to a woman victim in a particularly brutal rape. He's spoken to her on the phone, but when he tries to confirm a time, she won't commit, or commits to a time and then isn't home when he arrives. He talked with her this morning to let her know he will visit her home to show her a photo lineup.

So amped to get this done, McNeely has already taken the keys from the blue plastic coffee can where they are stored in Sergeant Eugene Young's office, the one McPike formerly occupied as the officer in charge.

McPike lingers in the unit for a while, chatting with different detectives about their cases. One detective thanks him for letting him take a training session on gang behaviors that was an especially eye-opening and educational experience. He and McNeely, who he trained eleven years ago when McNeely joined the unit and he was still a detective himself, talk for a few minutes outside of the lunchroom while they both wait for a fresh pot of coffee to brew.

McNeely explains that while one suspect's DNA showed up in the victim's rape kit, he was able to identify two other potential suspects simply "through great detective work." Turning to look at the bustling detectives' cubicle farm, he says, "Who did it for you?"

At 6'2", McPike resembles a rangy outside linebacker, so not the kind of officer a perp would try to mess with when he is patrolling in a zone car. With law-abiding citizens, he's quite affable, intelligent, and quick-witted. All kidding aside, McPike tells me that over the years, he's assigned several difficult serial rapist cases to McNeely, who tracked down and arrested all of the offenders.

Detective Brian Kellum joins us. McNeely needs a partner to serve as what's known as "a blind administrator" for the photo lineup. Kellum has plenty of cases of his own, so he doesn't know any details of McNeely's case and has not seen any of the information or photos of the potential suspects the senior detective has compiled. When I first met him a couple days before, McNeely gave me "a butler's tour, not a chef's tour" of the sixth floor, which included the city jail, where the no-longer-used lineup room is located. "We're not in Hollywood," he observed. "We're in the neighborhood."

A shade to the left of eccentric, McNeely keeps his active cases in a file folder on his desk behind a photo of himself playing one of the giant GuitarMania public art guitars in front of the Rock and Roll Hall of Fame and Museum. Almost-done files, however, are stored behind a photo of Van Halen. On his cubicle wall is a Nelson Mandela photo and quotation: "It always seems impossible until it's done."

Keys in hand, McNeely signals that we're ready to go search for the car down in the police section of the parking garage beneath CPD headquarters. The dynamic detective who hates guns and never fired one until he prepared for the police academy mentions that he has strapped his 9mm onto his hip. Typically, he never wears it around the office like everyone else but instead keeps it in his briefcase. "Victims are traumatized enough," he rationalizes. "So, I don't like to wear it when I'm talking to a victim or a witness, especially if it's a child. I want them to be comfortable, and I don't want them saying, 'Is that a gun?'" Plus, he wants to be comfortable, and a gun doesn't particularly go well with his trademark untucked sport shirt and slacks.

Detectives McNeely and Kellum and I take the elevator down to the adequately labeled bowels of the building, the parking garage, where we search for a license plate attached to an intentionally nondescript Ford Taurus. Unlike a zone car, the back doors have handles inside, so the officers don't need to let me out every time we come to a stop, although Kellum, who drives, can lock the back doors and windows from the front.

On our way to the victim's home in a tough, fairly run-down East Side neighborhood of Cleveland off Kinsman Road, I ask McNeely about how detectives partner and work together. On this day in late June, Detective Kellum is in his first six months with the unit, closing in on three months on July 8, so still on probation. He's thirty-eight, the same age as McNeely was ten years ago when he became a detective, as McNeely points out in an email a few days later. He also lives in the same neighborhood. With a little maneuvering by his father after he retired, McNeely wears the same number his dad did, #2217. All meaning? "Carl Jung and synchronicity got nothing on your Cleveland Police Department."

"There is no detective training manual and detective school," McNeely says, turning back to face me and my tape recorder in the back seat. "So, they leave it up to other detectives to train them. Like I was trained by McPike. I was trained by Lieutenant Dan Ross, and a little bit by Jim Butler, who later became my partner. They charged me with training Brian, so if he screws up, it's on me. Different people come to the bureau from different places, different skill levels, different tools. You can imagine the bureau for Sex Crimes and Child Abuse is not for everybody."

"Originally, I was in the 4th District, and then I was in Technology Integration Unit," says Kellum, eyeing me in the rearview mirror.

"Computer tech whizz. Galls him that my iPod still has a dial on it."

"And he still occasionally makes me use a typewriter."

"Yes! God bless him. What's enjoyable now is when Brian finishes his probation in one hundred twenty days, they'll evaluate him and, in the words of The Clash, should he stay or should he go?," explains McNeely, who loves rock music—He's got tickets to see U2's thirtieth anniversary of *The Joshua Tree* album tour at FirstEnergy Stadium a week later—and superheroes. His screensaver is the Hulk, and throughout the day he refers to Kellum as The Boy Wonder and me as Clark Kent.

"They'll come to the supervisors and they'll engage me: How was your young squire?" McNeely continues, as Kellum wends his way through streets he knows intimately from his time in the 4th District. "I will tell them what I like and what I don't like. Unless he's a complete screwball, he should be fine. A lot of it is the paperwork, but that's the simple part. A rhesus monkey can do the paperwork.

"Different things such as Brian sat in on interviews, does search warrants with me, you have to just learn from doing. So, I try to include Brian in many interviews. But he's progressed enough in just his first sixty days that he is already getting cases of his own.

"It's enjoyable to watch. I truly enjoy working with Brian. They update our shifts every six months, and Brian may get bumped off this shift. There may be someone with seniority that wants to come on this later afternoon shift. Which would be unfortunate because I want to keep working with Brian even after he's off probation. I'd like Brian to be my partner.

"Not just because of the training, but because I genuinely enjoy working with him. He's shown an aptitude for it. In addition, he's gotten to the point now where even with an aptitude for the paperwork and things around it, he's pretty engaging when it comes to talking with people. That's a kind of skill that if you have it, the more you do it, the better you will get at it. He's only going to get better."

"Do partners always go out together?" I inquire.

"It depends. Like yesterday, I was doing something, I think I was eating lunch, actually. And another detective asked Brian to assist her with an interview. I don't mind doing that. The more the merrier. He may learn something from another detective that I wouldn't teach him."

"I will never be able to get her style down," Kellum says. "Because she like kind of turns into a grade school teacher that you don't want to disappoint."

"It's an amazing interview [style] to watch," McNeely concurs. "People just want to tell her everything. You don't want to disappoint Sister Mary."

"Exactly what it is," Kellum avers.

"You'll see everybody else has their own style," McNeely continues. "Eventually, over a period of time, and it takes years, you will pick up your own style. Some people say very little. They simply ask questions and let these people babble on. It's their style, it works for them."

"What was McPike's style as a detective?" I ask.

"I picked up a lot from him. He was very engaging in the sense that he wanted people to talk to him. In a couple of statements when I would sit in with him, he would talk to [them]. . . . You want them to be comfortable. And that can be everything from how you talk to them, how you look, I mean little things you'll pick up.

"McPike was really good, he taught me a lot of lessons. He had a lot of teachable moments. He would tell you things. Like one of the things he always told me was 'never start with bullshit.' Maybe the case is a little sketchy, it's open. Don't start with bullshit. You'll get there soon enough. The truth stands on its own. If you start at bullshit, you never leave bullshit. Always proceed like they're telling the truth. And if you're doing your job, you're doing it right, and if it is bullshit, you'll get there. You'll figure that out. Never start there.

"Also, with child abuse cases . . . Over a period of time you'll pick up on different cues, like not every boy likes Iron Man, not every girl likes *My Little Pony*. But every kid likes breakfast cereal. I've never met a child in my life that didn't like breakfast cereal. You know, what'd you have for breakfast? *Oh, cereal.* What kind of cereal? I had Lucky Charms. *Oh, I had Cinnamon Toast Crunch. That's my favorite.* Then we'll start talking about Cinnamon Toast Crunch. Kids open up to that. Ever meet a kid that doesn't like breakfast cereal?

"You can sit there with a child of physical abuse and spend two hours talking about your cereals. Just to get them to loosen up. A little of that you just pick up over the years."

Turning to Kellum, he says: "I stopped at Taco Tontos. Last night, I'm not going to lie to you."

"Ohhhh."

"I was so pissed, on the way home, I stopped to get a burrito."

"Now you're not going to want one today."

"No, I'm going to want it today, trust me. You're buying. I definitely want my burrito today. We try to make it that whoever is in the office Friday nights will get burritos. We usually get the shrimp burritos. They have a Lenten special every Friday all year long. Shrimp and fish burritos and tacos."

We still need another ten minutes or so to get to the victim's house. I ask McNeely to discuss what he wants to accomplish on this run.

"So, we're going to a house on 146th Street. And this is the victim. Here."

McNeely hands me the report to read.

"She had made a rape report which appears to be an after-hours spot in a house near St. Clair and 93rd. She had hung out one night. She may have gone there willingly. When she's at this house, everything kind of turned on her. Based on the initial police report, she was attacked and sexually assaulted by up to three males. It's kind of hard to read the way the report is written, the police report is only a summary. It's just the first responders' summary account. That's why we like to talk to the victims in person. Formal statements. I've had a hard time getting ahold of her. I've been to her house twice. Then I found out she moved. Found the new address, went to that house, they've never heard of her. So, I found out she was having a custody hearing. She has some family court drama going on. So, I went to her family court hearing to try and meet up with her. For the only reason to make contact with this victim. And that fell through as well. But I was able to obtain some better info for her, and I've talked to her on the phone several times. I've tried to set appointments.

"I don't want to close this case. I can right now. I've done my certified letters. I've done my four to five phone calls. I've done my two to three home visits. I can legitimately close this case, but I don't want to. It's a pretty horrific rape when you read the report. So, I talked to her a couple of times and I let her know, hey, listen, you're not in trouble with me, I know I'm the police, but you're not in trouble. I talked to her last night before I left and let her know, hey, we're going to come by sometime after ten because she works three to eleven. I want to talk to her and show her some photo lineups. I've identified what I think are some of the perpetrators in her case. I want to show her these photo lineups. And since I'm going to have her on scene, try to minimize my time with this, I'm going to take a formal statement from her."

McNeely then explains how his preference is to take all interviews in the Sex Crimes offices. He believes detectives should always have the "home field advantage" when taking formal statements from victims, witnesses, or suspects, but sometimes situations dictate otherwise. One of the potential problems today is there can be a lot of noise and distractions at someone's home. He has a small digital tape recorder with him to record the interview, which he then types up into a narrative story form. Some detectives prefer to present it in an outline form. Interview and report style both vary, according to the individual detective. He then makes two copies of the MP3 file of the interview, one for his records and one to send to the prosecutor's office.

"I'd prefer home field advantage," he continues. "But you know what? I really want to get moving on this. These guys that raped her, these guys are pretty bad actors. There are some gang issues with them. Some photos of them on Snapchat, Instagram with guns, drugs, large sums of money. You don't have to be the second coming of Eliott Ness [the 1920s Prohibition agent who worked as Cleveland's director of public safety in the mid-1930s] to figure out what bad news these guys are. So, we're going to her house right now, I'm going to take the time to introduce myself and give her my card. And introduce you all. I'm going to tell her you're an observer just to make her comfortable. And I'm going to introduce Brian here to her. I'll talk with her. I'll tell her a stupid joke or something to make her comfortable. Then, 'Hey listen, let's get started now. I'm going to take your formal statement, okay?' Then I'll put my recorder on, and she and I are just going to talk."

He details what he'll be discussing with her, descriptions of the men, what they looked like, what they were wearing, what they said, descriptions of the home, anything she remembers, types and colors of cars they drove or that were in the driveway, and so on. "I want her to describe it as best she can," he says.

After that, he will have Detective Kellum sit with her in his role as the impartial or blind administrator and show her the series of photographs McNeely has assembled. He cannot say anything during this portion of the interview, so that he does not in any way tip her off to who he thinks are the suspects. Should she select any of the photos, Kellum will then ask her where she knows that person from and conduct a thorough interview about who he is and how she knows him.

"Then, when we're done talking with her, I'm going to give her my card, and I'm going to talk to her and tell her about getting some aftercare counseling at the Rape Crisis Center where there are victim's advocates and everything.

"I'm going to tell her what to expect. You know, I'm going to tell her I've developed some suspects, they may be arrested in the coming days. Once people start getting arrested, they're going to be charged with a crime. You should be hearing from the prosecutor's office in the coming weeks. After I arrest this guy, if you don't hear from somebody at the prosecutor's office in two weeks, give me a call. They get busy like we do. Now the wheels of justice are in motion."

McNeely says that the law now requires recorded statements, but when he started they used to sit at their typewriters and pound out typed statements from people they were interviewing. In classic detective style, he typed about eleven words a minute with ten mistakes, he confirms. The unit interview rooms have video recording, and some detectives use their laptops in the field to shoot video.

"I've done video recordings from time to time, but our video recording system isn't terribly reliable," McNeely says. "So, I prefer audio."

He turns to me in the back seat. "That good enough?"

"Yep."

As expected, the victim is nowhere to be found. When we pull up to where her house should be, the addresses are out of alignment. It's an odd number but on the even side of the street. The address is not visible on the house. McNeely first knocks on the door of the house next to where the number should be. When a woman comes to the door, he calmly informs her that he is a detective, shows her his badge, and says he's looking for a woman who is a victim and is not in trouble. He's there to help her. The lady comes out, and he sits on her front stoop as they chat for a few minutes. A younger woman who lives upstairs comes down. She thought it was someone else, but then quickly realizes he's a detective. Kellum and I stand in the driveway apron watching the three chat. He's a little quieter than the gregarious McNeely, and he is there to make sure his partner is safe. I tell him I can see McNeely opening a bar after he retires. He tells me he's already got a name picked out. (McNeely tells me later that his wife, Melissa Miller, has informed him she has different plans for their retirement.)

Eventually, we make our way across the street, where a woman had been sitting on a porch but went inside fairly quickly. They think she may have been smoking weed. McNeely knocks on the front door, but there's no answer. While he explains his friendly approach to talking with people and how he can't understand police officers who are cockier and more demanding (which does nothing but make people hate them and stay silent), Kellum goes around the side and talks to the lady through an open window. She is a caretaker and cook for an elderly man who lives on the first floor. She lets us in, and Kellum talks to her while McNeely and I go into the man's bedroom. He's lying on his side in bed with extra pillows, obviously uncomfortable, watching a TV on a dresser in the corner.

"How are you doing, how are you feeling, sir?" McNeely asks.

"I'm ninety-three. How do you think I'm doing?" the elderly man drawls.

"Ninety-three. God bless you, sir."

"God didn't bless me. He left me like this. If he blessed me, he'd take me outta here."

"Well, God bless you, sir, either way. Have you seen the young lady who lives upstairs today at all?"

"She took her baby, got in her car, and left about fifteen minutes ago," he says.

McNeely thanks him. He and Kellum thank the woman in the kitchen and wish her a nice day. McNeely decides to sit on the house for a while in case the young woman they need to interview returns, though he's not hopeful. After giving Kellum grief about how far from the curb he parked—"For quick getaways," his young partner quips— the senior detective instructs him to back up a few houses and gets into the passenger's side. Having piloted a zone car for many years, Kellum is an experienced driver, so he turns and puts it into reverse, and we pretty quickly and smoothly park several houses down the street. They joke that the man sitting on his front porch smoking a cigarette—or something resembling one—is going to call and let her know the police are waiting for her.

Since they can't really discuss the case, what follows is a reverential discourse on great actors in great detective films, starting with Steve McQueen in *Bullitt*. We all nod our heads and give our admiration of the universally acknowledged masterpiece that solidified McQueen's rightful place as the guy every guy wants to be. Kellum reveals that after he became a detective, he purchased an iconic tweed jacket like the one

McQueen sported in the movie. They both confirm that he was the reason they tried wearing shoulder holsters, which, both learned, look cool but are extremely confining and uncomfortable. "I was afraid I was going to shoot myself in the shoulder pulling my gun out," McNeely confesses. We share our adoration of several of McQueen's other cinematic tours de force—*The Great Escape, The Thomas Crown Affair, The Sand Pebbles*—and then move on to Marlon Brando and his two creative periods: the cool years and the fat and mentally unbalanced years.

After more than an hour or so, when it's clear the victim is not coming home, McNeely says: "She doesn't want to be found. Let's stop by the scene of the crime and then head back to *The Daily Planet*."

After lunch at the two detectives' favorite burrito joint, Taco Tontos in Lakewood, McNeely takes me to Commander McPike's office back at the downtown CPD headquarters. They discuss the case and the reluctant victim. McPike agrees that it sounds like she does not want to be found. There dilemma is twofold.

"If you're being victim-centered, on the one hand, you do not want to force a victim to go forward," McPike says. "Then, you want to find out what's going on. Is she being threatened by gang members? Intimidated? On the other hand, you've got the political process over here." He indicates the prosecutor's office in the adjacent part of the Justice Center. "They want to push through a case on some guy who's a bad dude in the neighborhood and a public safety threat. But you can't get a conviction without a cooperative victim."

"Right now, I only have DNA evidence of sex," McNeely adds. "I don't have evidence of rape. We don't know that it's not a consensual sex partner. He's a gang-banger, but he could be her baby's dad. He could have legitimately had consensual sex with her that morning, and then she got raped by three strangers that night."

"We tell detectives, don't get caught up in the fact that you've heard them lie to you," McPike says. "You need to find out why."

"Like I told you earlier, just because a person lies doesn't make them a liar," McNeely explains. "They may be lying for very important reasons: protection, vanity, humiliation. Doesn't mean they're liars, but they're clearly not telling the truth for some reason."

"There's a lot of second-guessing in the victim world," McPike says. "They start second-guessing the decisions they made that led to their assault. 'Maybe it's my fault. I shouldn't have gotten into that car.' Listen, we're all allowed to make poor decisions."

"When you're dealing with a victim of sexual assault, clearly, they're lying for a reason," McNeely says. "So he taught me when I first started, never start your interview with bullshit. Go right for the truth."

"Everything complicates the investigation," declares McPike. "We want the absolute truth. The reality is our criminal justice system, I don't think, is very kind to victims at all."

"Rape victims are the only victims that have to be vetted," McNeely observes. "If you are on the street and I stick a gun in your belly and steal your iPhone, the police don't come and say, 'Who were you talking to? What color was your iPhone?'"

"Why were you dressed like that?" McPike adds to the list of foolish, victim-blaming questions that only victims of rape and sexual assault are often asked.

"I don't care if she's dressed like Wonder Woman. She's still a victim," the victim-centered McNeely says, growing angry. "I don't care if she's wearing a garbage bag. She's a victim. That doesn't matter. She didn't ask for this guy to rape her. She didn't ask for this effing tree jumper to pull her into an empty building. She didn't ask for this."

The two discuss the need for detectives to be kind to people and to focus on the case with victims. McPike believes it's much better than it was twenty years ago, especially for first responders.

"Show me an excellent detective, and I'll show you someone who is good with people," McPike says. "You may be very good here," he says, indicating his computer. "But if you don't have people skills, you're going to struggle as a detective. You have to know how to talk to people. And that includes suspects. You can't go into a room with a phone book and start slinging it at people's heads."

"I engage them in a friendly way," McNeely says, referring to his front porch chat earlier. "That's how you meet with people. I'm a talker. I talk nice to people, people respond to me, instead of walking up and saying, 'Hey, get out here!'"

The commander and the detective discuss details of another potential case of an elderly woman who was possibly assaulted in a nursing home. Then McNeely says goodbye and heads back to the unit. Today, he's working until 8 p.m., but his regular shift is 2 p.m. until 10 p.m.

McPike fills me in on Cleveland's new Domestic Violence and Child Advocacy Center that is planned to open in the first half of 2018. It is intended to help children who have been or are being sexually abused or are victims of domestic violence. After his promotion to commander, he had to put his dreams on hold of opening a formal training program for detectives, but it's still in the works and he hopes to get back to it soon. The committee he formed hasn't met in several months, though. "Right now, with staffing issues, most of us are doing the job of two and three people," he informs me.

He knows Dr. Rebecca Campbell's groundbreaking work and has taken her training in the neurobiology of trauma and how it negatively impacts a victim's behavior and memory of a rape or sexual assault. He would like to do some in-service training with police in that area, but right now their focus is on the proper use of force to bring Cleveland police into compliance with the Department of Justice consent decree. The DOJ issued the decree because of a couple of several high-profile cases where the CPD used excessive force, including the 2013 shooting of two suspects in a car chase that resulted in their deaths after a hail of 137 bullets from officers in pursuit.

He knows it may take a while longer, but he does hope to see the Campbell teachings make it into the curriculum of the Cleveland Police Academy.

"Sometimes police might say, 'She's not a legitimate victim of rape. She should have been crying or hysterical about it,'" he says. "How dare you tell her how she should react to her traumatic event. But people will do that, and not just police."

In addition to the neurobiology of trauma training, he also trains his police officers to recognize how they make assumptions about and judge people based on their own experiences and how they were raised, which isn't fair to do.

"I'll tell you as a detective, I've seen the complete gambit of victim responses," he says. "I've had women who were like, 'Tell me who it is, give me a baseball bat, and get out of my way.' I also had a woman curl up in a fetal position, sob hysterically during her interview. In fact, we had to stop, and she told me 'I can't do this.' I never saw her again after that day. I've seen everything in between those two emotions, so it's not fair to judge a victim on how they react."

In addition to their high caseloads, he tells me, sex crimes detectives today deal with much more complex investigations than their predecessors. "Twenty, thirty years ago, you probably had to take pictures of a crime scene and interview people, right?" he says. "We did some biology testing for blood, fingerprints, and hair, but now we have DNA testing, fingerprints and touch DNA, social media, computers, security cameras, cell phones, and all kinds of accounts like Google and Kik and Snapchat, and Kik is Canadian, so that's a different process to get records from them. So, they're taking a lot longer to investigate because there are a lot more sources out there that you can get evidence from."

I ask him why he decided to get into sex crimes in the first place. While he loved being a patrol officer, after a while it started to wear on him. He wanted a job that was more intellectually challenging. "To this day, I can't tell you why I applied for that unit," he says. "But I just knew it was considered a high-profile unit with some pretty serious investigations so it sounded like something that would work for me."

He also wanted to enjoy the fruits of his investigative labors. First-responding police interview victims and file rape reports but then may never hear another word again on that case. As a detective, he knew he would have to immerse himself in the investigations and put the puzzle pieces together to get a picture. "If you work really, really hard on your cases, you're probably going to get a good outcome," McPike says.

McPike was such an assiduous sex crimes investigator, he eventually burned himself out.

"I liked it for a long time," he reveals. "A lot of people think it wore me out because of the cases I investigated, but it was the caseload. You come to work every day, and you have thirty cases on your desk, and you've got time to work on two, maybe, and it's just not fair to our victims. It stressed me out to the point where it was affecting me physically. I was intermittently on sleeping pills my last two years in the unit. The old joke was I slept like a baby, and when people said, 'Oh, you did?' I'd go, 'Yeah, I woke up crying every two hours.' As soon as I got promoted out of that unit, I slept great."

Ever since then, though, he's been doing everything he can to help the detectives in his old unit have the tools they need to work efficiently, including the best equipment and enough detectives to handle the immense and never-ending caseloads. For himself, he learned he needed to take better care of his body and find a good work–life balance. In the fall of 2015, he spent three months at the FBI training academy completing a special program for law enforcement officers, which required him to start running again. He has bad knees from his patrolmen days that required several surgeries, so he prefers to run on a treadmill these days.

He is confident things are starting to get a little better for the employees under his command, including the Sex Crimes and Child Abuse Unit, but it's still an ongoing challenge.

"I've learned in leadership that you have to figure out how to make things work with what you have, because sometimes you don't get anything else, at least not for a long time," he says. "So that's the challenge when the resources and the personnel decline, you still have a mission to complete."

It may not be easy, but nothing will divert McPike from his goal of keeping his Special Victims crew one of the best investigative units in the country.

Chapter 5

The Past Is the Future:
Richard Bell and the Cuyahoga
County Sexual Assault Kit Task Force

WALKING DOWN THE wide, white marble hallways of the Cannon House Office Building across from the US Capitol, Richard "Rick" Bell could feel the thick carpeting under his feet. He had just passed through an extremely tight security checkpoint, since it was two days after the shooting at the Republican congressional softball practice in June 2017. As congressional staffers escorted him and the rest of the panelists for the Bipartisan Task Force to End Sexual Violence hearing to their speaker chairs, he couldn't help but notice the ornate details of the room.

The representatives and cochairs entered just before the hearing started promptly at 9 a.m. The entrance of the tall, striking Mariska Hargitay, a.k.a. Lieutenant Olivia Benson on *Law & Order: SVU*, who established herself as a leading crusader against sexual violence with the work of the Joyful Heart Foundation, drew attention. Two key members of Hargitay's foundation were already seated in the roughly one hundred chairs for the audience: Sarah Haacke Byrd, managing director, and Ilse Knecht, director of policy and advocacy. Both have gotten to know Rick Bell well over the past few years because of the successes of the Cuyahoga County SAKTF in Cleveland, which he helms. They spoke briefly when he arrived.

After collegial introductions and hand-shaking, the reps took their seats around the tight horseshoe-shaped dais with their staffers in tow behind them, and the panelists sat at the speakers' table facing them. Each expressed his or her sympathy for the tragic and senseless shooting. Then Rep. David Joyce (R-OH), who had invited Bell and Cuyahoga County Prosecutor Michael C. O'Malley to this first hearing of the task force, introduced the panel: Hargitay, Emmy Award–winning actress; Lavinia Masters, victim advocate and survivor of sexual violence from Texas; Dr. Jenifer Markowitz, past president and government affairs committee chair of the International Association of Forensic Nurses; Nathan James, analyst in crime policy for the Congressional Research Service; O'Malley; and Bell, assistant prosecuting attorney for Cuyahoga County and special investigations division chief.

Composed of eleven Democrats and eight Republicans, the task force was created "to raise awareness and propose solutions to the challenges posed by sexual assault." I prefer Bell's take on their mission: to determine what the course of the nation should be in ending sexual assault against women.

Rep. Joyce's cochairs are Ann McLane Kuster (D-NH), Patrick Meehan (R-PA), and Jackie Speier (D-CA). The task force's areas of focus include K-12 education, campus sexual violence, the rape kit backlog, military sexual trauma, improved data and collection, online harassment, and law enforcement training. Together, the diverse congressional cadre plans to "advocate for legislation to support victims and their families, educate communities to prevent violence, and implement solutions to end sexual assault."

All good. All difficult, but doable. Certainly "aspirational," as Bell would say.

Last on the speaker's agenda, Bell sat back and listened closely to each person's testimony. He was especially impressed by the inner strength and grace demonstrated by Masters, who had endured much as a survivor. It struck him that the speaker lineup was reminiscent of many rape and sexual assault trials: opening statement, victim account, medical expert testimony, and closing arguments. Today, the representatives and audience of press and media and interested individuals would serve as the jury.

The high-profile nature, however, was a little different, with a cameraman seated on the floor to the left and slightly in front of the panel table, with two other cameras in the room, including a remote-controlled boom instrument that hovered above and below them like a UFO and swiveled to the left and right to capture all angles.

After Prosecutor O'Malley has completed his presentation, Bell is up. He's sporting his trademark prosecuting attorney attire: suit and tie. What else? After all, it is a congressional hearing. Also, for fifty years, he watched his father dress in a suit and tie as manager of the General Electric Nela Park plant in Cleveland. Every day. Suit and tie. A company man, he traveled the world—Brazil, China, England, Hungary, India, Paraguay, Uruguay—setting up factories to manufacture light bulbs or, Bell corrects himself, lamps. "So, I tell my people even on dress-down Fridays, I'd like them in suits and ties," he tells me another day.

He echoes O'Malley's comment that the increased opportunity to use DNA in solving crimes (the Combined DNA Index System, or CODIS, came online in 1998) has outpaced resources to law enforcement. Ohio alone has nearly 14,000 untested rape kits from 1993–2009, with more than 6,700 from the Cleveland/Cuyahoga County area. Because of the twenty-year statute of limitations, the prosecutor's office knew it had to move quickly to investigate the kits, and forming a task force with its own funds on Valentine's Day 2013 with several agencies detailing personnel to one location—a couple of floors in the Courthouse Square building across from the prosecutor's headquarters in Cleveland's Justice Center—was the best way to maximize a multi-disciplinary approach that would yield the best results. The Cuyahoga County Sheriff's Office and Ohio Bureau of Criminal Investigation joined the task force within a month of its founding.

He doesn't get down to this level of detail, but Cleveland's approach to sexual violence all changed on Halloween 2009, when, somewhat fittingly, the local police arrested Anthony Sowell for what would become the most brutal serial rape and murder spree in the city's modern history. In the days following his arrest, crime scene investigators unearthed the bodies of eleven women the "Cleveland Strangler" had wrapped in plastic garbage bags and buried in his backyard or left in crawl spaces within his house, a few directly across from his third-floor bedroom.

On the strength of an embarrassment of evidence, Sowell was convicted and sentenced to death on August 12, 2011. His Imperial Avenue home on Cleveland's East Side, which had become known as the "house of horrors," was razed on December 6, 2011.

Deeply disturbed by the crimes, the major institutions that combat sexual violence began to implement fundamental changes. Two months after Sowell's arrest, Cleveland Mayor Frank Jackson formed the Special Commission on Missing Persons and Sex Crimes Investigation. Issued on March 30, 2010, the report proposed twenty-six recommendations for handling these cases differently, including a countywide Missing Persons Bureau.

Back to Bell's report. Facing an extremely high volume of cases, the county SAKTF prioritized each case by age to prevent losing any to the statute of limitations deadlines. Fortunately, for those defendants whose DNA showed up in a rape kit test but did not match anyone on CODIS, they could employ another weapon in their legal arsenal: John Doe defendant or DNA indictments. This tool enables prosecutors to indict the DNA profile; should that person eventually be identified, most likely for another crime, their offense will not be lost to an expired statute of limitations. To date, Bell's crew has indicted 122 defendants. As of January 2018, they have indicted 656 defendants and convicted 328 of them for a conviction rate of 92.1 percent. They are serving an average sentence of 10.1 years.

The revelations of this SAKTF for Cuyahoga County have been extraordinary, according to Bell. Of the slightly more than 6,700 rape kits investigated, 670 serial sex offenders were identified. In reviewing their criminal histories, they found other arrests and convictions for rape or sexual assault or other sexual offenses that were not a match to one of the 6,700 kits in the rape kit project.

During the hearing, he doesn't detail all of the statistics from the most recent SAKTF Scorecard, which has graphs, pie charts, and call-out totals, that they keep as part of their meticulous record-keeping and research in partnership with their embedded researcher, Rachel Lovell, PhD, and her team from the Begun Center for Violence Prevention Research and Education at Case Western Reserve University. But I will. The June 27, 2017, card indicates they have closed 3,816 of the cases with fewer than 3,000 cases left to finish. They have opened 543 prosecutions and closed 313 prosecutions with 282 convicted defendants at a conviction rate of 92 percent. The average sentence is more than ten years. Of the 670 serial sex offenders, 428 were serial rapists, and 57 of those were identified in both stranger and acquaintance rape cases. The number of victims those predators raped and assaulted totals more than a thousand.

In one of my earliest conversations with Bell a couple of years ago, he told me that those DNA hits prove that serial offenders are not locked into one type of victim or one method of operation, as was previously believed.

"If you're a jerk enough to rape a stranger, you're probably not compassionate or empathetic towards the women in your life, so you're likely to assault an acquaintance," he said. "Doesn't seem like it should be, but that was an epiphany to prosecutors and police alike." Of course, they can often deploy the proof of a stranger rape to destroy the credibility of a defendant in an acquaintance rape case.

In his comments to the congressional task force, Bell talks about the benefits of forming the partnership with several cities. "The essence of the multidisciplinary approach is sharing ideas amongst the task force members as well as sharing with other jurisdictions," he informs them.

Under the previous county prosecutor, Timothy McGinty, who recommended the SAKTF partnerships, there were four best practices summits, beginning in Cleveland (2014), then Memphis (2015) and Detroit (2016), with the next summit planned for Portland, Oregon, in November 2017. The cities all use the same task force name—SAKTF—to encourage uniformity, and they all keep statistics to measure their results for comparative purposes. They all work closely with RTI International, which is tracking and recording the Sexual Assault Kit Initiative project, and the organization collects and correlates all of the SAKTF data. RTI joined with Cuyahoga County's SAKTF research partner, the Begun Center, to hold a meeting of SAKTFs from several cities, including Dallas, Detroit, Houston, Memphis, Washington, DC, and others, Bell explains, primarily to discuss what statistics should be collected across all task forces.

One of the most significant outcomes of this collaborative interaction, Bell reports, is the establishment of the four pillars of best practices that they all share:

- Test all kits: By testing all kits, you can develop leads that solve the identity of stranger rapes.
- Swab all felony arrestees: The more arrestees swabbed, the more robust the CODIS database is and the more victims' cases you solve.
- Investigate all positive or negative rape kit reports: Don't rely solely on the rape kits, but review police reports to determine whether any secondary evidence can be tested.
- Investigate with a victim-centered approach: Victim advocates should be used to notify and remain in contact with victims, using protocols reviewed by the Cleveland Rape Crisis Center and Joyful Heart Foundation.

Swabbing has emerged as a weakness in the system, because not all law enforcement professionals are swabbing all felony cases for a variety of reasons. In fact, Bell returned to Cleveland to headlines spurred by his testimony about an estimated six thousand–plus offenders from the region that had not been swabbed and so were not in the database. His office is working closely with the CPD and Cuyahoga County Sheriff's Department to ensure that they implement proper procedures to swab all felony arrestees. Later in his presentation, Bell explains how his office is instituting a new policy to ask the court on each case to make sure that defendants have been swabbed before they lose jurisdiction over that person. Assistant prosecutors will run criminal record checks at the initial charging hearing, before guilty pleas, and at sentencing or expungements.

Another hot issue is taking a proactive stance to acquiring "owed DNA" from offenders who should have been swabbed upon arrest (in the same way they were fingerprinted) but weren't. There are still financial and logistical challenges to accomplishing that task, but both Bell and O'Malley see testing rape kits as one branch of the CODIS tree and swabbing felony arrestees as the other. It's crucial to solving many stranger rapes. Obviously, more money will be necessary to hire investigators who will serve as DNA hunters for those missing six thousand–plus profiles.

Next up in his presentation, Bell explains the importance of not just testing the kits, but then following up with a detailed investigation. You don't just indict a case when DNA is identified in a kit, he says. "You need investigators, prosecutors, and victim advocates to locate witnesses, reports, and evidence and to bring the cases together."

In other words, you need serious funding to pay all of those people and obtain the resources they need. Ohio has done just that by furnishing significant funding for the whole endeavor: Ohio's attorney general, Mike DeWine, invested $4 million in robotics and personnel to increase the capabilities of the Ohio Bureau of Criminal Investigation (BCI) laboratories that test all backlogged kits for the state; the AG's office also contributes approximately half a million annually to the effort; the Cuyahoga County Prosecutor's Office invests $1 million a year; the Cleveland Police Department budgets more than $100,000 per year; the Cuyahoga County Council has invested $679,000 per year; and the county's SAKTF received $2 million in 2015 and again in 2016 from the Department of Justice to investigate and prosecute the cold case rapes. The initial DOJ grant to Cuyahoga County in 2006 established their Cold Case Unit that later morphed into the SAKTF.

"The DOJ funding on three separate occasions over the last ten years has served as the foundation for all of these partner contributions," Bell says, adding, to emphasize the underlying point of this hearing, continued funding. "Without it, our structure could not sustain the work we do."

Bell proudly rattles off some of the impressive statistics that have made their SAKTF one of the most successful in the United States, but it boils down to the 661 victims' cases solved that never would have been prosecuted without their efforts. At this time, he estimates that about a thousand defendants will be indicted. Facing the task force's 92.6 percent conviction rate, those defendants probably shouldn't be making any long-term plans for their futures.

Bell has turned the corner now, from the benefits of the SAKTF endeavors to how much they cost to how they can be justified. One of the other fundamental revelations for the SAKTFs is the amount of additional crimes the rape and sexual assault offenders commit and the exorbitant associated costs for communities. He cites statistics using National Institutes of Health studies to calculate the economic harm caused by the subsequent crimes committed by rapists who were not investigated or prosecuted and put in prison because the backlogged rape kits weren't tested.

"We added the cost of each indicted rapist's subsequent crimes that they have been convicted of since the rape they committed," Bell explains. "Our first 593 defendants have caused $440,256,512.89 in economic harm to the state of Ohio. This harm would not have occurred had these rape kits been tested and these victims' cases been investigated and prosecuted."

Now the good news, especially for fiscal conservatives. The savings calculated by Lovell and her CWRU research team underscore the substantial financial benefits communities realize by prosecuting cases. Cuyahoga County's SAKTF is projected to produce a net savings of $38.7 million to the community by removing dangerous offenders from the streets before they commit additional crimes. These findings indicate that for every rape kit tested, the community saves $8,893 in future economic harm.

"Testing is important," Bell reiterates, after a review of the importance of expanding the CODIS database by swabbing felony arrestees. "But the real work and real commitment and the savings to the taxpayers is only realized when funds are committed to funding investigators, advocates, and prosecutors."

Throughout his talk, Bell felt confident that his arguments would appeal to just about everyone. "Those that would be interested in the economic harm or the savings—conservatives," for example, he tells me the following week. "Those who would want to have these bad people in prison—conservatives. Or those who were interested in the study of the victims, the victimology, and the harm that this has done to the victims. Anybody that was across the board, across the aisle, would have an interest in some of what we had to say."

Bell then breaks down next steps for the representatives. As more states get onboard by legislating to test all rape kits and swab all felony arrestees, four key areas will require funding to complete the remaining prosecutions from the 1993 to 2011 cases: submit pre-1993 backlogged rape kits that by law must now be sent to the lab for testing (according to Bell, in Cuyahoga County alone, the SAKTF will need to hire five temporary clerks to assist the Cleveland Police Department in collecting the pre-backlog backlog); detectives to investigate those pre-1993 cases to solve the John Doe and old cases that solve stranger rapes; hire advocates to notify victims and provide counseling and support; and hire investigators to locate and swab felons who were never swabbed at their arrest to help solve crimes and deter future crimes.

Finally, after thanking the task force for allowing them to testify, Bell wraps everything with a neat, little bow: "Our task force has reached a high level of success in prosecutions and convictions. Other task forces will be sure to follow in these same footsteps as long as they have the proper resources. On their behalf, we would like to recommend that this body continues to fund this effort to end sexual violence against women."

He was slated to speak for three minutes, but the impassioned prosecutor ended up talking for twenty minutes. At the end of the hearing, Bell, who heard the door opening and closing throughout the two-hour proceedings and thought people were leaving, turned around when he heard a clamorous applause erupt. He saw that all of the chairs in the room were full, and people were standing along the back walls and in the aisle.

When we meet in his office a few days later, he is obviously satisfied with the outcome of the event for which he and his staff spent several weeks preparing. "The representatives asked insightful questions, and their comments expressed a true commitment to end sexual violence against women," he summarizes. "Afterward, the reps and audience members approached and asked more questions. All politics are local. It was clear the same issues that mean so much to our constituents matter to those in New Hampshire, Florida, Pennsylvania, California, Maine, etc."

Rep. Joyce informed Bell and O'Malley that he would like to meet again. He's interested in the swabbing initiative to collect owed DNA. He told them he would convey this information to the appropriations committee to make sure that the funding continues. The two prosecutors suggested that he reference the RTI International composite data from the various SAKTFs for additional research information. The bipartisan task force hearings will continue so that they can discuss other issues with a variety of experts on sexual violence.

While he maintains high hopes for what could come from the congressional watchdogs, one of his biggest concerns is that many law enforcement agencies and police departments across the country still don't see the need for these efforts or fully understand what's on their shelves. Each kit is a victim. Each kit is a rapist or sexual assailant that may still be on the streets and a public danger, unless they've since died or been incarcerated for another offense.

For Bell, along with pretty much everyone else I interview or talk to along the way about the backlogged rape kit testing project, it all starts with that essential American right to the pursuit of justice so eloquently articulated in the Declaration of Independence. Every victim his team has ever interviewed had no idea their rape kits were never tested. They just assumed that if they had endured a sexual assault examination that can take four to six hours to complete—in some cases longer than the subsequent investigation, Bell notes—and can be fairly invasive, even when performed in the humane, compassionate manner that SANEs do, and if they then file a police report, that their kit *absolutely must* have been used to prosecute their assailant. When they learn that was not the case, it is an awful surprise.

"The fact that they are shocked should shock all of us," Bell avers.

The SAKTF prosecutor was raised to help those in need. Definitely a home-grown prodigy, Bell grew up in Cleveland Heights, an East Side inner-ring suburb of Cleveland. He is the eighth of ten children, with six older sisters, all of whom have gone on to careers in nursing, teaching, or social work. As his father was toiling and traveling the globe for General Electric, his mother handled all the chaos of ten children with aplomb. She earned her nickname, "The General."

While he attended a one-storied Catholic school, Cathedral Latin, it closed because it was located in the city at a time when most citizens had fled to the suburbs. Bell transferred to another, Benedictine High School, located on the outer edge of the city. He then enrolled in nearby Kent State University thinking he would become a graphic artist because he was so adept at drawing with pencils or charcoals.

Suddenly, he switched to prelaw. "There was a girl involved," he admits. He graduated from Cleveland-Marshall College of Law. The "take-home value" his sisters enjoyed from their commitment to serving others as part of their careers did not go unnoticed. He also had observed "The General," after all the kids were raised, return to college to get a second degree in counseling at John Carroll University and go on to earn her certifications as a licensed professional clinical counselor who guided rape victims and families that had suffered from a loved one's suicide.

"I guess the apple didn't fall far from the tree," the soft-spoken Bell affirms in his resonating voice that would sound great on radio.

He practiced as a criminal defense attorney for six months but after being hired at the Cuyahoga County Prosecutor's Office in 1990 discovered he "could do a lot of good on this side of the practice." He could bring the cases that should be brought, or if there was a weak case that was not just, he could dismiss it.

"We call it wearing the white hat," he says. "I'm sure a lot of good people wear white hats in their jobs, but we take special pride in the work we do, and this office allows you to do the right thing ethically. It's been a fit that made sense, so I kept with it."

He and his wife encourage their three girls and one son to do whatever they want to do, as long as it's not law-related. "Not a single one of them will be a lawyer. I won't let them do it," Bell says with a laugh. "They're gravitating towards medicine anyway, and helping people. If they help people, they can work hard no matter what the money is and they'll be satisfied."

In 2001, County Prosecutor Bill Mason assigned Bell to lead the Major Trial Unit to prosecute rapes and murders. Shortly after, he was tasked to investigate the Catholic Diocese of Cleveland when twelve hundred victims stepped forward to accuse priests of raping or molesting them. "Putting together investigations is something that I've become accustomed to and am drawn to," he says.

In our discussion, Bell tells me that having the partner cities has been extremely beneficial. For example, Cuyahoga County changed its protocols to investigate all kits, not just the positive reports of DNA hits, because Memphis communicated their success in doing so. He also reviews a few of the protocols that he labels "aspirational" now but could become reality in the near future. One of those is finding an optimum way to electronically track kits. They had bounced around the idea of putting bar codes on the rape kits, but there were several concerns, including possible violation of HIPAA privacy regulations. However, he believes the kit manufacturers are exploring placing computerized chips in each kit so they could be immediately located and tracked.

"Right now, we're shadowboxing," says Bell of how the chips could help. "We should know where kit number one from 2017 is and where kit number nine hundred thirty-three is. We should know whether it's been utilized or if it's sitting on a shelf somewhere at the police department or prosecutor's office or still at the hospital, whether or not it's been tested. Otherwise, it's a guessing game." The chips could help with auditing, too, to provide more complete information about the status of the kits. "Auditing is crucial to know just how bad the problem in your city is," he adds.

Of course, making sure kits are legally mandated to be audited is another primary objective of the Joyful Heart Foundation, which Bell looks to when identifying other objectives to aspire toward. Such aspirational goals may take those in law enforcement and prosecution on the "practical level" a little longer to plan, fund, and implement, but it can happen. It happened with the Cuyahoga County SAKTF's decision to add a fourth best practice of making all activities victim-centered, another central tenet of Joyful Heart Foundation's mission.

When I ask Bell what has been most fulfilling about guiding the SAKTF for the past few years, he cites two things. First, seeing victims satisfied with the work of his team of investigators, advocates, and prosecutors and gaining some sense of closure on their long-ignored cases.

"In my career, I haven't seen victims be this engaged ever before," he says. "They see that somebody actually cares enough to come back and talk to them and wants to resolve something that needed to be resolved."

This is especially satisfying for him in the cases where children had been abused, to see how resilient they are in going through the enervating process of a rape investigation and trial, emerging on the other side and becoming successful citizens.

The other satisfaction he "personally, selfishly" has gained is seeing all the people he has worked with on this innovative new approach become so much more informed over the past three or four years. Watching new investigators, advocates, and prosecutors blossom into experienced professionals has been particularly fulfilling, too.

"I know that this legacy of being compassionate towards victims and our office going after the bad guys in the right way, wearing the white hats, is being passed on to the next generation," he says. "Now we need to figure out how to bottle it up or put it in a capsule for other task forces to use in other places. How do we take these cases and then educate not only our office but the different agencies and continue on? Because we know there will be victims in the future that will need to be helped. We know it will continue to happen."

For the immediate future, Bell estimates that this portion of the project with kits from 1993 through 2010 will be completed within four years, or around 2021.

Packing up my tape recorder and notebook, I ask him about a stunning black pencil drawing of JFK that hangs on the wall behind his desk. Bell relates the story of how he often let the previous county prosecutor, Tim McGinty, know how much he admired the thirty-fifth president's portrait that appointed his office. When he left the position in December 2016 after losing his election to O'Malley, McGinty presented it to Bell with a signed personal note on the back. Obviously moved by the artistry behind the intricate penciling, Bell also happened to be born in April 1963, just months before Kennedy's assassination.

"History certainly showed he was far from a perfect human being," Bell comments. "But none of us are."

On my way out, he pulls a Xeroxed photo of the hearing off the back of his door to show me. When Rep. Joyce introduced Bell, he referred to him as his boss's "super sidekick." The photo shows Bell leaning in to consult with O'Malley at the speaker's table. Several of his assistant prosecutors lovingly captioned it, "Super Sidekick" and left it as a surprise for him when he returned from DC.

"At least they put it on the back of my door," Bell says with a smile.

Chapter 6

The Science of DNA Profiles for CODIS: Lewis Maddox and the Richfield OBCI Laboratory

W HEN YOU ENTER the Evidence Receiving Unit of the Ohio Bureau of Criminal Investigation (BCI) laboratory in Richfield, Ohio—just inside the door near parking spaces reserved for police and law enforcement agents dropping off evidence—you know immediately who runs this place. You have to walk across the welcome rug featuring the seal of the attorney general of Ohio, as you look at the wall with the portrait of Ohio Attorney General Mike DeWine smiling at you.

But far more important than the official attorney general interior design appointments is the fact that in Ohio, unlike many states, the state crime lab falls under the attorney general's auspices. That is one of the reasons Ohio—and specifically Cuyahoga County and Cleveland—has had model success in identifying DNA profiles from the backlogged rape kits that are part of the national SAKI project.

"When we made the decision to test the kits, we had no clue how many there were," AG DeWine says when he calls me from Columbus in June 2017. "We thought it might be five hundred, maybe a thousand, maybe fifteen hundred. But I was able to make that decision, because I run the state crime lab."

After the initial shock wore off in 2013 when DeWine learned that the statewide total was an astonishing 13,931 kits submitted by 294 police departments out of about 900 jurisdictions, he made the decision to "do what was right." On the practical side, he substantially upgraded and augmented the state lab's capabilities. He hired ten new scientists/analysts to work on the backlogged kits. His predecessor, Richard Cordray, had installed robotic testing equipment in the BCI lab. DeWine added newer equipment, resulting in Ohio's current state-of-the-art lab and expediting DNA testing even further.

The lab also handles rape kits from new cases submitted by law enforcement, and DeWine reduced the turnaround time from a one-hundred-twenty-five-day wait for DNA testing at the time he took office to about twenty-three or twenty-four days on average.

"DNA is a huge part of our job today," he says. "We're doing about six times as much DNA work as we did six years ago when I took office. That just shows you how it's grown as a huge part of our job today, and the police departments' need for it, the public's appetite for it, prosecutors and juries wanting the DNA evidence, so we're just doing a ton more of the testing than we've ever done."

In addition to the BCI Laboratory Division, the other half of the building houses the Ohio Peace Officer Training Academy. BCI Richfield offers a full range of lab and crime scene investigation services to the northern Ohio region, including DNA testing; firearms, ballistics, and toolmarks examination; forensic biology; gunshot residue analysis; criminal polygraph examination; a crimes against children unit; a cybercrimes unit; and forensic accounting.

Richfield is not quite twenty-one miles south of Cleveland, so it's an easy commute for the Cuyahoga County SAKTF investigators who transport rape kits and other evidence to and from the lab when necessary. Inside the lobby, there are four open reception bays at a diagonal where law enforcement agents submit evidence to office assistants. They then barcode the rape kit and assign it a case number in the BCI's laboratory information management system. The LIMS database stores all of the lab's documentation, record of chain of custody, and testing records.

All of this is explained to me by DNA Technical Leader Lewis Maddox, PhD, who helms the lab, as he leads me on a tour of this center of the increasingly elegant technology of forensics.

The lanky Maddox guides me through the entire science of deoxyribonucleic acid testing, and he's a perfect DNA docent: articulate, able to convey it all in layman's terms, but able to easily elevate his commentary into high, complex science, if needed. As he explains it, DNA now stands as law enforcement's greatest weapon to convict rapists and sexual assaulters, since, if properly handled and presented as evidence, it is about as effective a "reasonable doubt" eliminator as possible, especially in cases where the sex was clearly not consensual.

It's not a huge surprise when the native of North Augusta, South Carolina (across the river from the home of the PGA Masters Tournament in Augusta, Georgia) rattles off his impressive science credentials: microbiology degree from Clemson University; doctorate in medical genetics from the University of Alabama at Birmingham; postdoctoral studies at Duke University. His first job in forensics and applying DNA science was at Cellmark Diagnostics (now Cellmark Forensic Services), where they processed evidence for the O. J. Simpson case shortly before he got there in 1999. In 2005, he went to Myriad Genetics in Salt Lake City. A colorful Salt Lake City poster on the bulletin board above his desk is the only artful appointment in his office. Mostly, he's surrounded by a desk and shelves full of black binders with STF (significant thud factor) containing copies of DNA profiles and other information used primarily for the lab's accreditation requirements. He joined the BCI in 2007.

"I just didn't see myself being an academic and having to write grants and publish or perish," he says of his career choice, with a minor twinge of disdain. "I wanted to be an applied scientist, so that's what drew me to forensics. I've always liked the crime aspect of it, and since

I've been here, I like knowing that we can help people, because you usually know that you're helping solve their cases."

Like the attorney general, he was a little startled by the total number of kits that came in when DeWine first requested that police departments submit them, and then Senate Bill 316, which took effect on March 23, 2015, made kit submittal an Ohio law. The bill requires law enforcement agencies to submit the contents of backlogged untested sexual assault examination kits to the BCI for DNA analysis within one year. Law enforcement agencies must also forward kits from new crimes to the BCI for DNA analysis within thirty days after the offense. In addition, Senate Bill 316 prioritizes the order in which submitted DNA specimens undergo DNA analysis.

"It was a lot more than we first thought," says Maddox. "It definitely exceeded what we first thought for staffing and equipment pretty quickly. I was shocked by the numbers that came in, and then we saw that it was not just here in Ohio, but across the country as well."

We continue our tour. After the office assistants receive rape kits into the lab, whether they are backlog kits that are part of the SAKI project or from new cases, they transfer them into the evidence storage rooms. These are sealed vaults that require not only a key card but a fingerprint reader for access. To preserve the security of the evidence and prevent contamination, unauthorized visitors are not welcome in the vault, which has only chocolate brown walls to mark its location. Inside, to protect the evidence in case of a fire, the vault features a fire suppression system that pumps an oxygen-removing gas into the room instead of water that would soak the rape kit boxes, cause mold, and degrade and ruin the evidence.

The SAKI kits, Maddox explains, became the priority because they came with the burden of the race against statute of limitations deadlines. Initially, the BCI lab started with kits with offense dates prior to 2000 to give law enforcement time to prosecute and investigate those cases before their twenty-year time limit expired. The lab then moved on to cases with offense dates of 2010 and prior. Some of the backlogged kits from more recent offenses have been waiting in the evidence room until more recently.

As of June 1, 2017, shortly before my lab tour, Ohio recorded 13,931 backlog kits submitted by 294 law enforcement agencies, and had tested 12,559 of those, with a total of 4,587 hits in the FBI's Combined DNA Index System (CODIS). Of the 4,996 kits submitted by forty agencies in Cuyahoga County, representing 36 percent of the statewide submissions, all had been tested, resulting in 2,211 CODIS hits; the county SAKTF continues to investigate and prosecute those cases.

In addition to prioritizing the order of testing, the lab also decided to forgo the traditional serology testing for blood, semen, saliva, or other bodily fluids and go straight to the DNA testing. The goal is to upload DNA profiles into CODIS to see if they match to any of the criminals already in the database or add a new one for future reference. They discussed this choice with others, and the Cuyahoga County task force, for example, was all for exploring ways to speed up obtaining lab results, according to CPD's Rick Bell, in the same way the BCI wanted to increase its turnaround times. Cutting out the serology step and going right for the genetic gold made the process more efficient. AG DeWine agreed with the lab's recommendation.

Before testing for DNA with the SAKI kits, however, the Richfield lab sends them to the BCI laboratory in London, Ohio, where the ten additional scientists added by DeWine work. They open the rape kits, cut the swabs into small tubes that are individually labeled and later used in the DNA extraction process, enter that information into the LIMS database, and return them to Richfield for the DNA testing.

Although the priority has shifted to developing DNA profiles as the most effective way to eliminate a suspect or identify an offender and upload their profile into the CODIS database, the lab does accept secondary evidence such as sheets, underwear, or clothing, and the rape kits include envelopes for submitting such items.

Still, when I ask Sara Kester-Florin Horst, a forensic scientist at the lab who specializes in inventorying the contents of a rape kit, whether forensic nurses or examiners can fit a pair of pants into the relatively small box (approximately ten inches by six and half inches by two and a half inches) with all the other contents, she deadpans: "They try." After we all laugh, she adds: "Yeah, we've had kits so stuffed, packed with a whole outfit sometimes, underwear, bra, pants, all in the kit sealed with lots of extra tape. But it's perfectly fine to collect them in the bags and then submit those separately."

Alright, technically, they are also sometimes referred to as a Sexual Assault Evidence Kit (SAEK), so that's all fair game. But the focus remains on the items that may bear DNA samples. Thus, the first three envelopes in the kit are from vaginal, anorectal, and oral samples the SANE/SAFEs have taken on a swab and rolled across a slide, so that the lab analysts have both to examine for semen and DNA samples.

Other envelopes include fingernail scrapings, dried stain combing, and combs from a pubic hair combing and a head hair combing; sometimes the nurses will also submit a clean paper towel or sterile wipe with the combings. Hair clippings themselves are no longer included, since they didn't yield much reliable evidence and are currently not given much weight in the courtroom. The newer kits collect more samples than those from the 1980s or '90s.

The newest kits contain six swab boxes and six sets of swabs for potential dried stain collection. These are typically collected if the victim informs the SANE that the offender ejaculated somewhere on their skin or if the nurse detects the presence of a stain with the aid of an advanced light source, which resembles a black light and is used during the examination. The type of light source may vary from a Wood's lamp, the cheapest tool, to a more advanced source using blue light, and the examiner wears orange goggles. The light can also reveal scratches, abrasions, and bruising. Swabs dampened with sterile water are used to collect the sample, and then all swabs are dried in a swab dryer so that they don't become fertile grounds for bacteria growth that would degrade the DNA sample. Many SANE/SAFEs employ synthetic swabs made of flocked nylon that are more efficient at releasing cells during the extraction than cotton-tipped swabs.

The lab analysts also use the checklist and victim account of their assault included in the kit to direct their testing. For instance, if the victim reveals the assailant ejaculated into her vagina, then they will start with that sample. Also, if she reveals she had had consensual sex prior to the assault, that affects what they collect and send forward for testing.

The kits themselves have continued to evolve, Kester-Florin Horst says, as the labs have learned which samples produce the maximum yield. Ohio's health department meets with SANE nurses and others such as BCI's director of research, development, and training, Elizabeth Benzinger, to review the contents and organization of the standardized kits that the state issues to SANEs and SAFEs. Currently, the state of Ohio pays a flat rate of $624 to reimburse for the costs of the kit, antibiotics, and the examination. Another recent change was a redesign of the box so that less evidence seal tape is required to secure it.

"I've been here six years in August," Kester-Florin Horst says, "[and] we've been through three different kit styles."

The lab analyst works on only one case at a time so there is no chance of contamination from another kit. Once they have completed the inventory, labeled each tube, and generated a barcode for each one to track them, they insert the tubes into a storage rack and return them to the secure storage vault until the DNA extraction team is ready to test the samples.

The London lab handles this entire preparation process for the SAKI kits. For new rape cases, however, the Richfield lab analysts process the kits and complete the traditional serology or blood and blood product screening that is not done for the SAKI kits, for which DNA testing is the priority. The screening includes a test for acid phosphatase (AP), an enzyme produced by the prostate gland that is found in seminal fluid, so it indicates the presence of semen and sperm cells on a slide or swab.

The rest of the items that aren't being sent forward are returned to the kit, which is resealed and sent to a separate secure location. There it awaits a police officer or detective from the law enforcement agency that submitted it to return to evidence receiving, so they can retrieve it to place in their permanent evidence storage facility.

Now for the hardcore science geeks among us: How is the DNA testing done? Once a lab analyst brings a set of the evidence sample tubes in the racks into the DNA extraction laboratory, they enter what's known as a clean space. Not that the others are actually dirty, but Maddox says they go through a lot of bleach in these rooms to clean the surfaces and instruments to protect the samples from contamination.

A DNA analyst who performs the DNA extractions will take approximately twenty-four tubes of samples. Typically, that batch represents samples from two to three rape kits. The analyst will then add chemicals that "pop open" the cells, says the scientist, keeping it simple for the nonscientist. The first chemicals are less harsh than what follows, but they open the non-sperm cells and release that DNA into the solution. They also employ heating blocks to incubate the enzymes and break down the proteins. That tube is then placed into a centrifuge and spun until it culls the sperm cells, which have a thicker surrounding, leaving a pellet at the bottom of the tube. Using a pipette to reach down into the tube, the analyst will remove the liquid sitting on top of the cell pellet. They place that liquid containing the non-sperm DNA into a new tube, which is part of that case, and that becomes the non-sperm fraction for that sample.

Taking the tube that contains the sperm cell pellet, the analyst will add a harsher chemical known as phenol-chloroform to extract or remove proteins, releasing the sperm cells and the male or the sperm DNA and purifying that DNA or sperm fraction to be tested. The phenol-chloroform is such a powerful chemical that lab analysts applying it to the samples must do so using a piece of equipment known as a chemical fume hood, a large, glass-enclosed cabinet with an exhaust system that protects them and everyone in the lab from the noxious fumes the chemical releases.

Next, the tubes move down the line to the robot operators who take three batches of extraction tubes to form one group of samples. One of the robot operators, Tom Williams, is there to demonstrate for us, as we watch through one of the well-placed windows at each station in the process. The lab gets a lot of requests to observe or photograph, but having people traipsing through the actual laboratories guarantees interruptions and contamination. They recently shot a thorough video of the processes for media use, finally eliminating the need for anyone besides lab personnel in the lab.

Their twenty-first-century workhorses, Maddox informs me, are the Tecan Freedom EVO 150. The number refers to the size of the deck of the robot's working space, which is 150 centimeters long. Other analysts work on their batches of twenty-four samples. "One advantage that we have that has been key to our success in this project [is] our automation," he observes. "So from the manual steps of three individuals to prepare those three batches of samples, they'll all get combined onto one ninety-six-well plate on our robot, so we've increased our efficiency. The robot basically does what humans have done for the most part, a lot of manual transfers, but it does it consistently. You basically hit 'Go' to go through the process. You need to watch it to make sure nothing happens, and there are certain checkpoints we have throughout the process."

We watch the analyst through the window. "Tom's got a rack there," Maddox points out. "He opened them up and placed them into those racks. They are in a predetermined order. You see him looking up at the computer for that. If we can get them into the robot, then the robot will take it from there."

I'm going to let Maddox explain the purpose of this step in the testing process: "We need to quantitate the amount of DNA that's in the sample of human DNA. So, we'll take a small amount of each sample, and we'll set up a qPCR, or quantitative polymerase chain reaction test. Basically, it works like a photocopier. We want to amplify specific regions in the DNA when we have a very small amount. We want to make millions of copies, so that we have enough copies to evaluate and determine the genetic DNA profile."

The quantitative procedure determines how much total human DNA the sample contains, Maddox patiently explains. It also allows the lab to see whether the sample has a lot of female DNA, if there is no male DNA, or if there is a small amount of male DNA, so they can decide whether they need additional testing specifically for male DNA. An instrument provides the quantitation data, which is then entered onto a spreadsheet in the computer system.

"All of the calculations are done to tell the robot, 'Okay, we need to take X amount of this DNA extract and dilute it with this amount of liquid to mix in with our actual PCR to make a target," Maddox explains. "The robot then uses that information to dilute the samples onto a new plate, and that plate goes to the thermocycler, where the PCR is performed."

We watch the robot go to work, its arms quickly and smoothly progressing through several steps. Each of the eight tips on the arm dips down into one of the tubes and removes and holds one sample. That process is referred to as pipetting, and the robot is so sensitive that it is able to pipette one microliter (one millionth of a liter) of material. The tips are constructed of a special material that can sense whether or not there is any liquid in a tube and the conductivity of the liquid samples in the tips. The tips then deposit the sample into one of the wells on the deck. Again, to prevent contamination, tips are only used once, so after use, the robot arm glides near the front of the deck, drops them into a disposal receptacle, slides to a different position and then picks up a new tip for the next round of pipetting.

A second arm with automated grips moves the plates that hold the samples dropped into them from each of the tips, which rotates somewhat akin to a record turntable. The deck is heated as well to incubate the genetic material further. A T-shaped object serves as a shaker with little grips to lock it in place as it vortexes, in labspeak, or shakes the material to mix it together.

Another piece of equipment has magnetic beads that the DNA will adhere to. For its automated procedure, it draws the DNA to the magnetic beads at the bottom surface, and the robot then uses suction to remove that collected DNA from the beads.

After the material is transferred from the tubes to the wells on the plate, the full plate is taken to the next lab, where the qPCR reaction test is performed. There, an instrument called a 7500 Real-Time PCR System collects the necessary data on the DNA sample that is used to create the DNA profile and inputs it into a computer database.

The qPCR system uses an instrument known as a thermocycler, and BCI's lab has five. The thermocycler provides conditions similar to a human body for the DNA to replicate, heating and cooling the DNA so that it implements the process to make copies of itself.

"It heats. It makes a copy. The pieces come and plug into the two strands. The pieces referenced would be the primers that target a specific location in the DNA to amplify the small number of initial copies to millions that can be analyzed. Then it just elongates and forms an exact copy. So PCR can be compared to a simple photocopy machine: you start with one or a few copies and can generate millions of exact copies,"says Maddox, keeping the fairly complex process simple.

The PCR makes millions of copies of specific sections of DNA that have a fluorescent tag on them added by the lab to identify the twenty-four locations mandated by the FBI to create a DNA profile. So, they are distinguished by color and size. That plate containing the amplified and marked DNA sections is then placed inside the lab's genetic analyzer.

The lab also utilizes an instrument known as a Tecan Freedom EVO 100. "After it comes off the thermocycler, we only need a small portion of that sample to go into our genetic analyzers," Maddox explains, proudly indicating another piece of equipment we're looking at through the next window that we've moved to down the hall. "This is our 3500 Genetic Analyzer, which allows us to type twenty-four samples at one time, so we increased our productivity from the previous 3130 model.

That robot will take from that plate and move a small amount to another plate, and we can then load it into the genetic analyzer."

The genetic analyzer uses an electric kinetic injector that injects the DNA into a column. Think of it as a straw, Maddox recommends, that has a polymer inside the straw. When the samples are injected into that straw or capillary, they flow through based on size, with the smaller fragments of DNA passing through the column faster than the larger pieces. The pieces pass by an instrument known as a capillary electrophoresis instrument, which is a small window in the capillary with a tiny camera and laser that records a signal when the laser excites the fluorescent tags on the pieces as they pass. If there's a small amount of DNA, the camera will record a small peak. A large amount causes a more intense signal, thus recording a larger peak on the graphic depiction.

The camera separates all of that information into colors to generate an electropherogram, which shows the tiny peaks, colors, and locations that comprise a DNA profile. Each of the locations has a letter and number, such as G3, A16, or C7. DNA has four base pairs: A, G, C, and T; the letter indicates the base pair in the DNA, and the number indicates which location. The electropherogram presents a picture of the DNA sequence genotypes that are based on the length of the specific DNA fragments. The software of the instrument will compare each location to what's known as an allelic ladder—sort of a Rosetta Stone for DNA—that contains the most common known types at the various locations in DNA.

"The locus (single location) or loci (several locations) are specific sites on the DNA, and what we look at is called short tandem repeats," Maddox says. "Those are segments of DNA typically four base pairs long, so it will be some combination of the four base pairs (A, G, C, T). That gets repeated over and over again within a population. So any one individual inherits two copies of the gene or the allele at a location in the DNA. They get one from their mother and one from their father, and these are based on size, that is, the number of times each pair repeats. I may have gotten one location that's twenty repeats from

my father, and then another location in the DNA I get twenty-five copies from my mother."

Here is the analogy Maddox draws to explain how the twenty-four
different locations mandated by the FBI help identify an individual. It
starts with me asking Maddox to find my car in the parking lot around
FirstEnergy Stadium where the Cleveland Browns play—or try to
play—NFL football. If I tell him my car is red, that's not going to help
him much, since there are so many red cars. "But if you tell me you
drive a red car with Pennsylvania license plates and a chrome bumper
with a dent on the left side, the more individualized you make it, the
easier it is to find," he says. "With DNA, the more locations you get, the
more specific you're getting. That eventually translates into where your
statistic is for how common you expect that DNA profile in the population." In other words, there's a one in one million chance that this DNA
profile matches another person besides the suspect.

Before we leave the lab area, Maddox adds that what I've seen are
the most current generation of these particular robots, and the lab just
switched over to the 3500 series in December 2016. The older instruments were somewhat larger, so the lab has more space now. They also
needed to recalibrate all of the equipment, which happens whenever
a sensitive testing or measuring instrument is moved to ensure that it is
functioning properly.

At that point, we walk down the hallway and through the laboratory
doors into a moderately sized but comfortably and nicely appointed
office cubicle farm.

"From there, the data comes out into the network, and then our
analysts in the cubicle area can pull up the data on their computers,"
Maddox says. "They can print it out and start a case file, comparing
their known DNA profiles and unknown DNA profiles, or determine
what they got from the evidence and generate a report."

Christopher Smith, CODIS administrator for BCI Richfield, tells me
that, basically, the immense and constantly proliferating FBI database

contains all of the existing DNA profiles in different categories so they can be compared to each other.

"The database will pull up a profile and display all of the pertinent information regarding what information was entered, who entered it, how long it's been in there, when it's been searched, and so on," he says. "It will search against other DNA profiles based on our search parameters, and then it can generate a match or a comparison that we can make. Then we'll evaluate it and determine if it's a hit or a positive match."

Before sending that information to a police department or law enforcement agency to investigate, however, the BCI implements an additional verification process to ensure the DNA profile is correct and whether or not it was a correct match to a known or unknown offender.

"You can see it's nothing big and flashy like on *CSI*," Maddox says, referring to the flickering images of criminals' faces on a screen, when in reality, it looks more like an EEG reading at a hospital, with peaks and valleys and multiple colors. When doing a CODIS search, all of the numbers from the DNA profile must be typed into the computer database. As a check and balance system to ensure accuracy, they also perform an administrative and technical review for each DNA profile. The entire process usually takes twenty to twenty-five days, according to Maddox.

"It's pretty boring," Smith allows. "It's a lot of number-crunching and algorithms that evaluate everything and put it together. But it's very useful. That collection of numbers will identify the repeats for sequences and that's how we'll compare them. Each marker has a set of numbers that's based on your genome, and we now have twenty-four locations to look at, so our certainty is getting better and better."

It may not be very exciting, but it sure has been accurate for Cuyahoga County. "About 39 percent of all the cases tested get a CODIS hit," Maddox says. "Of the ones that we get a profile for CODIS upload, it's been about 65 percent or 66 percent, so it's pretty high. I would not have predicted it would have been that high."

Maddox is particularly excited about learning the results of a joint study with the Ohio Attorney General's Center for the Future of Forensic Science and Bowling Green State University in Ohio. In June 2016, the Laura and John Arnold Foundation awarded the two institutions a two-year grant of $144,000 to use statistical modeling analysis of the abundant data gathered by the BCI from the SAKI project to help identify ways to streamline the analytical process of testing sexual assault kits.

"I know there's been a lot of research into the social aspects and some of the impacts on law enforcement," he says. "But this will give us a chance to do a deep dive into our data, to evaluate the most appropriate number of samples to give us the highest success rate for getting male DNA profiles, so we can better use our resources."

He anticipates more labs going straightforward with DNA testing. The equipment continues to get more sensitive and accurate, allowing identification from smaller and smaller samples, even "touch DNA" gathered from where a victim was grabbed or choked by an assailant, for example. If we know anything about technology, that trend is only going to continue.

"Our statistics for a single-source profile are already in the septillions, which is twenty-four zeros," the scientist says with glee. "The number of locations we can identify, that's just how powerful and specific these evidence kits are getting. There are also tools now with software that helps us with deconvolution to better analyze these DNA mixtures we're testing." Deconvolution, Maddox further explains, is breaking down a DNA mixture to identify the possible genotypes of each contributor.

As for how prosecutors leverage that number in a court case to demonstrate that the odds of that DNA profile matching another person in the population besides the offender are beyond infinitesimal, Rick Bell explains: "We write the number on the board with all the commas and zeros, and the DNA analyst explains just that. Since the numbers now are usually in the trillions, sometimes up to twenty-four zeros, it couldn't possibly be anyone else on the planet. Sometimes, you would need eight planets before it could be anyone else."

Chapter 7

The Research Partner: Rachel Lovell Disseminates Best Practices for the Future

L OCATED INSIDE THE historic former headquarters of the Goodyear Tire & Rubber Company erected in Akron in 1920, the Goodyear Theater is now a concert venue and beneficiary of a multimillion-dollar renovation. On Saturday, May 20, 2017, an engaged, inquisitive audience of more than 1,400 people has gathered to learn and be impressed by a baker's dozen of innovators in health care, business, art, media, and other fields for TEDxAkron.

Today's theme is "One Day." In his welcome address, Mayor Daniel Horrigan apprises everyone that today, they will hear about a number of important issues for the Rubber City, from homelessness and opioid addiction to sexual assault.

At just before 2 p.m., the third speaker, Rachel Lovell, PhD, senior research associate at the Begun Center for Violence Prevention Research and Education at Case Western Reserve University, takes the stage. She's slightly nervous but quickly relaxes into the topic she has immersed herself in for many years, particularly the last few, as the embedded research partner for the Cuyahoga County SAKTF. She's raring to add her talk on the task force's challenges and successes to the ninety-thousand-plus TEDx Talks regarding "ideas worth spreading to the masses" currently available online, as Sam Falletta, CEO of Incept and founder of TEDxAkron, says in his introduction.

"Jane is thirteen years old," Lovell opens. "She's walking home from middle school one day. And she sees a car behind her, sees two men in the car. The car stops. The driver gets out and asks her, 'How old are you?' She says, 'Thirteen.' The driver then grabs her, forces her into the car, where there is a second man in the backseat. The man in the backseat immediately starts to fondle her breasts and her groin. Then she begins to cry, and he then pulls off her clothes and begins hitting her because she's crying and screaming and fighting. That man then rapes her in the back of the car."

She proceeds to synopsize the rest of the young teen's ordeal. Jane was then taken to "what she described as a white house," where she was again repeatedly raped for the rest of the day and night before the men told her to get dressed and back in the car. They then dropped her off at a convenience store at 4:30 a.m.

Lovell continues to unfold this tale of unconscionable inhumanity, where the second layer of victimization was about to unfold. Jane's mother took her to an emergency room, and a Sexual Assault Nurse Examiner gave her a thorough sexual assault kit, or rape kit, examination. All good. The rape kit was then deposited into a storage container. That's where it remained for twenty years. Not good. She was about to fall victim to a system that didn't care about her. Or other rape victims. In what was typical at the time, nothing happened after she reported her brutal rape. No testing of evidence. No investigation. Until two decades later, when it became one of the first kits tested by the Cuyahoga County SAKTF initiative immediately after it was formed in 2013. The task force fast-tracked Jane's kit because the crime had occurred in 1993, and it was approaching the statute of limitations deadline.

In 2014, the then–Cuyahoga County prosecutor Timothy McGinty decided to allocate $100,000 to hire a researcher from CWRU's Begun Center. He had the foresight to commission a one-year pilot study generated by an embedded researcher, Lovell, who would document the processes, failures, successes, statistics, and data analysis of the task force's efforts to investigate and prosecute rape cases so that others could share what they had learned. The Begun Center later won additional grant monies of $858,324 to add three more years to the study. In a field marked by a dearth of significant literature, her groundbreaking research documents are all available to anyone in the world at begun.case.edu/sak.

"Jane's story is the first one I read as a researcher working with the sexual assault kits in Cuyahoga County in early 2015," Lovell tells her TEDx audience. "Her story stood out to me because I just couldn't imagine what she had gone through. But what I came to find out was that Jane was only one of so many victims in Cuyahoga County, across the nation, and in Akron whose rape kits were taken and never tested."

In Cuyahoga County, she says, there were approximately five thousand kits collected from 1993 to 2009 that were never tested. Currently, they also believe there are six thousand more pre-1993 kits in Cuyahoga County that have never been tested.

"What most people think happens," Lovell continues, "is that you go to a hospital, and you have a sexual assault kit taken, and then the police come, they pick it up, they take a report, they submit that kit to be tested. Then the results come back from that test, and then you use that for prosecution, and you thoroughly investigate it. But if you thought that, you'd be wrong, because life is not *CSI*, and it doesn't work that way."

Logically, whether you watch television crime programs or not, that is what you'd think would happen. You've collected evidence. You test it, right? Otherwise, it's not really evidence. You investigate. Do interrogations and interviews. Canvas the neighborhood. Get a warrant for the suspect behind the DNA. You take the offender to trial, and you get that person put away in prison. For many years. Right?

"What actually happens across the nation—it happened in Cuyahoga County and in Akron—is that the kits simply went into storage," Lovell emphasizes. "Most of the time victims never knew if their kits were tested." Looking down at her monitor, she clicks to a slide on the large screen above her that shows a row of storage lockers. "They assumed that because they took it that something would be done with it, but instead they were just put into these compartments where they were stored."

When Jane was assaulted, she says, DNA testing was just becoming available, and it was too expensive for most police departments to use on every rape case. It cost approximately $5,000 to test one kit then, but with the improvements in technology it now costs about $500 to test a kit. They also need less DNA material to identify it, and the testing is much faster.

In December 2014, Ohio's legislature passed a law that requires law enforcement agencies to send rape kits to the Ohio Bureau of Criminal Investigation (OBCI) for DNA testing. At that time, only California, Colorado, Illinois, Michigan, Texas, and Wisconsin had mandatory testing laws. Since then, roughly 14,000 kits that were submitted state-wide have been tested, including 4,000 from Cleveland, 1,700 from Toledo, and 1,400 from Akron. Those jurisdictions have the results, but Lovell believes Akron and Toledo have not been as aggressive in moving forward with investigations. (She tells me later that Cincinnati and Columbus did not have backlog kits, since they continuously tested as kits were taken, but there are no clear results available for what they did with those test findings.)

After launching its SAKTF in 2013, however, Cuyahoga County has recorded the highest number of convictions from testing backlog kits of any jurisdiction in the US. As of the week before her TEDx talk, they had convicted 266 defendants from backlog rape kits.

While testing of kits is still an issue in many jurisdictions nationwide, the other pressing challenge is whether or not they pursue investigations and prosecution once they get the kit test results, and it appears to be nearly impossible to mandate follow-up. Having seen what comes of successful follow-up of kit evidence testing, Lovell proactively advocates for the investigation and prosecution of the kits. She continues today to talk about what task forces such as Cuyahoga County's have learned by doing so. She proceeds through several key lessons.

"One of the main reasons you should be testing all kits is because there are a lot of serial offenders," she says. "In Cuyahoga County, over one-quarter of all defendants are linked to more than one kit." Since the repeat hits were solely from within the pool of backlog kits, as a statistician she posits they probably had committed additional rapes and assaults.

"We also know that a quarter of the defendants in our sample are raping strangers and non-strangers, which is counter to what most people thought prior to this initiative," she continues. Rape accusations between people who are acquainted can become he said–she said cases. However, if the man is connected to stranger assaults, it helps prove he is more likely to have raped the acquaintance, too.

By studying the offending patterns of the rapists identified through the DNA testing, Lovell and the task force members could see that those patterns may vary. In the past, rapists were thought to have a typical modus operandi (MO) that they followed closely again and again. They now know differently.

"People thought they were well organized and structured and had a well-thought-out way of assaulting," she says. "But when you read the case files, you see that's simply not the case. For example, one offender had three rapes. He raped a sleeping neighbor, a sleeping friend—both females—and then he raped a sleeping male who was a disabled man living in a group home. Without the DNA testing, you would never have put those together."

The task force has also learned to investigate all cases, not just the ones with DNA evidence from the rape kits, she says, because many of the cases without DNA have named suspects already in the case files who can be investigated. Often, there is other evidence such as clothing or sheets that can be tested, so Cuyahoga County investigators review the entire evidence inventory to see if there's anything they can use to catch offenders.

One of the great disappointments in looking at old case files, according to Lovell, has been finding how many cases were closed almost immediately, with a quarter of them closed within one day of opening. Sometimes the victim chose not to help with the investigation. Frequently, however, victims weren't informed about the contents, nor were they provided with victim advocacy. "So, what we're learning is that we need to change the way we investigate cases and use current practices to look at the pieces back then," Lovell tells the Akron audience. "Testing is the right thing to do. "Testing helps you find serial offenders and get them off the streets."

Checking the monitor in front of her once again, she clicks to a slide that reveals details on one of the most powerful lessons they've learned: Testing is cost-effective.

"We also did an analysis to show that testing actually saves you money in the long run," she says. "So in Cuyahoga County, as of January [2016], testing and investigating the cases cost $9.6 million, and a lot of that came from you and all of us because the taxpayers pay for testing of that through the OBCI."

Looking up at the next slide, she continues: "However, the cost from actually following up on these kits saved the community $48.2 million, which is a net savings of $38.6 million, or if you want to think about it per kit, it's close to $8,900 for each SAK that was tested that saved the community by getting those offenders off the street."

Part of that savings comes from eliminating trial costs for future rapes or assaults; part of it comes from preventing other crimes those offenders commit, such as car theft, burglary, or vandalism.

"But more importantly, it saves money because you're doing something with the testing of the kit," she adds to emphasize one of her primary messages to any and all of her audiences. "It's not enough just to test. That's an important first step, but there's so much more that we have to do after testing the kit."

Lovell closes her talk by saying that if the material she's covered today "hurts your soul or makes you very sad," her listeners have several options for how they can mobilize to make a difference, which she goes on to list.

Before doing so, however, she acknowledges that it can be a bit of a depressing topic and that anyone who knows her knows she can bring down any conversation merely because of the passion she has for revealing the truths she's learned about how rape and sexual assault cases have been handled in the US and what's being done to correct and improve those processes.

"My husband always asks me, 'Can we please not talk about rape during dinner?'" After a brief beat while the audience laughs, she deadpans, "I try my best."

If you are the survivor of a sexual assault and you had a kit taken and were not specifically told the results, she urges the audience, contact the police department where the assault occurred to ask about the results, since they now have to test all kits. In Akron, they should contact the Major Crimes Unit; in Cuyahoga County, the prosecutor's office; or they can also contact her.

Her suggestions for others who want to organize and make a difference in their community for "all of those victims who never had a voice, whose kits were never tested, or whose investigations closed very quickly" include contacting their local prosecutor's office to ask when they will see prosecution from all the tested kits, and if they have offender's names, when those cases will move forward. As elected officials, she explains, they will be more likely to respond to the community.

They can contact their police departments to ask the same questions. They can contact their local county council to request financial support, just as Cuyahoga County's council provided $100,000 at Prosecutor McGinty's request to expedite the testing and investigation of kits. Finally, they can request their local media to start asking questions, in the same way Cleveland's newspaper, the *Plain Dealer*, assigned several reporters to investigate the backlog kits and helped motivate the formation of the task force by raising public awareness and pressuring public officials to respond.

"Lastly, we can't really test our way out of the problem, because testing isn't really the first step," she says, intimating the way victims are treated is where a successful investigation and prosecution process starts. Echoing the theme of the day, Lovell concludes her TEDxAkron talk: "Our research shows that we need to improve the way we handle sexual assault so that *one day* how we treat sexual assault will change, and nothing like this happens again."

She exits, stage right, to great applause.

——————

Growing up near Amarillo in the Texas Panhandle, as she prepared to attend college, Lovell pondered pursuing a career in law—her father is an attorney—or possibly history, a favorite school subject. Five days after her high school graduation, she was almost eighteen and the proud owner of a brand new two-door 1997 Dodge Neon, a gift from her parents that she'd had for about a month to enjoy her summer freedom and so she could get around at Baylor University in Waco in the fall. "It was a big deal," she recalls fondly.

What she wasn't able to get around on her way home from a babysitting job in May, though, was a gargantuan garbage truck with a careless driver who signaled one way and then took up both lanes turning the other, plowing into Lovell's car and forcing her to swerve into an embankment near a telephone pole. She had tried to brace herself by pushing her legs into the floorboard, but the impact was so forceful that the bottom part of her legs and her ankles broke and then fused into each other, disintegrating both ankle joints. When she looked at her legs, her ankles were facing each other, and she remembers thinking, "That's not good."

In the confusion of the crash and her severe trauma, surrounded by fractured glass and a totaled car, she thought about two other things: Could she get her new pair of Birkenstock sandals off before they got blood on them? And she needed to use her new cell phone, another off-to-college gift from her parents, to call her mother, not an ambulance.

By the time she got to the hospital, her lower legs were so demolished that her bone tissue had begun dying. She remembers that, although the pain was excruciating, she never lost consciousness, and it only caused her to scream when the paramedic or the X-ray technician accidentally bumped her legs. The damage to her legs was so significant that they missed the fact that she had also broken her arm, which she and her mom didn't figure out until six weeks later when she was home recovering, and they heard it break again when her mom was transferring her to a wheelchair.

An emergency room doctor informed her parents that there wasn't much they could do for her, since the legs were basically splintered beyond their ability to reassemble the pieces. Lying in a hospital bed and wearing a neck brace until they confirmed she had no spinal injuries, she could only focus on the ceiling. The emergency room doctor also believed she would never be able to walk again, at least not normally. Fortunately, the surgeons were able to perform a procedure to keep her leg tissues alive. After five days, they sent her home to recover, and she's been recovering ever since.

Her father chose to get a second opinion and flew her to see other doctors. An orthopedic specialist in Houston said they actually had a proven procedure to reconstruct her leg bones. The doctor assured them, "It won't be perfect. She won't be a leg model or play professional basketball, but we can fix this." What followed fairly quickly were six surgeries. She missed her first semester, but was able to wear braces on one of her legs to attend Baylor in January of the following year. Each summer for the next few years, she would have various surgeries to remove bone spurs or to repair her knees or remove a plate, all to reduce the amount of pain she still endured. All totaled, she has had twelve surgeries to date.

"I still have a lot of pain in my everyday life," she reveals. "I'm limited in what I can do. I can't run. I can't do anything high impact. I can only use that joint for a limited amount of time without it causing me any problems, but most of the time I do have pain, but not an acute, sharp pain, but a constant dull pain."

You'd almost not notice without a close look. In fact, when she first told me, I had known Lovell for more than a year and had seen her moving around quite a bit, so I almost didn't believe her. "I've been in this body longer than I was in the other body," she allows. "It's been almost twenty-one years, so it's just part of who I am now."

More significantly, she knows the accident changed the trajectory of her career. Though she ended up minoring in history, she chose sociology over law or any other major. At a crucial time in her life, the accident became a defining moment, during which she had realized that our purpose as humans is to try to help make the world a better place.

As a professional sociologist, she knows she came from a privileged life, referring to the fact that her family had enough money to assure her the best health care, and that her father specialized in working with or suing insurance companies, so he knew how to get reimbursed for the accident to help cover some of those costs.

"I was raised white, upper-middle class, so as a woman I never had to struggle," she says. "Well, everyone has to struggle, but it wasn't a core issue. Then I had this car accident, and very quickly I became 'an other.' I became disabled. I saw how people treated me differently, and I was trying to make sense of this inequality. In other words, a sociologist would say that once I lost it, I saw what my privilege was and was very interested in trying to understand more about that. So, people would always give me credit for doing as well as I had done recuperating. 'Oh, you must be so strong to do this,' but I always realized that I had all of these benefits that most people wouldn't have had."

All while recovering and regaining her health, Lovell earned her bachelor's and master's degrees in sociology at Baylor in three and a half years. In 2002, she moved to Columbus, Ohio, to attend The Ohio State University; she graduated in 2007 with her doctorate in sociology. She immediately landed a job at a survey consulting firm, but she quickly realized that corporate work in the private sector wasn't for her.

She worked at a large nonprofit research education consulting firm in Chicago for a year, and then accepted a position at DePaul University as a researcher and methodologist tasked with assisting faculty with their research.

In 2012, Lovell, her husband, and their eighteen-month-old daughter moved to Cleveland when she took her current job at the Begun Center at CWRU, primarily to be closer to her husband's family.

Toiling in the academic world, Lovell faces increasing pressure from the infamous "publish or perish" requisite for researchers and professors to rack up articles in peer-reviewed academic journals. Daniel J. Flannery, PhD, the Semi J. and Ruth W. Begun Professor at the Mandel School, director of the Begun Center, and co-lead researcher of the Cuyahoga County Sexual Assault Kit Pilot Research Project, a.k.a. Lovell's boss, regularly reminds her she has to be mindful of her time and how much she gives to the dissemination of the SAKTF initiative research.

"I definitely do need to publish, and it is important," she says. "But I also feel it's *more* important actually to get this information out and to make that difference. I would have to rework all of the material to publish in those journals. I guess I have to learn how to balance them both!" Much to her boss's delight, Lovell did get two articles about serial sex offenders she coauthored with Flannery et al. published in 2017, one in the *Journal of Criminal Justice* and one in *The Cambridge Handbook of Violent Behavior and Aggression, 2nd Edition.*

When people ask, "Where are your publications?" she likes to respond, "What about the $1.3 million in grants and the dissemination of our research?" That dissemination is worldwide in the same way anything published online is in this era. The extensive information about what the Cuyahoga County SAKTF has learned, including mistakes, is available to any jurisdiction, any professional, any teacher or professor of higher learning. Even you. Just visit begun.case.edu/sak or www.sakitta.org.

Lovell's typical day includes researching all the records of the backlog cases that the Cuyahoga County Prosecutor's Office keeps; interviewing the investigators, prosecutors, and advocates involved on their processes, experiences, and lessons learned; and socializing with the team that has grown close through this ultimate law enforcement bonding experience. Reflecting on her good fortune as a sociologist who gets to study and record the evolving process and groundbreaking successes of the SAKTF work being done in Cleveland, she says: "There's not a lot of research-based literature on sexual violence. So, our ultimate goal is to change the ways we talk about rape, treat rape victims, and support them."

"We're trying to help other jurisdictions learn from our mistakes," adds Rick Bell, who heads the SAKTF for the Cuyahoga County Prosecutor's Office, in an early interview I did with him a couple of years earlier. So, in addition to having the research partner and all that they've published, he notes that their task force members have talked in person or via telephone to prosecutors in at least twenty cities, and he's also testified before state legislators exploring similar initiatives in places such as Washington State, which helped them move their statewide task force effort forward. "We see the similarities in other places where kits weren't tested or not enough detectives were put on cases to investigate and find the victims, so cases were regularly shut down when they should have been kept open."

Despite the "Pen of Damocles" dangling above her to publish, Lovell speaks publicly whenever she can to special interest groups such as the Ohio Alliance to End Sexual Violence. She even gave an impromptu presentation to a group of attorneys her father assembled when she went home for Thanksgiving in 2016. "Cleveland is a unique success story in many ways," she says. "So if we can help other jurisdictions see there's great value in testing and investigating the kits, it's worth it. Yes, it's a resource drain. Yes, it's hard to look backwards when you have new cases all the time, but here are some of the great things that can come from doing this."

Lovell says they do always try to understand and incorporate the fact that the SAKI project significantly increased the workload of the investigators and prosecutors, and that law enforcement must deal with new kits on a daily basis in some jurisdictions. In a conversation with Bell one time, he gave her a perfect metaphor: a conveyor belt that's moving faster and faster, à la what many consider to be the most popular episode of the TV program *I Love Lucy*. Entitled "Job Switching," the September 1952 episode had Lucy and Ethel take jobs in a chocolate factory where the conveyor belt kept gradually accelerating to the point where they couldn't box the candies quickly enough, so they tried to stuff as many as they could in their mouths or their clothes.

Once all of the backlogged kits—or at least those that have been collected and submitted for testing—are processed completely through to indictment and prosecution, where possible, that load may lighten a bit. But jurisdictions such as Detroit and Cleveland still have from one to four years to go, as of June 2017.

On the bright side, Lovell believes, all of the new legislation and the change in cultural approaches to sexual violence will be in place so that this pathetic phenomenon of neglected kits does not happen again. She's also confident in the body of achievements in cities such as Cleveland, Detroit, Houston, New York, and Memphis and that the research that's come out of those will provide a significant counterbalance as well.

"We've proven it was not an insurmountable challenge," she says. "It's just a matter of how much pressure the public and victim advocates can apply on the right people and say, 'This may have been what was happening in the past, but it's not what's going to happen now. We care about rape. We want these rapists off the streets. We see how much they serially offend. We believe victims now and want to take care of them. We're not going to settle for what has been happening.'"

Chapter 8

Reclaimed Evidence:
Shondreka Lloyd, Part 2

WHOEVER IT WAS, the knock on the front door was hard and reso-lute. Warily, John Jones opened it. Two men stood on the porch. One, a middle-aged, medium-height guy wearing jeans, a button-down shirt, and a jacket against the March chill, stepped forward. John noticed the bulge of a gun on the man's belt as he flashed a badge.

"Good morning, sir. My name is Tim Clark. I'm an investigator for the Cuyahoga County Prosecutor's Office. I need to speak to Shon-dreka Lloyd."

"She doesn't live here," Jones blurted out, fearing his fiancée had done something illegal. That didn't seem like her, but she did have a pretty tough past.

Detective Clark knew full well that this was her residence. He smiled and glanced at the mailbox that said Shondreka Lloyd.

"She doesn't live here. We're not together anymore," Jones tried again. Actually, they were closer than ever, after the former NFL tight end with the Baltimore Ravens (2000–2003) had treated her to a romantic weekend that included dozens of paper hearts he hand-cut and scattered throughout their hotel room.

"Well, hey, listen, if you do happen to talk to her, here's my card," Clark said coolly, having played this game on numerous occasions over the past twenty years. The family is always protective and doesn't want to divulge anything to law enforcement officers. "Have her call me. It's very important."

"What's this about?" Jones inquired.

"I can't tell you what it's about. She's not in any trouble. She's the victim of a crime I'm investigating, and I just need to speak to her. Thank you." He and his partner turned and walked to their car in the driveway. Jones stared at the detective's back, his mind racing, then closed the door.

"I can't speak for what other investigators do, but even if it's their mom, their sister, aunt, uncle, grandmother, whoever, I would not divulge anything, especially because of the nature of the case; it's a rape," Clark explains when I meet with him in 2017, four years later. We're having coffee with Marya Simmons, a victim advocate for the SAKTF at Karl's Inn of the Barristers restaurant, better known as Karl's for the owner/deli man, a frequent haunt of law enforcement agents and attorneys who work across the street in Cleveland's Justice Center, a twenty-five-story monument to the New Brutalism architectural movement. Clark and Simmons work in Courthouse Square, a building owned by the county prosecutor's office overlooking Lake Erie that houses the task force.

"It's confidential," Simmons says, with Clark quickly overlapping.

"A lot of times victims of rape don't tell anybody because there's such a big stigma when it comes to rape and the public's perception. Typically, they won't tell their mother or anybody unless they were there or knew about it at the time. So, we just don't tell anybody," he confirms.

When Jones went back inside the house that day, he immediately called Shondreka at the Revenue Group, an accounts receivable management company where she worked as a supervisor.

"Shondreka, some detectives came by the house," she heard through the receiver.

"I ain't did nothing!" Shondreka shouted.

"No, no. He said it was like something that happened twenty years ago."

"Twenty years ago?" she thought about what it could be. Her juvenile record had been sealed. "The only thing that happened twenty years ago was I got raped."

Silence for a few moments. "What?"

"Yeah, I got raped when I was like fourteen." Silence. Jones knew she had been raped by someone she thought was her friend, but no details. They didn't talk about it much.

"That's not something I share with people," she tells me. "I don't tell anyone, because people are very judgmental when you tell them that you got raped. They look down on you like you're either fragile or tainted goods. So that's how John found out, but as soon as he found out, he's been supporting me ever since." Shondreka refers to him as her "support system."

Later that day or the next, she called Clark. He explained who he was, but then told her pretty much the same thing because he can't know for certain who he's talking to on the phone. "You're a victim of a crime. I can't discuss it over the phone. I need to meet with you."

A couple days later, she went downtown to the tightly secured task force offices, with lots of locked doors with pass card entry, no windows into the hallway on their floor, and a police officer performing security checks in the lobby. She definitely needed support. So, Jones accompanied her the first time she met with Clark and Simmons, who would be her advocate. Well, he made it to the lobby, anyway.

"No, you can't sit in on the interview," Clark informed him. He chuckles now about how protective Jones was over Shondreka, which he appreciated, since most women come in alone; but he could not violate the confidentiality protocol. "I'm sorry. If she wants to tell you whatever this is about afterwards, that's between you and her. But right now, I need to speak with her, and you can't be in the room."

He wasn't happy about it, Clark recalls, but Jones backed off and waited. He would accompany Shondreka on her first several meetings, until she was comfortable. She had no idea what this was about. It was twenty years later. Why bring up her rape now?

"I don't know what's going on or what I'm walking into," Shondreka remembers. "But after I got to know Marya—I love her so much! Then I got comfortable with the situation, and I was able to go on my own and talk to people and stuff like that."

Marya, the lone advocate then, Clark, and the two other investigators at the time had first met with the task force crew in late February 2013, but the team officially started processing kits and cases in early March. Shondreka's kit from 1993, however, was one of the first two or three Clark had to investigate immediately of the twenty cases dropped on his desk. Facing the looming twenty-year statute of limitations deadline, he had about a month to get her case indicted.

"She remembered every little detail about what happened to her when she was fourteen," Clark says with a bit of awe. "She's a grown adult now twenty years later, and she probably gave one of the better accounts of what took place than most of the victims I've dealt with."

"Very detailed," Marya interjects. Prior to joining the task force in 2013, the soft-spoken Simmons worked as a justice system advocate at the Cleveland Rape Crisis Center for two years and then as a chemical dependency counselor at the Hitchcock Center for Women in Cleveland for three years. Her work experience honed her predilection for helping women trapped in the often convoluted and confusing justice system, so she decided to earn an associate's degree from Bryant and Stratton College and a bachelor's from Tiffin University. She is now a Registered Advocate with Senior Standing (RASS) in Ohio.

"That's rare to remember that much detail, especially with trauma involved," Clark continues. "They forget things. They block things out. They can't remember faces. Then, on the other end of the spectrum you get some victims, a smell will trigger a memory. 'He smelled like piss,' or 'He smelled like marijuana.' They can't remember his face, but if they hear his voice, 'That's him. I know his voice!' So everybody deals with trauma differently."

Shondreka's memory was intricately and lavishly detailed. "It was almost as if she were reading the police report she gave twenty years ago," he says. With so many details, the seasoned detective remembers being suspicious that she was embellishing things a little bit. Like that part about getting second-degree burns when her assailant and his "friend" poured boiling water on her foot. He looked at her ankle and foot and thought it should show more scar damage had the burn been that severe.

"I was a combat medic for twenty years in the army," says Clark, who served six years active duty and fourteen in the reserves as a staff sergeant. The Cleveland native enrolled in the Cleveland Police Academy in 1996. "[Her injury] had healed very nicely to where it looked like a skin blemish." He even confided to Marya that he thought she had gone a little overboard with the level of details, and he wasn't expecting that.

Then he read the St. Luke's Hospital medical records from the time of her rape and sexual assault kit exam. They confirmed the second-degree burn. "Wow, I was kind of taken aback by that," Clark admits.

Next Clark met with her rapist, Darlell Orr. He was in prison. He'd been in and out of prison since the time of the rape in 1993. Clark knew him well. He'd encountered Orr and his siblings many times. First, as a boot camp instructor at a juvenile detention center in Hudson, Ohio, east of Cleveland, where Orr and his brother had been sentenced when Clark was still in the army but working as a drill sergeant at the boot camp in the afternoons and evenings. Later, he encountered the Orr family as a police officer in the 4th District where they lived.

Here's the best way I can describe Clark: intelligent, no-nonsense but polite, ample street smarts, and street tempered, having worked undercover narcotics for many years with CPD. Basically, he's the guy you want at your back on the battlefield or in a dark alley. He's not the guy you want coming after you. Orr knew that well from their boot camp days together.

There are two things Clark prides himself on. One is his "gift of gab." He tells new investigators that it's easy to go out and run around in the street and chase bad guys. It's hard to talk to people. "Ninety percent of this job as a detective or even as a patrolman is knowing how to talk to people, knowing how to relate to people," he says. "If you don't have that, you're never going to be successful in your career."

He also knows that you can't treat a victim like they're the ones who did something wrong. "They're a fucking victim," he says with the anger and injustice he feels when he thinks about how rape victims are treated. "They didn't do nothing wrong. They were raped. And it doesn't matter what she was doing." He's talking about when a prostitute or sex worker is raped—the ultimate test case for advocates and experts alike to determine how well our society understands that *no* truly, definitely, always means no.

"If a prostitute says to me, 'Well, it was my fault,' I tell them, 'No. No. I don't care if you had them lined up around the corner and were giving [sex acts] out like Halloween candy. It doesn't matter. That guy, you didn't want to have sex with. For whatever reason. He raped you. So, I don't care if you robbed ten banks the day before and killed ten guys the day after; on that day, you were raped, and that's all I care about. I'm not here to judge you.'"

His passion for justice is palpable. He also understands how difficult life is for drug-dependent people or the impoverished and disenfranchised citizens of the inner city. Rape, he says, is the one crime he will never understand, especially of a child, but any person.

He's currently handling about one hundred open cases related to the backlog rape kits for the task force. He's closed 178 cases, and has had roughly forty indictments; all but two have been convicted or took a plea. The two were found not guilty due to legal technicalities.

When they met this time around to discuss Shondreka's case, Orr had returned to his familiar walls-and-bars abode not long before Clark's visit. This time, he wouldn't be leaving. In 2011, he had committed a home invasion and murdered the owner. Orr chose to represent himself in a bench trial. He was convicted of aggravated murder and sentenced to life in prison without the possibility of parole. When

Clark visited him, he refused to answer any of the detective's questions about the rape and asked for a lawyer to end the interview.

Clark and Edward Fadel, the assistant prosecutor assigned to the case, had Orr indicted for the rape in 2013.

Orr's attorney from the Cuyahoga County Public Defender office argued that his constitutional rights protected his client from being tried as an adult for a crime he committed at thirteen. Additionally, Ohio law at the time he committed the offense stipulated that cases of young children could not be transferred to an adult court. That law changed in 1997 to allow trial in a common pleas or adult court for a juvenile crime if the offender was over twenty-one at the time of his arrest. Orr's attorney argued the revised statute could not be retroactively enforced, and that the penalties for Orr as a juvenile would have been much less severe than an adult court would have given.

On their side, the Cuyahoga County prosecutors argued that the case should not have been dismissed in the first place and that he had no constitutional protection to be treated as a juvenile. Having the case argued in an adult court only changes the venue and doesn't affect his rights. Primarily, the prosecutors argued they need the opportunity to pursue justice for victims of serious crimes such as rape or homicide. There are no definitive statistics available on how many of the sexual assault kit cases involve suspects or defendants who were juveniles at the time they committed the assaults.

In 2014, a Cuyahoga County judge dismissed the rape case, arguing the adult court did not have the authority to hear the case of a defendant who was thirteen at the time of the rape in 1993. Concomitantly, the juvenile court could no longer hear the case, because Orr was now in his mid-thirties. When the Cuyahoga County prosecutors appealed the decision, Ohio's Eighth District Court of Appeals in Cleveland upheld the decision to dismiss, so the prosecutor's office asked the Supreme Court of Ohio to hear the case.

Ultimately, after hearing arguments on February 7, 2017, the supreme court ruled on February 22 that it would not decide the case.

The court did not provide specific reasons for the decision, nor did it affirm the opinion of the district court. Orr, now thirty-seven, won the legal battle, so his crime against Shondreka Lloyd would not be officially recorded. A Pyrrhic victory at best for a lifelong criminal who will never experience freedom again.

Still, Shondreka, obviously, was greatly disappointed. No, she was downright pissed off.

"I never had a chance to testify," she says. "But I feel like he's already locked up. They know he did it. There's DNA. So why not charge him? He's already locked up for life. He said when he raped me he would have gotten a little juvenile time or whatever prison time, and it wouldn't have been as severe, and that he didn't rape me as an adult, so he feels like he shouldn't be tried as an adult from our rape case, but a rape is a rape, and you did it, so in my mind it's about how can my justice be served for what you did to me?"

"I just comforted her the best way I could, took her out to eat, got her flowers, kept everything as normal as possible," Jones recalls. "She's a real strong person naturally, so she was disappointed, but I just reassured here that God had already punished him through the justice system, so he was being punished for her, too."

She could have viewed it as another situation where the adults and officials in her life had let her down, just like they did after she was raped as a child. Maybe part of her did. However, she knew in her heart that this time she had an entire team working hard to prosecute and bring her brutal, seemingly conscienceless assailant to justice. She had a lot of people on her side that cared about her and were doing everything they could to help her. In the end, Shondreka's glad she participated in the task force efforts.

"I just thank God for Marya," she says of Simmons, who remains in touch with her, even though the case is officially closed. "She's a great person. Very understanding. She helped me get over my monsters, some of the things I was dealing with, so again, it was uplifting. She doesn't even know that she was my counselor, but she helped me get over a lot. I just didn't realize how much it had affected me to this day."

Both Clark and Simmons talk about how Shondreka was a special case because of her courage to confront her assailant from start to finish, whereas some start off strong and then fade as a trial date gets closer. She was also different because many of the women struggle and don't have a lot of family support the way she does, so they deal with the challenges of facing their past assault and the revived cases alone.

"You're not going to have a success story in every case," Simmons says. "You're not going to have a victim who wants to participate from beginning to end in all cases, but just watching that progression of confidence sometimes is great. Encouraging them and validating how they feel throughout the process and seeing how sexual assault affects people differently and seeing how they can overcome, and they don't have to be a victim. They can also be a survivor."

For his part as investigator in her case, Clark says he's disappointed Shondreka didn't get a chance to see her rapist sentenced for that crime or to give an impact statement to tell the judge and the court all the misery he had caused her. She never had a chance to finally break the silence and share her story on the record in a courtroom. He and Simmons agree that can be a very powerful and empowering experience for a victim, even twenty-plus years later.

"She didn't get the justice she deserved or wanted because of a technicality in the courts, but Orr's never going to get out of prison," he says. "She knows he's going to die in prison, so she doesn't have to worry about him getting out on the street or trying to find her. So, in a way, she did get some semblance of justice."

He also admits she's one of two victims he's grown attached to, mainly because of her courage and willingness to speak up, tell her story, and take on her offender.

"I have to totally separate myself, so I tell them, 'Listen, I'm not here to be your friend. I'm not here to be your social worker. I'm here to get justice for you and that's it,'" he says. "That protects her or him, the victim, and it protects me from being emotionally attached to the case. But Shondreka and another case, for whatever reason, I happened to get more emotionally attached, but for the most part, I try to separate myself from all of that."

Simmons, who developed a special fondness for Shondreka, says of the conclusion to her legal case: "She was angry, but as angry as she was, we had discussed the possibilities on several occasions, so she was prepared either way, and she didn't skip a beat. She yelled about it. Said how she felt about it. She said how she felt about her mom's participation in it by not supporting her initially, but at the end of the day, she said, 'I'm still here. I'm still going to do what I'm going to do. I'm still going to raise my kids. I'm happily married. I'm still going to school to get my degree.' She remains very positive and is not going to give up just because this didn't work out the way she wanted it to."

Indeed, the day after we spoke, Shondreka learned that she was pregnant as a result of an in vitro procedure she had recently undergone. She was already raising several of Jones's children, whom she never refers to as her stepchildren, calling them her children as well. He credits her for helping him gain custody.

"Me and my wife, Shondreka, we relate real well to each other because we both grew up troubled teens," says Jones, who grew up in Cleveland until he was ordered by a juvenile court judge to attend high school at the Glen Mills Schools, a court-adjusted boarding school near Philadelphia, where he flourished, playing several sports and studying journalism as a trade. He met Shondreka in 2009, a couple years after he returned to Cleveland.

She graduated with a degree in central sterile processing technology from Stautzenberger College in Brecksville, Ohio, just south of Cleveland, in August 2017. She will eventually become a surgical technician. "Right now, I can't stomach the guts and gore of the operating room," she admits, adding she has an internship lined up at the VA Hospital.

In a follow-up email about her current relationship with her mother, she replies:

> Our relationship improved because I probably forced it. Still not perfect, but what is? She's still in denial about the entire situation, but I have grown emotionally and mentally tired of trying to jog her memory. I don't think she actually forgot. . . . I just don't think she expected things to resurface. She refuses to really speak on it, which makes me upset. Since I'm now pregnant with a child of my own, I choose not to stress about it and love my child the way my parents DIDN'T LOVE me.

She was interviewed for the Joyful Heart Foundation's documentary about the sexual assault kit project, *I Am Evidence*. She and her husband thoroughly enjoyed meeting producer Mariska Hargitay at the foundation's annual gala a couple years ago. However, they did not attend the 2017 premiere because they didn't like the final edit, which left much of her story on the dreaded cutting-room floor.

"I believe they said the film had been taken over by the HBO people," she relates in her email. "I don't know the business, so . . . However, I have no regrets. My life and testimony are my own. I've grown to THANK GOD EVERYDAY for the life I NOW live."

She's ready to move on with her life and all of the good things she has going for her, but she's also ready to help others who've been raped or assaulted in any way she can.

"Everything I've been through just made me a fighter," says the gregarious and no longer silent Shondreka. "Now, I want to fight for everybody who can't speak for themselves or don't have the strength to stand up for themselves or who are scared to come out or say anything."

After a beat, Shondreka raises her finger and with all the attitude she has stored from her years living the precarious street life and all the bad breaks and blows she has endured, she assures any victim of sexual assault, "I got ya, babe. I'll speak for ya. I got ya."

PART 2

Detroit Digs Out from a Pile of Darkness

Chapter 9

The Enforcer:
Kym Worthy and the Decision

ABOUT 4:42 P.M. on a Wednesday afternoon in April 2017, Wayne County Prosecutor Kym Worthy enters the swirling chaos of the Madonna University television station on their campus in Livonia, Michigan, to film an interview segment of *Celebrate Michigan*. She purposefully strolls past three floor cameras as their nervous operators position themselves according to the stage manager's instructions in their headphones; a boom camera guided by students in the control room hovers and whirls overhead. A small but mighty studio audience, including two visiting Dallas police officers, applauds as Worthy enters and takes her seat opposite the show's hosts, Chris Benson and Dennis Neubacher.

The two seasoned TV pros introduce their guest, define the mission of the Wayne County Prosecutor's Office, and ask what they label "probably the most frequently asked question you get": Why did she become a county prosecutor? She jokes that it's the "most frequently asked question I can never answer," and then tells the story of how, even though her parents didn't let her watch much TV, when she was in middle school she religiously watched the show *Julia*, starring Diahann Carroll as the eponymous lead, Julia Baker, a nurse whose husband died in Vietnam and was trying to raise a son. She points out that it was the first show starring an African American woman.

Later in the program, she talks about how important her mother and father were as role models, too. Her father was the first African

American from Michigan—and one of the first twenty-two African Americans ever—to graduate from West Point. Her mother had a master's degree but never worked outside of the home. Both always told her how proud they were of her and encouraged her to pursue the career that she wanted.

"I always wanted to be a lawyer," Worthy says, relaxed in a comfortable suit and enjoying the interview, but speaking in her characteristic quick clip. "I noticed that there was never any African American representation in that field ever at that time. Now it's of course different. No lawyers in my family. Didn't know any lawyers. For some reason it popped into my head and hasn't changed since."

When they ask what her job entails, she responds that her basic job, though there's nothing basic about it, is to serve as the chief law enforcer of Wayne County, the largest, most populous, and busiest county in Michigan, where 87 percent of the criminal cases in the state are handled. Her office is responsible for case intake. She explains that she has to take her job very seriously and be highly ethical and unbiased in her decisions, because the prosecutor, in deciding who's charged and who's not, is the gatekeeper to the criminal justice system. People who watch TV often think the prosecutor's most important job is trials, but it's actually case intake.

"When you have the awesome power of signing your name to an arrest warrant and changing someone's life forever—in all cases, you hope it's for the right reasons—you have to be very, very deliberate," she explains. "You have to do what's right. You can't take forever, certainly. But you have to make sure that you are making the best decisions you can make with all the information that you have at the time, and sometimes decisions can't be made overnight."

It was her ability to make and enforce tough decisions expeditiously, however, that established her as a legal warrior against sexual violence, when she was cast into the national spotlight a decade ago. She's on the TV show today to disseminate the pathfinding work she, her office, and the Wayne County SAKTF have accomplished since that toasty summer day in 2009 when Worthy received a phone call from her Wayne County assistant prosecutor, Rob Spada. He was standing in the Detroit Police Department's property and evidence warehouse in the Poletown East neighborhood, dozens of sealed and untested rape kits at his feet and more piled on shelves rising in steel storage racks all around him. She could hear surprise and urgency in his voice.

He was there because the prosecutor's office was investigating evidence from old Wayne County cases in which there were questions about the accuracy of ballistics and other testing done by the recently shut down DPD crime lab that potentially required reopening the cases for new trials because of their 10 percent error rate. Now, evidence analysis statewide was conducted by the Michigan State Police crime lab, which had requested an audit of all evidence that Detroit police had in their property storage facility.

During his audit, Spada stumbled on thousands of white cardboard file boxes sealed with yellow or red tape; a few even lay open. The police officers guiding him through the nondescript concrete and brick building informed him they were rape kits. When he asked how many there were and whether they'd been tested, the officers could not give him an answer. Spada's quick scan, his boss heard through the receiver, indicated somewhere in the neighborhood of ten thousand kits or more.

"It doesn't take much to surprise me in this business," Worthy tells me when we first talk in May 2016. To say she is a seasoned pro in the criminal arena is beyond an understatement. "But I was shocked and horrified. That day I went home, and I Googled '10,000 rape kits,' and I found it was a national problem.

"I wanted to charge somebody with whatever I could charge them with, but very quickly I learned that playing the blame game is not going to help any of these victims, and it's not going to help our cause in trying to bring justice to these victims, so I had to abandon that and move forward. I couldn't focus on who was responsible. I had to go forward."

Worthy first ordered a complete inventory, and the correct answer turned out to be 11,341 kits, setting the prosecutor on a long odyssey that is only now drawing to a close.

"We had a bad mayor," she sums up the problem. But that was just the start of it. She had also learned that instead of the one property storage warehouse everyone thought the DPD operated, several other places were used to keep—maybe "hide" would be a better word—evidence.

While she has noticed gradual changes in police policies, Worthy says they've been very slow because of numerous changeovers in leadership in both the DPD and the mayor's office. With each new police chief, each new mayor, there are reorganizations and new practices implemented that retard significant improvements. She feels the current police chief, James Craig, has been "very, very receptive to the issue," but that doesn't mean she doesn't still see problems.

"The ownership has to be from the chief on down and not just the chief," Worthy explains. "We now have the protocol with them that every SAK has to go to the lab. They have to follow the new statewide law, but we—that being the collective and collaborative we of the entire team fighting sexual violence—have offered free training for them on how to deal with sexual assault victims, because there was a huge problem in how we got to where we were in how they discounted the claims of victims and didn't believe them. It's not the police's job to make that kind of decision. They are there to do complete investigations. It's our job as prosecutors to determine the credibility of witnesses and whether we have enough evidence to go forward with a case."

Worthy had long established a reputation as a great arbiter and litigator, but upon learning of the secretly and illegally hidden and neglected rape kits, she was about to substantiate her title of "the toughest woman in Detroit," as bestowed upon her by *Essence* magazine in February 2010.

A year before the rape kit revelation, five years after she was elected as the Motor City's lead prosecutor, she had filed charges against then–Detroit mayor Kwame Kilpatrick. The indictment of the corrupt city

official eventually resulted in a twenty-eight-year sentence for racketeer-
ing, perjury, and other crimes. However, the hidden rape kits pointed
to a potential addition to Kwame's litany of misuse of power offenses:
obstructing justice. In addition, the crime lab's inaccuracies and errors
under Mayor Kilpatrick had reached such an egregious level that the
lab had to permanently close in 2008.

When she did her simple Googling to see how Detroit's estimate
of ten thousand untested kits stacked up, she hit some mind-numbing
numbers recorded by other major cities throughout the US that indicated this was a national issue. New York, for example, had tallied a
backlog of seventeen thousand kits in 1999; the municipality then spent
$12 million to process them and cleared the backlog in 2003. She found
estimates totaling four hundred thousand untested rape kits nationwide,
a number she considers conservative.

On *Celebrating Michigan*, she tells the cohosts she remembers thinking,
"Those of us from Michigan know the Big House at the University of
Michigan. . . . If you attach—and you should—a victim to each rape
kit, to every untested kit across the country . . . it's enough to fill the Big
House four times. So take that visual in, because we all know how huge
it is. So we started from there. We didn't know where to go. We didn't
have any money. So that's when our journey started back in 2009."

The cost to test and then follow through was almost as daunting as
the number of kits, especially at a time post-industrial Detroit wasn't
rolling in Cadillacs and cash. Two of its largest employers had recently
been forced into bankruptcy. Chrysler filed for Chapter 11 reorganiza-
tion in April 2009 and GM in June; without President Obama's pending bailout, they faced the loss of a million jobs at a time when the city's
unemployment rate hovered at 22 percent. Among Wayne County's
other financial woes loomed the loss of significant property tax revenue
thanks to the nationwide housing crisis.

Worthy wasn't certain how she was going to pay for it, but her lion's
heart and prodigious legal mind told her the kits had to be tested. It
was the right thing to do. It was the just thing to do for all those victims,

mostly women, who had been wronged—twice. Assaulted by a rapist, then ignored by the law enforcement and prosecution system that was supposed to protect and serve them.

There were other spurs for her decision. Twenty-five years earlier, she had initiated her legal career at the Wayne County Prosecutor's Office, and in 1989, the office selected her as its first African American special assignment prosecutor. She quickly established herself as an assiduously tenacious litigator who specialized in high-profile murder cases, gaining convictions of Toni Cato Riggs (who had murdered her husband, a returning Gulf War veteran) and two Detroit police officers who had beaten motorist Malice Green to death.

In 1994, she was elected to the Detroit Recorder's Court (now the Wayne County Circuit Court), where she presided over hundreds of serious felony cases for nine years. By the time she was sworn in as the first woman and the first African American to hold the position of Wayne County prosecutor in January 2004, Worthy had seen countless cases during which sexual assault evidence was neglected or mishandled.

One other lingering, darker, more personal motivator to seek justice for all of these victims of rape and sexual assault: One late night when she was attending her first year of law school at the University of Notre Dame in South Bend, Indiana, Worthy was attacked while jogging. She reported the sexual assault to the university, but concerns that the case could interrupt or end her law career kept the young woman from reporting to the police. That decision, she says today, was one she later came to regret. The thought that her rapist may have gone on to hurt others still haunts her.

Fortunately, now she had a chance to seek justice for thousands of victims who'd been ignored, even after they submitted to an invasive sexual assault rape examination, and go after numerous predators who could still potentially rape others. Moreover, she would soon understand there may have been other reasons why she chose not to discuss her case publicly, as she would learn all about the neurobiology of trauma that impacts a rape victim's responses, memory, and behavior for decades.

———————

Firmly resolved to see the untested kits through and bring justice to those victims—since each of the 11,341 kits represents a victim—Worthy contacted then–Detroit police chief Warren Evans. She wanted to meet to discuss how to move forward, and she made it clear that, even if the DPD was conducting an internal audit of the kits, an independent auditing entity would be necessary at that point both for the Wayne County Prosecutor's Office and the criminal justice system. He did not respond. Nor did he respond to her second inquiry with further warnings, including this statement: "It is imperative that your department move on this as soon as possible." Enough years had already been lost in this travesty of timely, legal, and just due diligence for the rape victims.

On September 22, 2009, a headline appeared in the *Detroit Free Press*: "Rape Evidence Shelved?" And the battle waged through the media between Worthy and the DPD ensued. They tried to claim that the total of kits was *only* seven thousand, and that their sample audit indicated that there were good reasons that only one thousand had been tested; the others did not need to be tested because of other evidence or a known assailant had been identified and so on.

That was just the beginning of Worthy's uphill struggle to make sure the kits, clear and present evidence of a serious and violent crime, were processed and investigated. She was buffeted on all sides, from the police to Wayne County Executive Robert Ficano, who denied approval to her plan and budget to oversee testing the kits.

US Rep. John Conyers (D-MI) invited her to testify before the US House Judiciary Committee in May 2010. She informed the representatives of her experiences as an assistant prosecutor many years earlier when she had to prosecute rape cases without a rape kit as part of her supporting evidence. "We were told by the police department that often they were lost, they couldn't find them, they were denigrated—all kinds of things," she attested. "At the end of the day, the judges and the prosecutors, the other witnesses, and the police go home. But the rape victim or the child molestation victim lives with it for the rest of their lives."

However, the first major step in her indefatigable efforts occurred when Worthy, in collaboration with the Michigan Domestic and Sexual Violence Prevention and Treatment Board, obtained funding from the Office on Violence Against Women to fund what became known as Project 400. Detroit would process four hundred randomly sampled untested backlog rape kits to determine the impact of what could be learned.

Based on the significant results of Project 400, the National Institute of Justice selected two jurisdictions, Detroit and Houston, to receive thirty-month grants of $1.5 million each. The funding was intended to determine the full scope of the unsubmitted SAK problem and more completely comprehend the resources required to correct the problem. The grant allowed the testing of an additional sixteen hundred SAKs. Commenced in April 2011, the NIJ-funded Detroit SAK action-research project ran through October 2013.

Already in Worthy's corner, Hargitay, who had testified on the same day as the persistent prosecutor at the congressional hearing, had her Joyful Heart Foundation bestow $75,000 and staff support to assist in the launching of Detroit's fledgling task force.

The initial two-thousand-kit sample led to 670 hits in CODIS. That included hits linking to crimes committed in twenty-six other states and the District of Columbia. It also helped the Wayne County Prosecutor's Office identify 188 serial rapists and obtain 15 convictions. Throughout the ensuing task force efforts in Detroit and other cities, the volume of serial rapists has surprised everyone. For Detroit, the following are five brutal offenders they were able to remove from their streets because of Worthy and the work of her entire task force team:

- Reginald Holland abducted and raped four women before being identified through DNA testing. He is now serving a life sentence.
- Shelly Andre Brooks raped and murdered seven women. He is now serving a life sentence.
- Gabriel Cooper raped three women. He is now serving a sentence of thirty to seventy years.
- Eric Eugene Wilkes raped four women. He is now serving a sentence of thirty-two to seventy-five years.
- DeShawn Starks raped four women. He is now serving a sentence of forty-five to ninety years.

Detroit would need a lot more money, though, to keep their task force rolling. Worthy had estimated she would need $17 million to test all of the kits, which at the time would cost between $1,000 and $1,500 each for the lab work alone. She also planned to investigate every case, whether or not the kit produced any significant evidence. The other challenge was limited personnel, with only three investigators on her staff and six available from the DPD.

So, Detroit definitely needed more money, and it wasn't the best time to request municipal funds, since the city had declared bankruptcy in July 2013. But when the financial going gets tough, the tough get fiscally innovative. If they needed to do bake sales, they would, because nothing was going to stop Worthy now. So, she was not averse to a little grassroots fund-raising. Fortunately, due solely to the success of the first two thousand kits tested, private donors gave $150,000. Nevertheless, a bigger windfall was needed.

Fittingly, the nonprofits Michigan Women's Foundation and the Detroit Crime Commission stepped forward and founded Enough SAID (Sexual Assault in Detroit), which they believe is the first crowdfunded campaign for a government program. Donations came from a wide variety of groups and individuals, from a local canasta club that threw into the coffers at weekly games to a local book club that gave money. Capitalizing on the fierce rivalry between the University of Michigan and Michigan State University football teams as their theme, a group of African American businesswomen organized a fund-raiser that brought in more than $30,000. One individual, Facebook COO Sheryl Sandberg, contributed an unsolicited $25,000, and an Australian company chipped in another $100,000 and lobbied all of the presidential candidates to inform them of the problem.

"Since we've been doing this, about $1.9 million private sector money has leveraged about $8 million of public money," says Peg Tallet, chief operating officer of the Michigan Women's Foundation. "Our donations have ranged between $500,000 and $5, and we've gotten money from all fifty states, eighteen foreign countries, and a number of service people around the world, so this effort resonates with many people."

Tallet went into the fund-raising campaign with three concerns: If they spent the next five years raising the money and got the backlog kits resolved, would another ten thousand untested kits show up at some point? The law change in Michigan eliminated that concern. Her second concern revolved around the dubious status of Wayne County government, where Ficano had become embroiled in accusations of corruption around misuse of public funds. The partnership with the Detroit Crime Commission should shield them from money "disappearing into an abyss," she says. Third, she worried about double-dipping with taxpayers who had already paid to have kits tested that weren't because of what she refers to as "bottom-line government failure."

Initially, she was also "surprised and disappointed" by the decision of Detroit's corporate community and foundations, known for being philanthropically generous and community-minded, not to support the backlog kit testing initiative. "They told us, 'The minute we pick up after the government's mistakes, that's what we're going to be asked to do. We're not going to be able to do things that are additive,' and I understood. That made a lot of sense. With the foundations, it didn't fall within the legal parameters of what they could support."

A couple of other things happened in Detroit's favor. In 2014, the Detroit Crime Commission, working on behalf of the Wayne County Prosecutor's Office, negotiated the cost of lab testing down to $490 per kit. Realizing more substantial money was required to continue the SAKTF endeavor, public entities including the Michigan Attorney General's Office ($3 million), the state legislature ($4 million), and others granted $8 million to Enough SAID. Six DPD officers dedicated to rape kit investigations joined the task force in Worthy's office.

Ironically, Ficano, the county executive who stymied Worthy's initial plan, lost his reelection bid in November 2014 to Warren Evans, the police chief who wouldn't respond to her requests to start an independent rape kit audit. Always the pragmatic politician and prosecutor, Worthy had endorsed Evans, and it paid off a year later when he pulled $1 million from Wayne County's delinquent tax fund for the ongoing SAK operations. He also relocated the SAKTF into the Guardian Building, an historic art deco skyscraper not far from Worthy's downtown headquarters.

At the time Spada discovered the rape evidence boxes, the dates on some kits went back almost thirty years. With a twenty-year statute of limitations for rape, there were quite a few that had expired. Worthy made the bold decision to test all of the kits anyway, whether or not the statute of limitations had run its course, whether or not the defendant may be deceased. She had many more-than-valid reasons.

"There may be cases that we tried without having the rape kit results or even knowing if there was a rape kit, so potentially, we could have someone exonerated from a case we have already tried," she explains. "It has not happened yet, but it's always a possibility, so I thought that important to have them all tested."

There is a federal rule of evidence that most states follow that allows evidence to be used in a case, even if the statute of limitations has expired for a specific crime related to that evidence. In other words, Michigan and many other states apply the Rule of Evidence 404(b), as she explains: "In certain cases, after there has been a judicial review, we can use that evidence, that victim in another case where the statute of limitations is not an issue." Basically, if a defendant is on trial for a rape and there is a kit from a previous rape where the statute of limitations has expired, he cannot be tried for that previous rape, but the kit results can be used as evidence to prove that the defendant has a history of rapes. These are particularly useful in he said–she said acquaintance rape cases, in which prosecutors can use a previous act of rape to show the defendant is not just a nice guy caught in a misunderstanding.

Worthy also believes it is always good practice for law enforcement to populate criminal databases. "If we test all of the kits, even the ones beyond the statute of limitations, we may get CODIS hits," she says. "We many not be able to use them in a trial, but the CODIS hits may identify someone who committed other sexual assaults or other crimes, so they can assist in the arrest of those suspects."

So, yet another reason is that by testing, you can help solve crimes in many other states. One thing Detroit has learned is that rapists don't restrict themselves to one city. Looking at their SAKTF's statistical information, she relates that they've mapped out offenders from Detroit who are connected to rapes in forty other states. (As of June 4, 2017, they've identified 797 suspected serial offenders and have recorded 95 convictions with 335 cases being actively investigated and another 1,692 awaiting investigation.) "It's not really accurate when it comes to Detroit's city limits, but everybody here knows what I'm talking about when I say, 'Rapists travel beyond 8 Mile Road [a major thoroughfare delineating the start of the suburbs].'"

After pushing through the initial shock and horror of what they had uncovered, she determined what she needed to do by drawing a perfect analogy with the most heinous of crimes.

"Everybody understands a cold case homicide," she says. "Nobody investigating a cold case homicide in this country, if they found a smoking gun, would ignore that case, no matter how old it was. So we want to bring justice to as many of these as possible, not just testing, but the investigation and prosecution as well. Testing is just the first step. It's an important first step, but certainly if you just test them and do nothing else, then that doesn't bring justice to any victim. They still have to be investigated as if it happened yesterday—or how it should have been investigated when it first happened—and also they must be prosecuted."

Worthy knew she needed to ensure that this would never happen again. She and her team took three steps to do so: First, they initiated a protocol mandating that going forward all kits must be sent to the lab. "It took us a long time, and it was not easy getting that through to the police department," Worthy recalls. "There were several starts and stops, but we eventually got that done a year or so later. So they are supposed to send every SAK to the lab."

Second, she researched legislation across the country to determine which states had laws enacting standards for getting sexual assault kits to a crime laboratory for testing, such as Illinois and Colorado. There weren't many. They used those models to develop legislation for Michigan that Governor Rick Snyder signed on June 26, 2014, as House Bill 5445, sponsored by John Walsh, Michigan state representative, and known as the Sexual Assault Kit Evidence Submission Act. The law stipulates time standards for the testing of kits statewide. If a SAK is completed, police in that jurisdiction must pick up that kit within fourteen days of the sexual assault exam, and then that police department has another fourteen days to get it to the lab. Every kit. The lab must have the correct resources to test the kits, and they have a time requirement for testing also. Now, all kits must be tested, so that there is and will never again be a backlog in the state.

Worthy's team went one vital step further. "We said from the very beginning that if you can track a package that you order from an online company, so that at anytime after you purchase it you can go online and see where that package is, then we should be able to track a SAK through the criminal justice system in Detroit or anywhere," she says.

They recruited the people who track packages for a living—United Parcel Service, or UPS—and worked with their logistics specialists and formed a partnership with UPS and businessman Dan Gilbert, founder of Quicken Loans. Thanks to those two, DPD secured funding for a more-than-year-long pro bono pilot project to test out the specially designed UPS package scanner that is used at each point in the process, from the time police pick it up at the hospital or medical center to when they deliver it to a lab, pick it up at the lab, and deliver it to the prosecutor's office. Detroit can track every single SAK that has been generated since February 2015. Michigan is also exploring how to track SAKs statewide, whether using UPS or another system.

Even though prosecutors work with victims of crime on a daily basis, the backlog rape kit project was a beast unto itself. Worthy instinctively knew they would need a different approach for victims who had been raped five, ten, twenty years ago; they may have never fully recovered or may have moved into a new phase in their lives, gotten married and had families.

"We have to be very careful and very diligent in how we approach our victims," she says.

Worthy and her team enlisted the help of the Joyful Heart Foundation, the organization founded by *Law & Order: Special Victims Unit* television star Mariska Hargitay, to monitor the backlog testing and processing and pursue more effective legislation against rape and sexual assault in the US. "They helped us throughout the entire process," Worthy states. "I can't even tell you how monumental their support has been from then until now."

Additionally, they formed a team that included community-based advocates, court advocates, members of the DPD, prosecutors from her office, and Debi Cain, executive director of the Michigan Domestic and Sexual Violence Prevention and Treatment Board. One key partner from the start was Rebecca Campbell, PhD, professor of psychology at Michigan State University, who as a community psychologist had performed extensive research into the neurobiology of trauma and sexual assault to evaluate how victims were treated or mistreated by law enforcement and others. The team spent nine months developing an effective victim notification process that became one of the nation's first formalized best practices for compassionate, respectful treatment of victims that provides the foundation of a victim-centered approach to sexual violence.

"I'm very proud of our team and the work they've done on victim notification," Worthy says. "We knew fairly early on that we had to turn to some victim experts and advocates in how we dealt with women in these cases. I say 'women' because most of the victims overwhelmingly are women, and most are women of color as well."

"We are very deliberate, very sensitive with how we do that, and it's paid off dividends because overwhelmingly our victims have wanted to cooperate and keep going."

"This was Cuyahoga County Prosecutor Tim McGinty's idea several years ago. . . . He relied a lot on the work we were doing, because they discovered their kits several years after we had our issues here . . . and he had the benefit of us having started the work, as opposed to when we were doing our work. We really didn't know where to turn, and we had to make our way and did. So we share our information and resources."

They learned about Memphis's initial SAKTF efforts and, at McGinty's suggestion, collaborated with them as well. At that time, the then-mayor of Memphis, A. C. Wharton Jr., issued an executive order instructing the police to devise a plan to clear the backlog as quickly as possible. "They had more kits than we did, with more than twelve thousand," she says. "But it wasn't the DA in that case. It was the mayor who was spearheading and trying to get things done."

Ultimately, she says, the point of the summits and three-city collaboration is simple: "Sharing ideas, networking, and trying to help each other get through all of this, because we all have the same goal, and that's to bring justice to all of our victims, so that's what brought us together."

After reflecting for a few moments after my question about what the entire experience has been like for her, Worthy concludes: "It's been difficult. Our whole culture has to be changed, not just the police, but with the way this entire nation looks at sexual assault. So, that is another added benefit to all this happening, all that we've learned, so we've really been focusing on that as well."

Chapter 10

Coalescing Forces:
The Fall 2016 SAK Task Force
Summit with Cleveland and
Memphis

THE CONFERENCE PACKET for the 2016 Detroit Sexual Assault Kit Summit—a white folder featuring the seal of Wayne County Prosecutor Kym Worthy—is jam-packed with information about the agenda of a half-dozen plenary and more than twenty breakout sessions, speaker bios, and a sixty-page booklet published by the Joyful Heart Foundation entitled *Navigating Notification: A Guide to Re-engaging Sexual Assault Survivors Affected by the Untested Rape Kit Backlog*.

The three-day event is housed in the Detroit Marriott at the Renaissance Center and the Courtyard by Marriott Detroit Downtown across the street, the hotels connected by a second-floor pedestrian walkway. With its soaring seventy-three-story central cylinder, the futuristic, mirrored glass and steel Renaissance Center's cluster of corporate buildings is the most frequently cited landmark by Detroiters giving directions downtown.

As striking as its architectural exterior is, however, the circular, symmetrical interiors, while attractive and comfortable, are at once bemusing and perplexing to navigate. Thus, the folder also contains maps that resemble the axonometric floor plans of Darth Vader's Death Star.

Wisely, the hotel assigns direction-givers who point people toward the elevators to the conference rooms and other key locations.

Despite any navigational challenges, Prosecutor Worthy's team has organized a truly impressive schedule of panels and experts for this distinguished collection of investigators, prosecutors, sexual assault nurse examiners, sexual assault forensic examiners, rape crisis and victim advocates, psychologists, therapists, and educators in attendance.

Rick Bell, who heads the Cuyahoga County SAKTF, tells me the first summit held in Cleveland in 2014 had about fifty people from the three partnered cities—Cleveland, Detroit, and Memphis—in attendance. The Memphis summit the following year had roughly one hundred people and several more cities that had joined the SAKI project coterie.

The 2016 summit counts roughly three hundred attendees from more than thirty cities, so the movement is growing fairly quickly. More than thirty cities have applied for and received SAKI grants. Some have received financial support from the district attorney of New York (DANY) funding or other sources supporting the new victim-centered approaches to rape and sexual assault cases and the aggressive law enforcement and prosecutorial efforts to leverage DNA evidence collected and extracted from sexual assault kits.

At the welcome reception on Sunday night, September 25, 2016, in the Granite City Food & Brewery on the Renaissance Center's first floor, Bell tells me and others that he hopes the next summit will be out west, in Seattle, perhaps, or Portland. We're talking with Tina Orwall, Washington state representative, who had Bell come out to testify to promote one of her bills to combat sexual violence statewide.

Around 8:30 a.m. on Monday, we begin with two special guests from Washington, DC: Kristina Rose, then-senior policy advisor on violence against women issues in Vice President Joe Biden's office (now Rose is the executive director of End Violence Against Women International), and Caroline "Carrie" Bettinger-López, White House advisor on violence against women and senior advisor to VP Biden.

Rose calls Worthy "indomitable" and "fearless." No argument there. She talks a little bit about the National Institute of Justice action-research project on sexual assault kits that she was involved in when it launched "six years ago this week," and proclaims that what Detroit and Houston accomplished as the beta testers "led the way for everyone else" who followed as SAKI sites.

Bettinger-López informs everyone that VP Biden had planned to attend the summit, but he ended up at a golf event in memory of his older son, Joseph R. "Beau" Biden III, who died of brain cancer at forty-six in May 2015. She reiterates Biden's passion for this issue, and she adds that although the federal government has disbursed $86 million to help cities fight sexual violence by processing and investigating SAKs, and hopefully more in the future, there's more work to be done.

"Although we have made extraordinary gains, we have much to finish," she says. "We encourage you to be bold with your ideas, connections, and initiatives." Citing author Malcolm Gladwell, she says the "tipping point" concept he coined will happen when sexual assault becomes a regular topic of conversation in schools, the media, policy, and legislation. Finally, she assures the audience that President Barack Obama, VP Biden, and their team will continue to fight violence against women long after their administration is over.

Next, Kym Worthy takes the microphone to welcome everyone and kick off the summit. The first thing she does is recognize Cuyahoga County Prosecutor Timothy McGinty for proposing in 2014 that Cleveland, Detroit, and Memphis partner their SAKTFs so that they could share best practices and support each other's SAKI endeavors. McGinty, seated in one of the first few rows, stands and acknowledges the applause.

The lame duck prosecutor who lost his reelection bid earlier in March and will serve through the end of the year remains for the first days of the summit before returning to Cleveland. The gregarious McGinty either knows the key players or readily introduces himself for a chat. His tenure in the last couple of years became controversial because of two dubious police shootings of unarmed suspects in an era in which such incidents have become epidemic. There is little question about his adamant support of the SAKI project and his open approach to working with other cities and maintaining an embedded researcher to share the Cuyahoga County task force's successes, failures, and lessons learned with the world.

Prosecutor Worthy then retells the story she's been telling for six years of how Detroit was drawn into the fray with the revelation of more than eleven thousand kits that had been "lost," that she chose to test and investigate the cases, even though it took her six years to raise all of the money necessary to fund the task force. Worthy comments on the approximate nationwide total of four hundred thousand untested SAKs, which she and most in the field believe is a gross underestimate. "The scandal is that it shouldn't be that hard for this country to say these women should be helped," she concludes.

Next, Steve Garagiola, popular newscaster from WDIV Detroit and son of baseball player and broadcasting legend Joe Garagiola Sr., who had passed away six months earlier, hosts a session with a diverse range of speakers giving brief comments. Other speakers include the Detroit-based FBI special agent from the violent crime task force Ray Johnson and Congresswoman Brenda Lawrence (D-MI).

Wayne County Executive Warren Evans, a former Wayne County sheriff and later controversial Detroit police chief, reminds everyone that we have a system that doesn't always value these crimes or these women. "Even though we are in debt, we have to find the money to test the rape kits," he says. "On the other end of that kit is a human. We need to empower the victims to feel like they count. We need more people to become advocates for supporting prosecution."

The brief introductory comments end with Michigan's attorney general Bill Schuette, who says of the statewide initiative to provide justice and a voice for victims of rape and sexual assault, "We have a new culture and approach now. We have unity in our approach, funding

from the state of Michigan, and a shared commitment to provide justice to women, solve the crimes, and have a safer Michigan."

The morning plenary session of Day 1 highlights research and training "rock star," as she is introduced, Rebecca "Becki" Campbell, PhD,
who will review the latest findings on "the neurobiology of trauma and
the criminal justice system response to sexual assault" that have completely transformed the way law enforcement agents interview victims
of sexual violence. Her five-hundred-page report about the topic, the
unsubmitted and untested evidence in the sexual assault kits and lessons learned from the action-research projects in Detroit and Houston
published by the National Institute of Justice, was a bombshell that
completely exploded the ancient, conventional first responder and
investigator habits of abusive victim-blaming and treating them as if
they were all liars.

On stage, she looks and sounds very much like a, well, professor of
psychology at Michigan State University, only with an astute sense of
humor and an acute awareness of knowledge that will impact everyone
in the audience, no matter their field of expertise in sexual violence.
The room is completely overloaded, and everyone's attention is glued
on Campbell or scribbling copious notes.

So critical and of such universal interest to the attendees is her work
that she has been given more than two hours for her entirely engaging
presentation. The conference agenda blurb says "she will explain the
underlying neurobiology of traumatic events, the emotional and physical manifestation, and how these processes can impact the investigation
and prosecution of sexual assault cold cases." And she does.

She reminds all that she is a scientist, first and foremost, and that her
research is peer-reviewed. Research, she declares, can help connect the
dots between how the brain and body react after trauma. By focusing
on the victim's emotions, behaviors, memory formation, and recall, and
by examining how the victim's trauma response affects reporting of
their assault, initial responders and enforcement professionals can better comprehend the significant implications for cold case investigations.

Campbell proceeds to take the audience on a journey through the relevant neural anatomy and how each part of the brain responds to trauma. For instance, the prefrontal cortex becomes quiet, also referred to as "hypoactive" or inhibited, and shuts down in the face of trauma. Although it's impossible to obtain functional MRI slides of a person's brain while an assault is occurring, victims have granted permission to have their brains scanned within a few days of their assault.

As Campbell explains the images on the fMRI slides of one victim, I notice Commander James McPike from the Cleveland Police Department, who's taken training courses with Campbell and is a steadfast proponent of her trauma-informed approach, sitting next to Joseph Hoffer, assistant district attorney general from Athens, Tennessee, who worked in Cleveland as a prosecutor earlier in his career. Another former colleague, Rick Bell, had introduced me to Hoffer at the Sunday night reception, and the affable barrister described how his jurisdiction has applied for a SAKI grant and is proactively pursuing a reformed approach to addressing rape and sexual assault cases.

Campbell then explains the amygdala, the walnut-sized gland that processes our emotional reactions and memories, which is part of the limbic system deep in the brain close to the hippocampus that plays a role in the formation of memories. One key responsibility of the amygdala is to assess the environment constantly for potential threats and then remember them so the individual can avoid or escape them in the future.

She next details how hormones affect victim behavior and the complex brain–body processes that can lead to fight, flight, or freeze. While society may expect a fight or flight response, that is an unrealistic expectation, she says, because freezing is also a normal mammalian response. Additionally, the opioids block more than just pain; they also blunt emotional responses, the lack of which may be misinterpreted by police as the person not caring or being unresponsive and uncooperative.

After explaining "tonic immobility," or rape-induced paralysis, a reflexive mammalian response to extremely terrifying situations,

Campbell says, "We can't misinterpret the neurobiological responses to trauma as the choice of the victim."

Campbell then takes the audience through the role of the hippocampus in collecting, encoding, and storing memories. Though it's a fairly complex subject, Campbell has a keen teacher's gift for conveying the information in a way lay listeners can absorb and apply. She includes the damaging impact of alcohol on memory, especially since memory loss and compromised decision-making are two of the reasons why perpetrators like to ply victims with alcoholic beverages in the first place.

"Trauma creates fragmented memories, so a victim's story may come out fragmented and sketchy, nonlinear and cycling back and forth," she says. "They may have difficulty piecing the story together, hedge about details or be uncertain, and have memory gaps or make inconsistent statements."

After she lets that settle in for a moment with the law-enforcement-heavy onlookers, she adds, "Outdated training can lead detectives to not believe or press too hard, because they don't understand how memory is affected by trauma."

Toward the end of her talk, she reveals some newer research related to memory that she cautions she is still analyzing and evaluating. For graphic emphasis, she uses a Post-it note analogy to explain how we record experiences, sensations, and memories, slapping different Post-it notes on boards on either side of the stage.* Her takeaway again is that a victim's memory doesn't always work the way an interviewer might want it to, so detectives should be careful not to misinterpret gaps or inconsistencies as lies or withholding information. Additionally, she advises giving the victim two or three days of rest to let their memories consolidate before questioning them.

---

* After receiving some criticism from other scientists that the Post-it note analogy was an oversimplification of memory, Campbell decided to no longer use it in her training.

In sardonic summary, Campbell says, "The human brain is the world's messiest desk."

Referring to the research of David Lisak, PhD, a forensic consultant who studies the motives and behaviors of rapists and murderers, she says later that law enforcement needs to remember a key motivation for sexual offenders. "Assailants pick their victims based on vulnerabilities, because it increases the likelihood they won't discuss the details, will be embarrassed, or won't reveal everything to the police."

Detectives also need to remember that sexual assault is a violation of trust, so the victims typically do not yet trust their interviewers and will be embarrassed and ashamed to discuss the intimate details of their attack.

"Just because you are who you are doesn't give you an automatic pass," Campbell chastens any unenlightened law enforcement agents in attendance. "Especially because of institutional racism or sexism, etc."

She covers a number of other topics, including how interaction with the criminal justice system can cause its own forms of trauma, and reveals a survey that indicated contact with the system had caused 81 percent of victims to feel bad about themselves. A further 88 percent were depressed, 94 percent felt violated, and most were reluctant to seek further help.

"We have to change this. We can change this," Campbell declares.

Focused almost entirely on protecting the women who comprise the majority of sexual violence sufferers, Campbell discussed the impacts of PTSD on cold case victims who were assaulted years or even decades ago. They may easily be retriggered through faulty notification or investigation, if theirs is one of the backlogged kit cases, sending them tumbling once again into a self-perpetuating maelstrom of guilt, humiliation, depression, physical ailments, and self-medicating substance abuse.

"The victim's choice, safety, and well-being are the focus," she says, after proclaiming the importance of a victim-centered, survivor-centered, patient-centered, and trauma-informed approach. "The victim must be at the center of all decisions regarding recovery and any involvement with the criminal justice system."

Choice reinstates control for victims, as we know from fundamental psychology, she informs the group. Choice improves mental health, and improved mental health facilitates decision-making while promoting planning and support-seeking. This approach will also increase the likelihood that victims will participate in the criminal justice system, rather than dictating that they must help put away a bad predator.

"Addressing their health and well-being is the way to get you where you want—engaging them in the criminal justice system," Campbell says. "It's a very simple, direct route."

Before referring everyone to several resources for more information, such as the National Criminal Justice Reference Service or Keith Clark, lead attorney for the Wayne County Prosecutor's Office for a copy of the best practice protocols, she concludes with a comment from a rape victim she had interviewed that adeptly summarizes the fundamental guideline for everyone in the room: "Everything you say, everything you do is a chance to help me or to hurt me. Make the choice to help me. Please help me."

I have to admit, it's the most energized I've ever seen a group of people after a nearly two-and-a-half-hour presentation. Like Commander McPike, many of the people had heard Campbell or taken training sessions with her but still remained attentive throughout. Most are trying to implement her message of compassionate, respectful care and treatment of victims and recognize victims must be the center of everything that follows an assault to have any hope of achieving a more comprehensive, holistic outcome on both the healing and the prosecution sides of their case.

It's almost noon, and everyone heads off to lunch on their own. At 1:15 p.m., attendees must choose from a selection of wide-ranging breakout sessions that includes "Failure to Pay—Addressing Prior Victim Blaming Practices at Trial," "Where Are They Now?—Advanced Investigative Techniques on Finding Someone," "Best Practices in

Sexual Assault Medical-Forensic Exams: An Update—Sponsored by Oakland University School of Nursing," and "Direct to DNA Approach for Sexual Assault Kit Testing." Though I'm not much of an IT-phile, I head to a conference room on Level 5 to attend "Case Management Systems," a huge issue in the SAKTF world.

Moderated by the Memphis SAKTF coordinator Dewanna Smith, the panel includes Brett Kyker, Cuyahoga County's Prosecutor's Office; Richard Lott, Prosecuting Attorneys Association of Michigan; and Ed Arib and Susan Lehman from the Portland Police Bureau, which has pioneered an innovative database system that they've donated to several other jurisdictions. I don't fully understand all of the technical intricacies of data points and adding data fields, but the relevance of "jurisdictions finding effective document management solutions to help automate workflow, data collection, and information-sharing between agencies" is clear. In fact, it is a recurring topic of numerous conversations and interviews I've had over the past few years.

At 3 p.m., I attend a session on the same floor entitled "Anatomy of a Cold Case Investigation: Case Study." I choose this session because Bell also introduced me to James Markey, a former detective sergeant for the Phoenix Police Department who now works as a private consultant and, along with Campbell, a member of the federal Bureau of Justice Assistance's training and technical assistance (TTA) team that travels to any of the SAKI sites requesting support. I've heard about the well-liked Markey from several others. He's a really bright, knowledgeable, energetic guy who became one of my key advisors on this project.

I'm out of my depth in this police investigation–focused, interactive case study of a rape case that Markey and his detectives in Arizona investigated that had gone cold, until several years later DNA evidence linked it to another case. Markey establishes the pertinent case details first, then asks attendees to give their analysis, make investigative decisions, and try to resolve the two cases. Guiding us through all the twists and turns of the convoluted investigation, Markey connected each of their steps to the new victim-centered approaches at the foundation of the summit that he and his team were already implementing in the early 2000s. A sex crimes detectives' forum—fascinating. Who needs *CSI* or *Law & Order?*

On Day 2, the lunch break happens after a media roundtable session billed as "for members of the press only" with two courageous sexual assault survivors who've gone on to become public advocates: Kim Trent, Wayne State University Board of Governors, and Natasha Alexenko, Natasha's Justice Project. Despite suspicions that this session was offered to appease the fourth estate because we were excluded from a concurrent panel with survivors whose cases were part of the Detroit SAK project, Trent and Alexenko are more than captivating in their presentations, and moderator Maria Miller, assistant prosecuting attorney for Wayne County who helped organize and manage the summit, keeps the session flowing smoothly, including a stimulating Q and A segment.

On the way out, I grab Jim Markey, who snuck into the session about halfway through, and ask him if we can chat for a little while. He joins me at an empty table as everyone else heads off for lunch or stands around analyzing and discussing the content of the previous session, at times rather loudly. I ask him if the Detroit summit has been beneficial for him.

"It's been really eye-opening," he responds, "even though I've been doing this work for a long time, to really see this movement of passionate, convicted people that have the same mission and goal in life, to make their community safer, to hold offenders accountable. So, it's been energizing."

One of the perks of attending these conferences, meetings, and training sessions, he clarifies, is it serves to recharge everyone's batteries. "We still have to go out and do the work, so sometimes we get lost in the pile of paperwork or the number of cases we're working, and we kind of lose focus on the big picture," says Markey. "So to know other people are doing the same work with the same resources or lack of resources or without the experience or they're just starting out, it kind of energizes you to see these people working together."

From talking with different people throughout the event, before sessions, in the hallways, at lunch, at the Detroit Tigers v. Cleveland Indians baseball game at Comerica Park that about twenty-five people attend on Tuesday night, it doesn't take me long to figure out that no one is participating in this summit because their boss told them to; each is here on a mission. They've been involved in the movement for many years or they just got onboard recently when their jurisdiction applied for a SAKI grant, but they're all here to learn and share and build their networks.

Moreover, the seasoned veterans from Detroit, Cleveland, and Memphis, which Markey at one point labels "the holy trinity" when introducing a panel, go out of their way to offer their business cards, cell phone numbers, or website addresses or to converse and connect with neophytes to SAKI and the new approaches who are looking for information. Several times I hear one of these folks like Bell or Mark Farrah, investigator for the Wayne County SAKTF, or Anna Whalley, administrator of Crime Victim Services at Shelby County Crime Victims Center, say something to the effect of, "There's no reason to reinvent the wheel. We've made the mistakes. We've figured out the processes. Talk to us."

"You've got a lot of sites and jurisdictions that have been doing this for a while," Markey comments about the priceless peer-to-peer exchanges. "So they know what's worked, what hasn't, what's a good approach, what's a bad approach, how many resources are required, how long it's going to take, so there are all of those things involved that for the jurisdictions just starting on these projects, it's good to see that vision, get a feel for what's going to happen in three, four, five, ten years."

Markey and his Phoenix PD Sex Crimes Unit started improving their practices as far back as 2000, when he launched one of the first cold case sexual assault teams. They landed an eighteen-month grant to address the cold cases. Today, he remembers thinking they'd be done in eighteen months. "Everything will be tested. Everybody will be in custody, and we'll move on to our regular cases, right?" he says with a chuckle. "It's fifteen years later, and we're still working cases. We're still testing kits. We're still getting hits and doing follow-up."

Although he retired in 2012, after thirty years with the Phoenix PD and fourteen years as supervisor of the Sex Crimes Unit investigating more than six thousand felony sexual assault cases, including eighty serial rapists, he will always feel actively involved with police work.

"I wish I had known all of that and some of the things we struggled with early on with notification and follow-up, some of the technical things of process evidence," he continues. "Half of the kits don't have any evidence, so we had to decide to close the case or find something else we wanted to process, so a lot of the investigative stuff we just didn't know at the time."

Referring to Dr. Campbell's trainings on the neurobiology of the brain after trauma, he recalls, "We didn't know a lot about victimology back then, but I knew there was something different about rape victims than victims in any other cases I worked. I didn't have a name for it. We learned early on we had to deal with their trauma, though we didn't call it 'trauma' or 'victim-centered.' I didn't really understand it, but I knew we couldn't approach them the same way we did everyone else." During his session the day before, Markey discussed how one of his detectives took a very patient approach, allowing the victim to tell her story, not interrupting or bombarding her with questions as police interrogators prefer to do. That became their standard operating procedure.

He cites the onset of DNA technology as the major turning point that gave law enforcement a sharper tool to solve these cases. He shudders, though, when he remembers the complicated bureaucratic process Arizona had initially to approve cases for DNA testing, since it cost more to process kits in the early days, and the equipment wasn't as high-performing as it is today. Referring to it as "the Death Panel," he remembers a lot of police not even bothering to deal with it because of the time lost appearing before the approval board.

While he's seen Campbell's lessons being adopted in many law enforcement agencies, Markey's realistic enough to understand the challenges ahead. "When you think that there are sixteen thousand law enforcement agencies in the country and trying to reach out to each to give them this knowledge base, these skills to be able to work these types of cases, especially those that only deal with a few sexual assaults a year, they may not have that skill set or be able to understand victims in the same way."

The best way, he believes, is to make the testing of kits and the follow-up investigations the law. "What cops respond to is oversight and accountability," he says. "With everything police are asked to be responsible for, priorities become a huge issue and a concern in these agencies, so taking some of the discretion away by mandating testing evidence in a rape is helpful to law enforcement agencies, too."

When CODIS came online in 1999, he says, that opened the way for DNA testing to really take off, as more city, county, and state labs were going online with processing evidence for DNA profiles, so there was no longer an excuse not to test. Though many agencies still did not. Most labs can now test at least the most probative samples from the rape kits for about $500. Seven years ago, Markey made the somewhat unpopular decision to test all of Phoenix's kits. At $1,000 each to test the entire kit, that cost the city roughly $200,000 a year, but he felt that expenditure was miniscule considering the multimillion-dollar budget for the police, and the productive evidence yield the SAKs provided.

There is one component that continues to disturb Markey, and it remains a continuing topic of conversation in his travels to numerous jurisdictions from Alaska to Florida: the lack of a comprehensive national or even international database of sexual assault case information that any law enforcement agency can access. He's also troubled by the number of jurisdictions that don't track or manage their own case statistics to understand the scope of the crime and indicate trends.

"With technology now, we should be able to track it all much better, communicate with each other more freely," he says. "When you have offenders moving from jurisdiction to jurisdiction, you need to know that information in law enforcement."

I could talk to Markey for hours because of his depth of experience and expertise, but when we realize we don't have much time left in the lunch hour, we head in different directions to find something to eat. For the next day and a half, I attend as many sessions as I can, sometimes popping in and out to sample diverse topics from "Meeting the Complex Needs of SA Survivors: Addressing Intersectionality of Poverty, Mental Health, and Intergenerational Trauma in the Healing Process" to "Advanced Prosecution Strategies in SAK Cold Cases" to "Working with an Embedded Researcher," a panel featuring Bell and Cuyahoga County's researcher, Rachel Lovell from Case Western Reserve University.

When the summit ends around noon on Wednesday, September 28, I've got a legal pad full of notes, a sport coat–pocket full of business cards, and, as one of my college English professors used to say, a commotion of cogitation charging through my gray matter. Prosecutor Worthy's closing remarks furnish a rousing call to action that fires everyone up as they linger for brief goodbyes or immediately dash through the Marriott lobby doors with their roller suitcases clacking behind to grab cabs, Ubers, or airport limousines.

I'm not in a big rush, since I've asked the two survivors who spoke on Tuesday, Natasha Alexenko and Kim Trent, if I could interview them later in the afternoon. So I saunter back across Renaissance Drive during a dry moment when the torrential rains of the last couple days lighten up.

Alexenko and I meet first at the Starbucks inside the Renaissance Center, temporarily located around an elevator bank in a cavernous hallway that burrows through the building's open warren of tunnels, spiral staircases, and sky-lit atria with elevated and transparent-floored pedestrian tracks so you can enjoy looking down to the other levels, if you dare.

Born on Long Island, Alexenko grew up in St. Catharines, Ontario, Canada, where the family relocated after her father's death when she was a young child. Like Detroit, the city had a GM plant that shut down, causing major employment challenges and a depressed economy. Her dream, however, was to return to New York to attend college, and at nineteen, after completing Canada's grade 13, she returned to her home state in August 1992. One year later, on August 6, 1993, she was raped, sodomized, and robbed at gunpoint.

Her male roommate gave her a shot of Jack Daniel's to steady her nerves, as she was shaking and hyperventilating. Her female roommate convinced her not to take a shower and go to the hospital to get a rape kit done. She wasn't sure what a rape kit was, but they called an ambulance. Rudely, the paramedic pressed her on whether she had the drink before or after the assault. Looking back, Alexenko says, "Even then I knew how women were judged in that situation. It was ridiculous. Who cares if I had it before or after? It doesn't matter."

In the emergency room waiting area, she sat shaking, as the other patients all held their stomachs, heads, or blood-soaked bandages. "I just felt like everyone in the ER knew why I was there," she recalls. She did the rape kit. Four hours later, she left. She can't remember exactly how she was dressed, but she left her underwear there for evidence, as she retells in the HBO documentary, *I Am Evidence*, produced by Mariska Hargitay and the Joyful Heart Foundation that Hargitay founded. "I tell college students I speak to, 'Your mom says always wear clean underwear.' It's true," she quips to me. "It might end up in a movie!"

The police interviewed her, and she tried to help them create a sketch of her assailant. "I close my eyes right now and see the gun as if I just saw it yesterday, but in terms of what the man looked like that's really vague to me," she says. "So, it was hard to create the composites."

Shortly after the incident, her mother, a petite woman, pulled up to her Upper West Side apartment building in a big U-Haul truck to take her home to Canada to heal.

"It was good for me because everyone I knew from childhood, all of my very good friends were there to help the healing process," she recalls. "My mother had good resources, too, since she worked in social work and could connect me with people so I could heal, and I just kind of went on."

In the mid-1990s when personal computers were just emerging from the wings, the New York Police Department would snail mail her photo arrays of possible suspects. She never recognized any of the faces and would mail them back. One day, she called to check on her case, and they told her it had been closed. Her stomach dropped. "There are no leads," they said. "We won't throw it out, but we're not actively pursuing it."

"How is it possible for him to get away with something of this magnitude?" she wondered. "It's my fault. I didn't memorize his face. I thought I was going to die, so looking at his face wasn't a priority."

Ten years after her assault, Alexenko was living in Virginia when she received a call from the district attorney's office in Manhattan. She wasn't exactly sure what they were talking about. They had gotten some grant money, created a DNA testing lab, and connected to CODIS? Anyway, they were going to test her rape kit. Finally. Could she please come to New York to testify before the grand jury? The law now allowed them to use the DNA of the as-yet unnamed suspect from the kit to obtain a John Doe indictment and stop the clock on the statute of limitations.

In 2007, when she was living in New York again and a detective knocked on her door, the investigation of backlogged kits was an entirely new phenomenon that law enforcement and prosecutors were still stumbling their way through. She found his sheepish approach endearing when he notified her they had arrested her rapist and asked her to call the DA's office, but it brought everything about that day in 1993 rushing back to her, retriggering her panic. "I even called my rape crisis center because I started freaking out," she recalls. "Where is he? Is he in jail? What's going on?" Unfortunately, the people at the center didn't have a clue how to handle this retriggering caused by a backlog kit notification, either. They questioned why she would contact them about a rape that happened more than ten years ago.

Alexenko learned from the police that her assailant had been arrested shortly after assaulting her for possession of an illegal weapon, served a short amount of jail time, then was released on parole. From there he went on a "one-man crime spree," as Cuyahoga County Prosecutor Tim McGinty had called it when she met him at a conference. Her assailant had been arrested in Las Vegas for jaywalking, of all things, and extradited to New York. The police matched his DNA on CODIS on August 6, 2007, fourteen years to the day of her assault.

Her experience testifying at his trial was at once horrible—she fainted when she saw him; it felt like she had gone through a wormhole, and it was just the two of them, alone on the street again—and empowering, because she finally learned her assailant's name, something she hadn't known all those years. Victor Rondon was sentenced to forty-four to one hundred seven years in prison.

Fortunately, her experience with the NYPD was good. They always treated her with respect and kindness, she says. She knows that's not how all victims have been treated, and today she has a close relationship with the DA's office, which often invites her to speak at conferences to relay her message that all rape victims' experiences are different.

"There's a lot of suffering going on in other communities, and it's a catastrophe," she says. "My concern is that people think this is a women's issue. Yes, when a woman is raped, she goes through so much. But what they're not getting is the people that commit these crimes are a burden on everyone. They're a public safety issue. So even if you don't give a hoot about the women that are being affected by this crime, they're endangering everybody out there."

In 2011, Alexenko solidified her role as a national advocate, speaker, and expert by founding Natasha's Justice Project. "Fund-raising hasn't always been easy, but it's been life-changing and surreal in how it's taken on a life of its own," she reveals. "Every time I'm ready to say,

'That's it!' something awesome happens or I see what's happening in Detroit or in Cleveland. I'm like, 'I'm in it. I'm doing it. I'll do anything anyone needs me to do to help!'"

After saying goodbye to the indomitable Alexenko, who is headed to another meeting before returning to New York, I bought a green iced tea and met with the equally energetic Kim Trent. Born and raised in Detroit to a family whose roots there go back to the 1830s (her great-grandparents were founding members of the church she attends), Trent was a "huge bookworm" as a child, so naturally, she wanted to become a writer. During a proactive push to employ more people of color in newsrooms, she scored an internship at the *Detroit News* after graduating from high school. She received a full scholarship to the Journalism Institute for Minorities (now Media Diversity) program at Wayne State University, where she is now on the board.

While interning at the newspaper, an older—maybe thirties or forties—parking lot security guard befriended her. He charmed the nineteen-year-old and gained her sympathy with a tale of how his fiancée had been murdered, to the point where she agreed to let him buy her a cup of coffee at a favored place in Greektown. When he arrived to pick her up at her grandmother's house so she wouldn't have to "be out in the dark," he asked if he could use her bathroom. When he came out, she started walking to the door, and the next thing she knew, he was attacking her. "What is happening? Why am I on the ground?" the shocked Trent thought. After he finished, he stood up, collected himself, and walked out.

She chose not to report to the police. When her grandmother returned from a summer trip to China, Trent told her. And no one else. Her grandmother advised her to seek counseling, but the only treatments she took were hour-long showers during which she told herself not to think about it. Trent did start parking in a different lot to avoid her rapist. When she saw him one day, he smiled at her; she responded with a scowl. "I never saw him again," she remembers. "He quit right after that, because I wasn't going to go to the police, but he realized it was going to be uncomfortable for him."

She worked as a reporter for eight years, and her first assignment was covering yet another of Detroit's controversial mayors, Coleman Young. During a strike in 1995, she left the paper. She moved to South Africa to study at the University of Cape Town; worked for a paper in Toledo, Ohio, for a little while; moved to Washington, DC, to work for a member of Congress; then returned to Detroit, married a fellow member of the National Association of Black Journalists in 1998, and settled down in her hometown.

"It's so crazy because I felt so numb and confused that I just shut down and it didn't even occur to me to report," Trent says today. "I just said, 'Okay, I've got to move on.' My life didn't fall apart. I was functioning. I still went to work every day. I was still going to school."

She remembers falling "into a very dark place and [being] severely depressed" in July 1991 when heavyweight boxer Mike Tyson was arrested and later convicted of raping Miss Black America pageant contestant Desiree Washington. "When that happened to her, and the way people talked about her, I remember just feeling that's why I never told anybody, because it was my fault," she says of the guilt and self-blame that victims of sexual violence often experience. Whenever people criticized Washington's choice—"Why would she go into that hotel suite with Tyson?"—Trent felt it confirmed she never should have let her assailant into her grandmother's home.

When Detroit's rape kit backlog began to hit the headlines, Trent says, she didn't feel any connection as a rape survivor. But she did feel a connection as a citizen and a feminist. "When the kits were discovered, to be honest," admits Trent, who was the director of then-govenor Jennifer Granholm's Southeast Michigan office, "I probably had the same reaction as other people: 'That's terrible. We want to solve or address the problem, but we're trying to keep GM, because if it collapses, that would be the end of the state of Michigan.'"

She really didn't reflect on or talk about her rape until nearly thirty years later, when she participated in a Take Back the Night event in April 2016. She had resisted for a long time, turning down offers from the chief operating officer Peg Tallet to work with the Michigan Women's Foundation on the issue. Then she read reporter Nancy Kaffer's article "How Detroit Cop Culture Hindered Rape Investigations" on June 20, 2015, in the *Detroit Free Press* that revealed the abusive treatment rape victims received from police officers.

"I was really pissed to read that," Trent says of learning all those women had been treated so poorly by police on top of the fact that their 11,341 rape kits were left collecting dust on police storage shelves. Then, after getting into multiple heated arguments with women who tried to defend Bill Cosby from accusations he was drugging and raping women and feeling deeply disturbed by the way women spoke nastily about his accusers (reflecting the prevailing rape culture), she reached her boiling point. "That's when I said I've got to do something with all of this anger I have," she recalls. "I called Peg the next day, and we've been working together ever since."

Tallet tapped Trent to galvanize black women leaders and help raise money to support the backlogged rape kit testing initiative. Learning that 81 percent of the victims were African American, Trent jumped onboard to create an organization to collaborate with Enough SAID (Sexual Assault in Detroit) to raise funds to cover the $650,000 needed to test the remaining kits and help prosecute any ensuing cases. In October 2015, a group of more than one hundred high-profile and grassroots black women Trent recruited stood in front of the Detroit Association of Women's Clubs to launch the campaign they named African American 490 Challenge, referring to the $490 it costs to test one rape kit.

Today, Tallet remembers how the freshly energized survivor advocate devised a brilliant strategy that included sororities, service groups, politicians, and corporate leaders. "It was like someone opening the doors for us," Tallet told a *Detroit News* reporter for a profile of Trent that ran in August 2016.

Since then, Trent, who serves as president, and her organization have raised more than $300,000 with the driving goal of covering the kits of the African American victims. An example of one brilliant fund-raising tactic, she organized an event that capitalized on the well-established rivalry between Michigan State and University of Michigan alumni and football fans to establish an online wagering competition that raised $30,000. Wayne County Prosecutor Kym Worthy, an alum herself and friend of Trent's, served as "quarterback" of Team Wolverines and ESPN journalist Jemele Hill as QB of Team Spartans.

"Some of Detroit's problems are so entrenched and longstanding that they don't seem solvable," Trent says. "But the joy is everybody gets that this is a solvable problem. If you raise a certain amount of money, all of these kits will be tested. I also feel confident that at the very least there will be an investigation of every kit."

"Not every woman is going to get justice from this," she continues. "We know that. But at least there's the prospect of justice, rather than just having their kit sit on a shelf, which is so disrespectful."

We talk a little bit more about Worthy's unmatched tenacity, serving as a lone voice in the wilderness, until more people got onboard to build what has become a national movement.

"It just shows how little the lives of black women mean in this society, in general," Trent sighs, before giving me directions from the Renaissance Center back to I-75, so I can drive home to Cleveland. "To have this happen in my backyard was really unacceptable."

Chapter 11

The Scientist-Researcher Rebecca Campbell's Psychological Paradigm Shift

LYING ON A bed, waiting, uncomfortable and disoriented, the woman in her early twenties had been raped. She soon realized several physicians were quarreling in the hallway outside of her examination room.

"I don't want to do this kit," she heard one doctor say.

"*I* don't want to do this kit," said the other. "You're the lowest ranking resident. You go do it."

A woman of similar age, Rebecca Campbell, stood nearby, appalled, watching yet another such argument occur in a hallway of the facility where she volunteered as a rape crisis victim advocate. Located in Urbana, Illinois, A Woman's Fund offered a combined domestic violence (A Woman's Place) and sexual assault (Rape Crisis Services) program. Campbell was working on her bachelor's degree in psychology at the University of Illinois at Urbana-Champaign. She was there doing a women's studies practicum at the beginning of a decade of her initial research into how awful the community response—police, nurses, doctors, and other first responders—was to rape. Mostly, she felt this place was where she belonged; the work was what she had chosen for her career.

Still, it was nearing the tail end of the dark ages of rape and sexual assault twenty-five years ago, before there were sexual assault nurse examiners who were experts in treating victims of sexual assault and who knew how to perform the rape kit examination thoroughly, all while treating the victim with dignity and compassion. She knew the resident had no idea how to do the examination. Heck, he barely knew how to do a gynecological examination, which is not the same as a sexual assault kit exam, anyway. The latter is intended to detect and treat any injuries to the victim's genital area and collect forensic evidence of the sexual assault.

Striding into the room where the young woman lay, the resident proceeded to open the kit, remove and unfold the instruction sheet, and set it down to refer to during the exam. On the abdomen of the victim. As if she were a book prop. Looking on and now completely horrified, Campbell picked up the sheet and handed it back to him.

"No, you can't do this," she declared. "You can't do this."

Today, she chuckles at the resident's indignant response and angry look of "Who do you think you are?"

"I felt then and do now that I did have the expertise, even as a very, very young student of psychology, to say that behavior was not consistent with how you treat a human being," declares the "born and bred Midwesterner" from Champaign, Illinois. "It just wasn't."

When it was all over, the victim—hurt, confused, and just trying to get through this most recent humiliation—later "very, very sweetly" thanked her advocate.

"That was a pivotal moment for me, very early in my career," Campbell says, as we sit at a small conference table in her long, rectangular office in the Psychology Building at Michigan State University in East Lansing, Michigan, where she joined the faculty in 2003 as a professor of psychology. "It was during that formative time when I knew I was committed to psychology," she continues. "I was committed to doing research on trauma, but that was the crystallizing moment: This is exactly what I want to do. We have to make this better."

A self-confessed neatnik, as much as possible she keeps her office surfaces clear and organized to enhance her mental organization and as a reminder there is a way through the volumes of complex information she needs to digest to generate her research papers and articles. "I can find a narrative in this. I can make sense out of this incredibly messy data spreadsheet," she reasons. "There's a pattern here. I just need to find it."

Her desk is near a window overlooking the campus to the west. Running the length of her office stands a wall of bookshelves packed with titles pertaining to statistical methods and designs or sexual violence, including *Missoula, Sexual Violence, Violence Against Women*. "It's math and then violence, so there's nothing happy on this wall," she says. At the far end of her office, there's a row of file cabinets—"because I'm still an old dinosaur who puts things on paper"—serving as a trophy stand for her numerous teaching and research awards, including one from Eric Holder, the eighty-second US attorney general: the Department of Justice's Vision 21 Crime Victims Research Award.

Around the door is what everyone refers to as her "wall of children," which features years of progressively changing artwork provided by her son (now fifteen) and daughter (now twelve). "I like to have all of these pictures that my kids have drawn over the years as a reminder that I do this to make the world safer for them," she says.

Our meeting is in April 2017, and earlier this week she attended an ill-fated final gathering of the National Commission on Forensic Science (NFCS) in Washington, DC. Prior to the meeting that morning, they learned that their commission—dedicated to the fair and proper use of forensic science in the criminal justice system—had not been renewed by the US attorney general Jeff Sessions. Campbell was there to present about DNA and CODIS hits and explain the victim's point of view and how victim notification works when an offender is discovered after an untested kit has been processed. "What do we learn from research, what do we know about the best ways to communicate very complex DNA information to survivors when they're very likely in a state of trauma, because they were just recontacted about a rape that happened many moons ago," she explains.

The participants were all fascinated, yet the pall of an expected funeral settled over the collection of "the best minds in forensic science prosecution, defense attorneys, and law enforcement in the US" at the Office of Justice Programs. "They've been at it for years," Campbell concludes. "Now they won't be."

Her son happened to see an article about the closing of the NCFS in the *Washington Post* and asked her about it when she got home. "Now I can talk to them about it and hopefully raise them to be socially concerned, socially adjusted," she says. "But that's what I do when I'm not doing this. I just go with my family, drive children to soccer, drive children to swim meets, watch Food Network TV."

Over the years, due to confidentiality and parental sensitivity issues, she developed a handful of euphemisms for her topics of study when they asked "How was your day, Mommy?" As her kids get older, she can gradually be a little more detailed about her work.

As a community psychologist, much of Campbell's early work was focused on documenting the tremendous harm our communities were doing to rape survivors. Of the domestic violence and rape crisis center volunteer days, she says that while she was there solely as a victim advocate, it was not possible to turn off her research brain.

"As an advocate, I was there to support the survivor and ensure that her or his voice was being heard, their wishes being respected," she says of this early phase of her seminal studies of community response to rape and sexual assault. "But I could observe what was happening and think about it in a research study; how would I systematically capture the good and bad—it was mostly bad—of that? Then when I was there as a researcher, I was very clear I was not an advocate, but I was there as a researcher, and I could interview the survivor after his or her exam, interview the advocate after the exam, interview as much as possible the doctors and the police, what just happened, and I was able to document that what was happening was actually pretty darn bad.

"Our doctors and nurses were probably awesome, if you had a heart attack," she quips of her experience that echoes Liz Booth's ER nursing observations a decade ago in Cleveland. "But they were not so awesome in that particular sexual assault context. How the police were treating the victims in incredibly victim-blaming ways, because they weren't acting right, that kind of made me say, 'Okay, how can I start to move this in a direction that's a bit more positive, do some evaluation work on SANE programs and say, whoa, here's a model that works a heck of a lot better.'"

Since then, Campbell has done more than make it better. Thanks to her work, people in the field recognize her as one of the forces behind a great leap forward. Her trainings on the neurobiological impact of trauma on a victim's brain have significantly improved the way police, law enforcement, medical professionals, and others treat and interview victims in the days immediately following the crime or any time afterward, whether it's two months or twenty years later. Just as she demonstrated at the Detroit SAKTF summit in September 2016.

A quarter century into her career, Campbell experienced another defining moment. It slightly preceded Prosecutor Worthy's decision to participate in the NIJ's SAK action-research project along with Houston. Entitled the 400 Project, it was a small pilot project through the Michigan Domestic and Sexual Violence Prevention and Treatment Board and funded by the Office on Violence Against Women. The objective was to test a random sample of four hundred sexual assault kits from the more than eleven thousand kits Worthy's office had uncovered in 2009 to see what the effort might produce.

When it quickly became crystal clear from that random sample the vast majority of the kits had not been tested, Worthy knew they would need to devise long-range plans for next steps for the daunting task of processing those kits and notifying and helping all those victims who'd been in the dark about their cases for five, ten, twenty years. Around that same time, the National Institute of Justice released a national call for action-research projects on untested kits.

That's when Debi Cain, executive director of the Michigan Domestic and Sexual Violence Prevention and Treatment Board, recommended Campbell and her MSU team as a potential research partner to Worthy. She had done a lot of work for the Michigan board. Cain and others knew Campbell was equipped with all the ideal expertise and qualifications: exhaustive research on trauma, intricate familiarity with the justice system, acute comprehension of forensics practices. Campbell met with Worthy's senior staff and it seemed like a good fit, so she submitted an application.

"Prosecutor Worthy formally made me interview for it, too," she tells me, feigning indignation, in a statement fully freighted with our shared knowledge of the great colleagueship and accomplishments that ensued.

"Really?"

"Yeah. Oh yeah. Oh yeah."

"She's good."

"She is."

As part of her research partner responsibilities, Campbell read all of the reports associated with the sixteen hundred untested rape kits that were part of Detroit's immense backlog. The dubious police reports and poor quality of investigations or lack thereof quickly became obvious. But a distinctive critical revelation jumped out at her. Emphasizing that she is not a neurobiologist by training but a community psychologist at a professorial level who understands the impacts of trauma on the brain and the body, Campbell says that her research into the criminal justice response to sexual assault led her to an eye-opening realization.

"What I kept seeing really frequently was police saying things like 'this was an unfounded case,' 'victim is unreliable,' 'we're not going to pursue this.' The police report would say things like 'victim showed no emotion,' 'victim didn't seem distressed,' 'victim couldn't answer simple questions about what time the assault happened.'

"So, reading them as a PhD-level psychologist with training in trauma and understanding the neurobiology of trauma, my jaw sort of fell open," she continues. "Wait a minute. That's trauma, folks. So, in collaborative work with other researchers on understanding trauma, I knew there could be a real benefit in sharing that research with the law enforcement community. The practice of writing cases off, marking them as unfounded, not testing the kits or doing anything about the cases could be traced back to many causes, but one of the reasons was that [law enforcement] didn't understand trauma. They really didn't have any training into what trauma looks like."

In giving a PowerPoint presentation of her findings to the Detroit Police Department, she kept hearing the same basic narrative in response: "We just didn't have the resources." That may be true, but you did not fundamentally treat these survivors in any way resembling kind, empathetic, fair, just, or civil, she countered, as she tried to shift the narrative away from, "We just don't have enough money."

"Having to say that directly to the senior leadership at DPD and show them their reports was very much a defining moment in my career," Campbell reflects. "You know, putting up on the PowerPoint sample reports to say this is what you did, this is what your people did, and they looked at it and said, 'Yes.' They did not contest the findings. They said, 'It's not our best work.'"

The irony that the police chief at that time, Ralph Godbee Jr., was suspended and then resigned shortly afterward under a cloud of allegations that the married official had an affair with a female Detroit police officer is not lost on Campbell. However, she says at the time of her presentation, he showed "tremendous honesty and integrity" in admitting, "This is not right. This is not our best work."**

Although the formal component of her collaboration on the Detroit research-action project ended in 2015 and she has not met the current police chief James Craig, she did see a serious commitment to training. "Some of the key people, Sex Crimes Unit, and staff had participated in trainings I had done," she says. "The Michigan Domestic and Sexual Violence Prevention and Treatment Board was one of our partners on that project, and they brought in national trainers, so I want to give the DPD credit for that. I don't know what is happening currently, but they had made really amazing progress in terms of getting their detectives trained on current best practices."

When we meet in her office, she's on sabbatical facing the daunting task of reducing, refining, and reshaping all of her expansive work with Detroit's SAKTF and nationally as a member of the SAKI team. Her initial comprehensive report about what she had learned from her research and through her involvement with the Detroit research-action project was just south of six hundred pages, but it has become the Rosetta Stone for law enforcement, prosecution, nurses, advocates, and anyone else interested in understanding the impact of trauma on a rape or sexual assault victim.

Chipping pieces off that mountain, she and her research team have published roughly a dozen peer-reviewed articles. Some are already

---

** Author's Note: Despite repeated attempts to interview someone with the Detroit Police Department for roughly two years that included some of the silliest stonewalling techniques I've ever encountered as a journalist, I was unable to talk with anyone at DPD. I wasn't out to burn anyone. I just wanted to discuss their experience with the task force work and new approaches to sexual violence cases. Anyway, as a substitute, I decided to ask Campbell what her experience has been.

in print; others have been accepted for publication but are in what's known as "publication backlog" and waiting to be published.

"I can't get away from backlogs," she deadpans.

Since 2015, there's been a continual rollout of new articles each year. One of the "bigger, better" publications she's really proud of is in the journal *Criminology & Public Policy*, an official publication of the American Society of Criminology. The publication ran one of the articles born of the Detroit SAK Action-Research Project. Entitled "Should Rape Kit Testing Be Prioritized by Victim–Offender Relationship? An Empirical Comparison of Forensic Testing Outcomes for Stranger and Nonstranger Sexual Assaults," Campbell and four other authors examined the DNA forensic testing of 894 backlog SAKs from Detroit that had not been previously tested to determine how many of the kits would provide CODIS-eligible DNA profiles.

"There was a lot of discussion in Detroit, as there has been in pretty much every city I've been to, that we should test the stranger perpetrator kits or give them higher priority than the nonstranger perpetrator," Campbell explains. "We said, let's think about that, because the advocates, prosecutors, and nurses are saying there might also be CODIS hits on nonstranger rapes, and there might also be serial episode rapes associated with them. So we tested both types, and they have statistically equivalent CODIS hit rates.

"So, if you test a nonstranger kit, you get a CODIS hit and it matches to an unsolved rape case, you know who the perpetrator is. You pull the file and have a named perpetrator, you do the investigation and confirm that it's the offender, so then you might have just solved a rape case that's been sitting however long because everyone thought the nonstranger or acquaintance was probably not a rapist."

If you'd like to read it, and you probably don't have a subscription, you can "rent" it for $6, "cloud" it for $15, or "PDF" it for $38, or just preview it for free at the Wiley Online Library website. (Actually, Dr. Campbell has numerous research papers and YouTube videos online you can check out, and they're worth the search.)

Currently, she's got one publication pending about what she's learned from evaluating the Detroit task force's victim notification process, but she's spending much of her sabbatical writing and preparing new articles. She tells me I'm catching her in a weird moment, where she's not gathering more data, but trying to take all the research and countless interviews with police, prosecutors, nurses, and advocates—as well as some survivors, when possible—she's compiled to disseminate those statistics, lessons, and insights. Survivors may be difficult to interview because they don't want to speak publicly or, more likely in Campbell's case, they were still embroiled in litigation against their assailants who've been pulled back into the present through the emergence of SAKTFs around the country, so there are legal and ethical concerns both for the Wayne County Prosecutor's Office and her university's ethics committee. She hopes, however, to approach Prosecutor Worthy eventually about speaking to survivors whose cases have been adjudicated.

The biggest challenge in her personal publishing endeavor is there are still only twenty-four hours in a day. The second challenge is Campbell regularly finds herself bouncing through a number of airports in places as varied as Mobile, Alabama, and Reno, Nevada. As a member of the SAKI training and technical assistance team, she and several others, including Jim Markey, provide training in their various fields of expertise to task forces that have received SAKI grants to process their backlog of rape kits and enhance their approach to handling rape and sexual assault cases in a variety of ways.

At first, Campbell took to the road after word-of-mouth dissemination of her potent research findings began to reach other cities pursuing the SAKTF route. So she received requests to share her work from Detroit's efforts with other jurisdictions like Cleveland and Memphis, and to provide training to law enforcement on the neurobiology of trauma. "What I do in my trainings is weave together research that has been conducted by many scholars for decades, from many disciplines, to summarize key findings in this literature and to consider implications for policy and practice," she explains.

Despite the far-reaching admiration for her work I have encountered, the humble scientist says it is inaccurate to state or imply that her research on the neurobiology of trauma has affected policy and practice. She prefers that I say that her trainings, teachings, or review of the literature have affected policy and practice.

Then in 2015, the Bureau of Justice Assistance launched the Sexual Assault Kit Initiative to support cities with sizable amounts of untested kits. Under the Obama administration, Vice President Joe Biden and Attorney General Loretta Lynch announced the $41 million FY2015 SAKI program, which awarded twenty initial grants to jurisdictions across the country "to get more kits tested, improve investigations, enhance prosecutions, and develop victim-centered protocols for interviewing and notifying victims." Part of that initiative included funding set aside to create a national training and technical assistance (TTA) team. Campbell partnered with two colleagues at the Research Triangle Institute (RTI), which was managing the SAKI project, to assemble a multidisciplinary team of experts from different organizations across the US. The team is available to train and advise the task forces in any one of the now thirty-two cities that have received SAKI grants.

"Through that role, I've been able to find out what's happening in those cities and offer some feedback and training, and we learned from other cities, too," Campbell said when I first interviewed her by phone a week or two after meeting her at the Detroit summit. "There is a lot we still need to learn about this, and just because we have a lot of knowledge about what's happened in Detroit, Houston, Cleveland, Memphis, and some other cities, there's still a lot we don't know about this issue in smaller jurisdictions, what it looks like on a statewide level, what it looks like in rural communities, so that's what the national TTA team is hoping to do."

Typically, the team works collaboratively with the SAKTF in a city, first assessing what their situation is in terms of the backlog of kits, what resources are available to them, who their stakeholders are, what the key issues are for that community, and finally resources the TTA team can contribute to help them develop and implement a long-term plan for their kits. The team also provides specialized training in law enforcement (both high-tech DNA or good old-fashioned gumshoe investigation), effective prosecution techniques, compassionate victim notification, and advocacy practices.

"These are cities that cared enough to apply for the federal funding and have been receptive to these issues," Campbell says. "It doesn't mean they agree with some of the things we might suggest, but we've had a good dialogue of understanding what is happening in all of these different jurisdictions."

When I ask Campbell if there's anything within this gigantic, dynamic, fast-evolving subject that is at the forefront for her these days, she says the thing that wakes her up at 2 o'clock in the morning is the way society and public policy funders and others have defined a successful solution to addressing sexual assault very narrowly to testing kits. And, as we know, that's only an early step.

"I'm worried that we will see jurisdictions where they've tested the kits," she says. "Then they have one or two prosecutions from it, and they go, 'See. We told you it didn't make sense to test the kits.'"

For example, according to www.EndTheBacklog.org, a Joyful Heart Foundation website, upon completion of testing its 6,663 previously untested sexual assault kits funded by $4.4 million in federal and municipal funding, Houston officials reported the following results: Testing yielded 850 matches in CODIS, resulting in the prosecution of 29 offenders. (The Houston Police Department had outsourced all of the kits to two private labs for testing, along with 1,450 more recently collected kits and 1,020 samples of DNA evidence from other crimes.)

Even in kit processing situations with lower conviction rates, however, the upside is more DNA profiles of rapists have been added to CODIS from tested kits.

Pointing out the downside, Campbell says: "It won't go any further than that, unless we change the way we think about this to not just test the kits, but investigate the cases and prosecute the offenders and support the survivors. When we see jurisdictions that think about it in that broader, holistic way—Cleveland, Detroit, New York originally—we're going to see more and more where the benefit of testing the kits is not just in terms of CODIS being populated with more profiles, but prosecutions and survivors having the opportunity to testify if they so choose, to participate in sentences and hearings. But jurisdictions that think about it narrowly are going to test and then call it a day."

Testing the kits, especially the tens of thousands of backlog kits nationwide, is important. But if the effort stops there, if it doesn't become an ongoing best practice to test, investigate, prosecute, and provide a victim-centered approach to each case so that survivors can regain some control over their lives and what happened to them and possibly some closure by participating in their case and, hopefully, putting the offender away, then we haven't advanced.

Thanks to the efforts of Campbell and her research colleagues at other institutions in disseminating paradigm-shifting revelations about the impact of trauma on a victim of rape or sexual assault, law enforcement, prosecutors, advocates, and others now understand what had been a complete unknown.

Naturally, Campbell is psyched that after several decades of intensively focused study, her work is finally making its way down into the police academy in Michigan, and other states are slowly considering incorporating it in their academy curricula.

"There is now a broad, multidisciplinary literature on how trauma affects victims and the implications of that for first responders," she says, adding humbly: "I am one of many people who do research on this. I am one of many people who train on this, but having the research on trauma and its impact reach the academy level is really important because it's vital for all of our first responders, police, prosecutors, [and] advocates to have the most current information to help them do their jobs well."

———————

Throughout my interviews with everyone, I've asked what they think are the underlying causes for the horrific tradition of victim blaming and general lack of concern for victims of rape and sexual assault that law enforcement, and the human race in general, has practiced for millennia. Campbell, a member of MSU's Research Consortium on Gender-Based Violence, gives the following fundamental rationale:

"Sexual assault is a gender crime. It happens disproportionally to women. It does happen to male victims, and we've seen a very positive shift in the last five years in the growing recognition of the number of boys, young men, and grown men who also have been victims of sexual assault. But before that shift happened, it was broadly understood as primarily a gender crime against women. In a society that does not place the same value on women in terms of their health, their well-being, their equitable pay in the work force, all sorts of general indicators of women's status in American society, a crime that disproportionately affects them is just not simply going to get the same institutional attention. It's just not."

In the yin-yang situation that sexual violence remains, the recent changes and improvements across the spectrum for police, prosecutors, nurses, and advocates have given increasing reasons for hope. There is growing belief that cultural changes demanding more compassion and respect for victims and more aggressive approaches to taking offenders off the street for public safety will continue to become common best practices. For Campbell, the momentum of this movement originated in different places and for different reasons.

"There's a huge public safety component to it," she says. "One of the key things I talk about when I'm training multidisciplinary teams is we may not all necessarily be there for the same reasons, but let's try to find common ground and keep moving forward. For some people the momentum and their passion for this is understanding the public safety threat of having untested rape kits, so what happens if we can test these kits and start seeing patterns of serial offending, how can we keep our communities safer for our sons and our daughters, our teens and our adults and our elderly, how do we make the whole community safer through this?"

There are others who have a social-justice-focused approach as more people are realizing what victims have to endure after surviving a brutal, violent crime. They undergo a very invasive medical examination. They file a detailed report and often withstand a long round of interviews with police and detectives. They then have to sit through hours of grueling testimony and cross-examination in court, if they choose to testify. Frequently, though, their case may be neglected altogether by the criminal justice system and by society.

"I think we've gained momentum as more and more people realize what it costs a survivor to be raped and then to be neglected," she says. "So what can we do to try to make amends to the survivors?"

At the time she attended the first SAKTF summit in Cleveland with the Detroit and Memphis task forces in 2014, Campbell felt like the advances just might be permanent as the momentum continued to grow. "I never imagined I'd be sitting here with three states that really wanted to do something about this and feeling like, 'Oh my gosh, we're really trying to make a dent,'" she recalls. She was unable to attend the summit in Memphis the following year, but upon entering the Detroit summit, she was encouraged to see even more people and thought, "I never thought I'd be in a room this big with this many people committed to this effort," she thought. "We have hit some sort of critical mass in people caring about this."

Having gone from one room just two years prior to a full-fledged conference with numerous plenary and breakout sessions—"at the Renaissance Center, for Pete's sake!"—Campbell knew they were making marked progress, and everyone was on a mission to keep this movement rolling forward.

"I believe the folks working on this issue get out of bed every day because they really do want to help," she says. "They do it from different disciplines and different perspectives, but at the end of the day, it is about protecting, serving, and helping victims."

One of her biggest fears now is that if the existing resources for support—SAKI and DANY grants—disappear, a lot of that progress could halt and reverse itself. "These cases take time, they take energy, they require a lot of passion and compassion on the part of the service providers to keep doing this day in and day out," she says. "And there are still a lot kits to be tested, cases to be investigated, and survivors to be supported, so communities could still want to do the right thing, but just not have the resources to do it."

She believes there are several key ingredients necessary to continue the task force initiatives and all of the best practices that have come out of them. For Campbell, it all starts with having a champion. "Prosecutor Worthy's leadership has been rock steady, unwavering since the kits were discovered in 2009 and you and I are having this conversation in 2017," she says. "I don't think her position or her passion has changed in the slightest in all that time."

One of the reasons Campbell spends a significant amount of her time and energy writing and disseminating all of her research in high-quality peer-reviewed papers—in much the same way CWRU researcher Rachel Lovell does in Cleveland—is that it can help influence public policy decisions as well as best practices of professionals working in the field or participating on task forces. Part of her research through the SAKI project compares and contrasts how what was accomplished in Detroit may or may not replicate what was implemented and achieved in other jurisdictions.

She says she's excited by the work she sees being done in Kansas and West Virginia, which are both implementing statewide rape kit testing and investigation approaches to make the entire state safer, rather than specific cities or jurisdictions. There are always challenges when trying to coordinate multiple jurisdictions with divergent policies and practices, but several states are exploring it and developing centralized statewide databases, including Michigan. Washington State is moving in that direction, and Portland, Oregon, is making great progress as well, and served as the site of the SAKTF summit in November 2017. Campbell was one of fifty-one presenters at the summit, which had nearly two hundred attendees from all over the country, including law enforcement officers from twenty different jurisdictions, according to Susan Lehman from the Portland Police Bureau.

She also likes what she sees in Fayetteville, North Carolina, which had been struggling with the issue of rape and sexual assault; but the new police chief has already received positive recognition for the steps he's taking to correct their deficiencies. Mobile, Alabama, is a more recent SAKI site just getting up to speed.

"They have a number of kits, and they have really strong research partners, which helps," she says, since not all SAKI sites have chosen to involve a research partner to evaluate their methods and track their results. "Not to praise my own discipline out of turn, but having a research partner helps make things concrete. We count things, put them on paper, and send them across the table, so we can see if we're doing a great job or we're not doing as many things as we thought we should, so let's do more."

As for the fast-burgeoning movement to correct and improve the way we've handled sexual assault and rape cases that's been unfolding rapidly over the past five years or so, she says she's never seen anything like it. "I've been studying sexual assault and the criminal justice system for about twenty-five years now, and I've never seen anything grow and take root as quickly as this," she says. "I believe the visual of the untested kits is very powerful and unsettling, too. The public understanding of the power of DNA evidence to convict or exonerate someone wrongly accused has been important. Just the idea that these kits were sitting there and that people could have convicted or cleared with that evidence is troubling."

Pressed to talk about why she does what she does, Campbell cites the Girl Scout law: Make the world a better place.

"I think I've had a small but important role," she says in assessing her contributions. "I feel I've been helpful in the behind-the-scenes stuff of compiling information, sharing research, helping people understand about trauma and how that can improve things. I think I've been helping Detroit see a pathway to something better, and then on the national SAKI project I've had a bigger role helping there. Ultimately, I feel like I've had a positive impact. I'm very proud of the work we did collectively in Detroit and proud to have been part of that team that really made something positive happen."

Chapter 12

The Investigator:
Mark Farrah and the Wayne
County SAK Task Force

JUST TO THE left of his computer monitor, Mark Farrah, investigator for the Wayne County SAKTF, keeps a list of names, phone numbers, and email addresses of victims from the Detroit rape kit backlog whose cases have been adjudicated.

"On that rare occasion when there's a little bit of downtime—and we try to make this a general practice for everybody—just look over and dial up a number," he says. "It may be six months or nine months later, 'Hey, haven't talked to you in a while, just wanted to touch base. How are you doing?' That call just goes so far. We like to let them know that they weren't just a number to us, a statistic to say we wrapped up another one. We really become somewhat attached to them."

Occasionally, should a victim get into a minor legal scrape, detectives have accompanied them to court for support. Farrah's office maintains a "jean fund," so the normally suit-clad investigators can dress casually on Fridays and throw a few bucks into a coffee can. The funds are used to help victims if, for example, they need to drive downtown and end up getting a parking ticket, or if they just need a cup of coffee and a donut or lunch. On the eleventh floor of their building, the female detectives and prosecutors stock a closet of women's clothing, since the majority of the victims are women, in case they can't afford the proper attire for a court proceeding.

"We try to go the extra mile to make it as simple as possible and let them know that we're doing everything we can for them," he explains.

Another approach that Farrah believes distinguishes their work is what's known as vertical prosecution. In other words, the investigator, prosecutor, and advocate stay with a case from its inception through prosecution; they do not hand off cases to others. This continuity is something the affable Farrah says he's never seen done before in his previous law enforcement life. Sometimes there would be three or four different investigators involved in a case. The dedicated group approach helps the victims feel more comfortable as they proceed through the justice system. It's especially effective since the team members all become involved in the victims' lives. They know how their children are doing, when their birthdays are, or when one of their kids is in the school Christmas play.

"That really means a lot to them, so that's one of the unique aspects of the way that we do it here," Farrah says. "We do have an impact on their lives. We can't take them out of the neighborhoods; we can't provide them with a safe haven, but they have a name and a number of somebody they feel they can trust if they need help."

That empathy for victims is a key characteristic that distinguishes Farrah and the other Wayne County investigators. It's at the core of the victim-centered, trauma-informed approach they implement when working with victims, starting with their victim notification procedures as they initiate an investigation of one of the backlog kits. Within the SAKTF world, Farrah is considered an expert in notifications now. He has been doing them since he joined the task force in 2014 after twenty-five years on the police department in the Detroit suburb of Southgate. At the 2016 Detroit summit of cities, he served on a panel specifically to address notification techniques.

The panel discussed some of the varying approaches to victim notification. Unlike Cuyahoga County's task force, for example, Wayne County investigators never bring victim advocates with them as a safety measure, although their absence can add to the burden of what they're doing. He says they always look at Google Maps to get an idea of where they are going, though a neighborhood may have changed since the photos were taken. If the victim wants to move forward with the case, investigators then introduce an advocate at a second meeting, most often at WC SAFE, Wayne County's rape crisis and victim advocacy center.

They also do all notifications in person, whereas some task forces contact victims by telephone first. Those units prefer phone notification in case the person has moved on from their assault, which may have happened fifteen or twenty years ago, so the victim may not have told family members about what happened to them. Preferring in-person notification, Farrah explains that task force members always prepare for situations where the victim is not alone and someone else at the home does not know or may be a danger to them in domestic violence situations, for example. They always create an "alibi" to give the victim, if they need it.

"When I take that girl out onto the porch and we talk a little bit, we always give them a story. Generally, through our initial investigation, we'll know some things about them. We'll say, 'Tell them when you worked at Burger King seven years ago, it got robbed, and they just arrested the guy that robbed a whole bunch of Burger Kings, and we're trying to tie him into some old ones.' We'll give them something to go back in the house with so they're not getting questioned by their family as to why the police are here. You have to take every precaution. The safety of the victim is our ultimate concern."

Everyone has different successful methods, Farrah adds about Wayne County's procedures, but, "This is just the way we think it works best for us."

A tall, former high school football and baseball player and wrestler, Farrah possesses the kind demeanor and personality of the neighbor you always ask for advice on how to fix your car or find a good plumber. He believes the notification stage of an investigation is the most interesting aspect of the entire process.

"You have to realize that no two are going to be the same," he notes. "You don't know what you're going to get when you knock on that door."

The reactions they get from victims, who have typically given up expecting any progress on their cases after they initially stalled, include feeling excitement and joyful relief; needing time to think about it; expressing anger and frustration; and responding, "I'm past that. I don't want nothin' to do with it."

He can usually tell within the first two minutes whether a victim will become a willing participant or will clam up and choose not to assist with an investigation. He's also learned how while victims might have been deceitful in their initial reports or statements, it may be because they were embarrassed they chose to get into someone's car on their own and not at gunpoint. Or maybe they were forced to submit to humiliating acts, such as anal sex, that they couldn't get themselves to reveal at the time but it had shown up in their rape kit examination. Some are more willing to discuss those details many years later.

"Every visit is a learning experience," Farrah imparts. "You can't predict what's around the corner on any one of them. They're so unique in all of their collaborating facts that each one has its own intricate details that make it interesting to investigate and prosecute."

The master detective details how, based on that reality, they train their investigators to be completely ready before they ever knock on a door. They need to have medical release forms so they can obtain all original hospital records, for example, or they can obtain a court order, if necessary. Medical records, Farrah explains, may contain a vast amount of valuable investigative information. Records can help investigators document injuries that can change a criminal charging; verify times, dates, and locations; corroborate statements (e.g., the statement given at triage may have more information than the police report); determine the names of examining hospital personnel for witness testimony; and provide information on who brought the victim to hospital and possible witnesses. Medical reports may also have information on recent consensual encounters the victim may have had at the time of the assault.

Investigators also need to have lineup photographs of the perpetrator(s) ready to present to victims. "We never know, but that person might just want to open up right then and there and want to talk," Farrah says. "Ultimately, we want to make that initial notification, and then we want to schedule a full interview at the Wayne County SAFE advocacy center in Detroit that we do along with our advocates so that we have that support there for the victim, but that's not always the case."

After an extensive search, Farrah found one victim who probably would have benefited from some advocacy help immediately after she was first assaulted. After the initial interviews and investigation into her case, she had fallen back into drug dependency and disappeared. When he finally relocated her, Farrah knew they had to treat her a little differently.

"We wanted to make certain that as we move forward again, we don't send her back into the spiral that she was in when this incident occurred," he says. "So there are so many different personalities and aspects, the things we encounter on these is just incredible."

When I interviewed Farrah in April 2017, one recent notification lingered for him. He and his partner went to a house to notify a woman who had been raped multiple times. Her name was attached to three different rape kits they were investigating. She vividly remembered each. For roughly half an hour, she was talkative, engaged in their conversation, and was prepared to schedule an appointment to meet with the detectives and an advocate at WC SAFE to discuss the cases in more detail. Then, as they finished scheduling her appointment and prepared to leave, she got real quiet, Farrah recalls. "Is something bothering you?" he asked.

She looked him directly in the eyes and "dropped the bomb": "It just astonishes me that after all these years you've got all of this information about my rape, but nobody's ever called me about my daughter that was murdered."

Farrah remembers thinking to himself, "Man, what some of these people have withstood in their lives is just incredible. What could be worse than this? She's a victim of multiple assaults. She lost a child to murder. Never was contacted, no information, no follow-up from the police. She still knows nothing about the murder of her daughter."

He did contact an advocate immediately and suggested giving the woman a call even before they did the interview because of the amount of trauma she had endured. "This is one that's going to need support right out of the gate," he told the advocate. The case had not been adjudicated at the time I spoke to Farrah, so he couldn't discuss details, but another detective followed up to investigate the homicide.

"You just don't know what notification is going to bring," the seasoned investigator reiterates. "So, if there's anything we've learned, it's that it's such a critical aspect of this whole process that you have to be prepared for anything. If you can't work on your feet, if you can't be adaptable, if you don't have empathy and you don't understand these things, you're not going to be a successful investigator in this stuff."

No matter what the case is, the investigators doing the notifications never try to force or coerce the victims into participating in the prosecution of their assailants. They let them know what the statute of limitations deadline for their case is. They leave them information about Wayne County SAFE, should they want to meet with an advocate or seek counseling, and their task force contact information.

"We have an advocate follow up to make certain they're okay and that we didn't stir up something or some emotion that's going to trigger them or cause them further distress," Farrah explains. "We tell them, 'We know there is no better way for us to do it than to knock on the door. We know that's a lot to take in. We understand that you may be apprehensive. Here's my information. This case is a case where there's no statute of limitations or it's still open, so as long as this task force project is in effect, at any time you change your mind, feel free to give me a call, and we'll come back and start over.'"

"We leave everything open-ended in that respect," Farrah continues, before the fully converted victim-centered investigator declares the bottom line, "If they don't want to do it, they don't have to do it."

Farrah readily admits one of the factors that made him so much more acutely aware of the victim's vulnerabilities is the work of Rebecca Campbell, PhD. We briefly discuss her presentation at the September 2016 summit, and when I ask him how her findings in the neurobiology of trauma affected the investigators, he replies, "Dr. Campbell's work, in my opinion, may be the most enlightening training that I had in all my years of law enforcement."

He has heard the presentation several times and picks up something different each time. Campbell, of course, continues to research and refine her studies. Farrah, who sits on an advisory panel for the Michigan State Police with Campbell and other law enforcement specialists, says Campbell's ideas are now being rolled out in updated police academy courses as part of increased sexual assault training in Michigan. When he was going through his police academy training in 1986, he vaguely remembers taking a two-hour class on reading the statutes regarding what the differences were between first-, second-, and third-degree criminal sexual conduct. That was about it. He does not remember any training on why you get the unresponsive, flat affect, memory loss reactions that police get when dealing with victims of rape and sexual assault.

"Dr. Campbell's training is something that every law enforcement officer needs to learn, because she points out things that we used to see as deception: 'Why would she be laughing when she's talking about this?'" he gives as an example.

"I can't tell you a law enforcement person that has been in the game for twenty years or better," Farrah continues, "who doesn't sit through that, walk out of there, think back, and go, 'Oh, my God. Did I blow that case? If I had only known.' It's really that enlightening."

Obviously deeply impressed by what Campbell has revealed to police and happy to see it being taught and adopted in different jurisdictions and moving down into the academy-level curriculum, Farrah reiterates: "What she's done is really the best training I've had in my career."

Growing up in Southgate, Michigan, about eighteen miles south of Detroit, Farrah never contemplated a career in law enforcement. After enjoying his time in high school as a three-sport athlete, he enrolled in Central Michigan University, where he earned his bachelor's degree in business administration and dove into his career in retail and retail management. "Believe it or not," Farrah quips.

An opportunity arose when the Southgate Police Department announced it would be testing and hiring some police officers. Well, the hardworking twenty-five-year-old didn't see it as an opportunity, but his older and wiser father, who had a bunch of buddies who were Dearborn police officers, did. "My dad said, 'Listen, these guys are doing all right. It's not a bad job. You really need to think about it because all the hours you're putting in and everything,'" Farrah recalls of their fateful conversation. "He convinced me to take the test, and lo and behold, I got hired and worked in my hometown for twenty-six years."

After fourteen years as a patrolman, he was promoted to the Detective Bureau. As a detective-sergeant, he served as a lead investigator for the last several years of his career, focused primarily on high-profile municipal and judicial embezzlement cases. He retired in 2011, and basically, well, you know, lived the retiree's lifestyle. Travelled. Knocked around the house. Promised his wife to remodel the kitchen. He had told her when he retired he might be able to earn some extra money to pay for it, but he confesses now that it was a stall tactic. He did his darnedest to put it off. Until his sister-in-law noticed the home makeover contest on the back of a flyer she received in the mail.

"After being prodded for almost two weeks, I begrudgingly entered the contest," Farrah sighs. "Wrote a short essay and entered this contest for Lowe's, and lo and behold, I was one of four winners across the United States from almost a million people who entered. I won a $100,000 home makeover from Lowe's and was an employee spokesman for a year."

Summing up the experience, he says, "I come from a pretty lucky family. My brothers and sisters have won different prizes along the way, so we've been blessed."

Several years into his retirement bliss, when the Wayne County Prosecutor's Office tapped his shoulder to join the team, he became one of three investigators. They're now up to twenty-four, including six Detroit police officers assigned to the SAKTF. Because of his depth of experience and expertise, Farrah's role evolved to managing administrative duties and being involved in all of the cases rather than working a few individual cases. He's mentoring, assisting, and instructing other detectives as a "go-to guy" and overseeing his favorite task.

"I try to go on all new notifications to make sure the notification is handled correctly," he says. "Then I review all of the warrant recommendations before they go to a prosecutor to ensure that everything's done and crossed and correct."

According to Farrah, one of the biggest challenges they've encountered when processing the backlogged rap kits has been trying to track down old police files. While the kits were all found and identified, each has an accompanying police report that was kept separately, as were any medical records. Thus, he and his fellow investigators have spent a considerable amount of time searching through endless stacks of banker boxes and trying to decipher perplexing and antiquated filing systems in police warehouses and file rooms for past records.

"Ideally, we like to have as much of the original documentation as we can," says Farrah, who is scheduled to go police file hunting later this week. "If it doesn't exist or we can't find it, that doesn't stop us. We will still go out and talk to the victim, and we'll generate a new case number and a new report, and we'll move forward from there."

When I asked him about the benefits of the national collaboration engendered by the partnership with Cleveland and Memphis that continues to grow, he spent several minutes listing the colleagues he's met at the city summits and the resulting meetings, valuable communication, shared information, and cooperative experiences he's enjoyed. One advocate from Kansas that he met at the 2016 Detroit summit reached out to him to help her get their local law enforcement agents to buy into the victim-centered approach and process, of which Detroit's SAKTF and Farrah are avid proponents. He had a meeting with her scheduled for later that month.

"Law enforcement and advocacy have always been sort of an oil and water type of thing," he says. "But we've found that by making that connection we're much more successful. So that was a great connection that I made, and we're going to get an opportunity to share our stories and hopefully help Kansas get rolling on their program."

Farrah also had a case that took him west to Seattle. He was joined by two Detroit FBI agents. They not only had dinner with their Emerald City counterparts, and then met with FBI agents from Tacoma who assisted in their investigations. Farrah and his team gave a short presentation on cold case investigations and shared some stories with their colleagues that included a sexual assault investigator who was new to the process.

"Yes, just that few days at the summit led to us being able to reach out across the country on several occasions," Farrah relates.

In the end, though, Farrah always comes back to how much he enjoys working with and helping the victims.

"Even on a couple of cases that didn't end up in a guilty plea, the victims came to us and said, 'Thank you for taking on my case,'" he recounts. "They said, 'I feel so much better. I was telling the truth all along, but nobody believed me. But you guys believed me, and at least I got my day in court.'"

Chapter 13

The Motor City Healers:
Kim Hurst and Wayne County
SAFE

S OMEWHAT ASTONISHED, KIMBERLY Hurst stared at her attending physician, then stared at the rectangular box he had just handed her. "Here's a rape kit. This is your patient," he said before walking away. She was studying to become a physician's assistant and working in a busy urban hospital's emergency department.

The discomfited young victim lay on the bed in the exam room at St. John Hospital and Medical Center. Fortunately, it was a slow night in the ER, so she was given the "courtesy" of the only exam room with a door; the rest were curtained cubicles with beds. She was Hurst's first sexual assault patient. Hurst had never even seen a rape kit before. She was nervous. Afraid she would say or do the wrong thing. She hadn't received any training in sexual assault cases in PA school. She knew it wasn't offered much in med or nursing schools, either.

"There was not one word said about how to take care of a patient who's been sexually assaulted, how to talk to them, what questions to ask, and definitely nothing about a rape kit and how to collect evidence," she remembers of that day in 2001. "That's one experience I will never forget, because the attending didn't come in with me. It was just me as a student going in to take care of this young girl for the first time. I had this feeling that this is so wrong. I have no idea what I'm doing. I don't know how to open the kit. I was reading the directions as I was doing this exam. I had no idea."

Hurst remembers thinking she couldn't possibly comprehend what her young patient had just gone through, so she needed to get herself together, focus on the girl, and do the exam.

Born in Ann Arbor, Hurst grew up in Metro Detroit before earning her bachelor's degree at Michigan State University. While in pursuit of a master's degree in kinesiology at the University of Minnesota, she worked full time as an athletic trainer because she had an innate drive to help fix people who had been injured or suffered trauma.

Hurst had grown bored, however, and felt she needed more demanding tests than the ones presented to trainers on the fields and courts of athletic competitions. She soon realized she was drawn to the challenges and fulfillment of providing treatment in a place where patients need it most exigently: hospital emergency rooms. She returned to Detroit and enrolled in the physician assistant studies program at Wayne State University. Prior to her ER assignment, she had already completed one interesting student rotation.

"I worked in a morgue, where I was able to help with the autopsies, and the forensic side of it really, really fascinated me," Hurst recalls, quickly adding, "*But* I also like living patients and not spending my time in a morgue."

While on her ER rotation, she became intrigued with a subspecialty called sexual assault nurse examiner. A friend informed her there were training programs she could do, especially because of her burgeoning interest in forensics. Hurst thought she had to be a nurse first, but her friend told her physicians or PAs could train to become a sexual assault forensic examiner (SAFE). She found a program near where she lived, signed up, and was "just hooked."

"The program only validated what I had done wrong with that one patient who I just couldn't forget," she says. "I started working for the county I lived in as an on-call forensic examiner, so it was above and beyond what I did full time in the ER."

Working in the ER, Hurst saw sexual assault patients arriving all the time and tried to do what she could for them with her new SAFE training, but it wasn't her job there. Actually, there was no SANE or SAFE program at the hospital. Patients were treated by nurses or doctors without any specialized expertise or equipment, or they were sent to hospitals in Oakland or Macomb, the two counties north of Wayne County that had SANE programs. Many of the patients, she observed, had to take cab rides of roughly forty-five minutes to get to the hospital in Oakland County, and then the police were occasionally lax in picking up SAKs from outside of the forty jurisdictions within Wayne County.

Hurst started to ruminate on what services victims of sexual assault ideally needed and how the questionable care they did receive wasn't being provided in a safe, private setting. When she began to explore the optimal SANE programs for rape and sexual assault victims in Detroit, she realized that there really weren't any. Her conclusion?

"Well, just start one. Right? Easy enough?" she says with a laugh, crediting her youthful naivety for the decision. "Not so much. But one thing led to another, and I started figuring out what kind of model we needed."

To get direct experience with how a program should run, she started working with one of the programs, but even though it was busy, it wasn't busy enough to give her many on-call experiences. So, she started working as a SAFE for the programs in both northern counties. "That's where I thought, 'Yeah, this really needs to happen in Wayne County because that's the largest county in the state,'" she says.

She also started talking to some of the leadership in the Wayne County health care systems to learn more about becoming an incorporated entity and nonprofit. They guided her to Blue Cross Blue Shield of Michigan, which donated the start-up funding she needed. Hurst spent time with medical and victim advocates' stakeholders in the community to learn what they would most need from a SAFE program.

On January 1, 2006, Hurst, a handful of nurses, and a few other SAFEs opened a clinical space that she had gotten donated through the medical system she worked for, thanks to a medical director who also had an interest in providing these services for victims of sexual violence. They also acquired the appropriate special medical equipment necessary to perform the Sexual Assault Nurse Examinations. They called the new center, now the largest and busiest in the state, Wayne County SAFE.

"We provide medical and forensic care, as well as community-based advocacy and crisis intervention services," Hurst informs me. SAFE offers "a comprehensive and compassionate continuum of care in order to improve the community's response to sexual assault and set a higher a standard."

The first year, the group saw nearly two hundred patients. The number of sexual assault victim visits continued to increase in all counties. By 2008, it had grown to three hundred at WC SAFE. In 2009, the Detroit Medical Center, one of the largest and busiest of the four health systems in the county, after resisting Hurst's repeated requests to partner, came to her. DMC offered to donate space, supplies, and equipment to open WC SAFE's second of what would eventually be five clinic locations in one of its main hospitals, Detroit Receiving.

"The idea caught on with doctors, because many were relieved to no longer have to do rape kits in the emergency department," she explained in an interview with End the Backlog, an initiative of the Joyful Heart Foundation. "People saw that we were doing good work with good results, while we saw the number of patients coming to see us more than double annually."

When I first met Hurst at the Detroit SAKTF summit in September 2016, it was the morning of the last day of the conference, and she was rather harried. Later that day, she and Rebecca Campbell were flying to Denver to speak at the annual conference of the International Association of Forensic Nurses. Their presentation would encourage forensic nursing as a whole to understand the importance of their role in the unsubmitted kit issue and motivate them to initiate and promote the discussion in their communities. Campbell also presented her well-known training on the neurobiology of trauma and victims' responses to sexual assault that was generally unknown until the past few years. Campbell had an entire room of law enforcement agents, prosecutors, nurses, and advocates entirely engaged when she presented her plenary session on the first day of the Detroit summit.

The day before, Hurst prepped for the co-presentation by leading her own breakout session on the role of SANE and SAFE examinations and how the issue directly impacts health care's current work with these patients and the relevance of the unsubmitted kit issue nationwide.

"In many cases and many communities," Hurst told me at the time, "it's just looked at as a law enforcement issue and not a health care issue. We have ownership in this, as well, and a lot of really great input and great skill sets and great resources to help provide to communities as they're figuring out this issue."

Hurst first became involved in the whole unsubmitted kit undertaking in 2009, which turned out to be a transformative moment for WC SAFE. While on maternity leave, Hurst learned of the more than ten thousand untested sexual assault kits that had been uncovered in Detroit at the same time her fledgling organization was about to make several advances. One of her funders contacted her, inquiring whether WC SAFE could hire advocates for victims of sexual assault, since Wayne County did not have anyone serving that role, only a few advocates for domestic violence cases.

"There were no dedicated sexual assault services that we could really partner with to provide that advocacy component, to have someone who could be there as a safe person to talk to and provide emotional counseling," Hurst recalls. "Because in the medical field, we like to heal and we like to fix, but we're not always so compassionate, since our focus is making sure the patient is okay physically, evaluating their injury, and treating it."

The medical staff at WC SAFE also had to be conscious of the fact that all their medical records could become part of an investigation or be subpoenaed by a court. The advocate would have a confidential relationship with the victims and could assist them with follow-up medical services or transportation to help them participate in the criminal justice system to prosecute their assailants. Thus, WC SAFE's funders offered to pay for adding an advocacy piece to their programming, because they believed it was an essential component to providing a comprehensive response to the budding SAK initiative in Detroit.

"The advent of the advocacy program in 2010 was a complete transformation for us," Hurst informs me today. "It started to put us into this niche where we are the only agency in southwest Michigan that strictly focuses on sexual assault and can provide all of these comprehensive services around counseling and advocacy coupled with the medical forensics and everything else."

Shortly afterward, Debi Cain, executive director of the Michigan Domestic and Sexual Violence Prevention and Treatment Board, contacted Hurst. She was in the process of assembling the team that would take on what became known as The 400 Project, the first step of a multi-phase approach to eliminating Detroit's backlogged rape kit problem.

"It was really Debi's vision and foresight that brought all of us together to provide the services that were needed and start the discussions that led to submitting the application for the National Institute of Justice funding and all that followed," Hurst declares.

One of the biggest surprises for Hurst was they had all been laboring under the same presumptions as the rape victims for whom they were administering the sexual assault kit examination and evidence collection. "We turned the kits over to law enforcement, and our expectation was that they were being tested," she says "even though we had witnessed interactions with law enforcement that had us question how they were treating those victims without having that advocacy component yet."

WC SAFE started with two advocates in 2010, but six years later, with additional funding, they were up to twelve full-time advocates and three full-time program directors of their medical services. In November of

2015, after two years of planning, the organization added full pediatric services, which required specialized training and credentials in pediatric sexual abuse, especially since the SANE examination for a pre-menses girl of twelve or under is significantly different anatomically than for an older teen or adult woman, according to Hurst. Six of their nurses are trained in pediatrics, so there is always someone on call with that expertise.

"That pediatric population is a whole world unto itself," she says. "We needed to have enough forensic examiners with an interest in doing pediatrics, because we might have a two-year-old come to us after being assaulted. The work is not easy anyway, but sometimes with our little people, it's even harder."

The center also partnered with Detroit's nationally acclaimed Kids-TALK Children's Advocacy Center for helping children who have been involved in any kind of trauma, including victims of sexual abuse, sex trafficking, domestic violence, or having witnessed a homicide or violent crime. They employ individuals trained in performing what's known as a forensic interview with children in ways to elicit information without causing further trauma or with children too young to articulate fully what they experienced. The partnership with the CAC helps WC SAFE address complex related issues. For example, the CAC works directly with Child Protective Services to handle cases that may require the potential removal of a child from a home.

WC SAFE began working with the Chief, Child Protection Team at Children's Hospital of Michigan and Assistant Professor of Pediatrics at Wayne State University, Dena Nazer, MD, who also ran the Child Protection Center at Children's Hospital of Michigan, a 228-bed children's hospital that is part of the Detroit Medical Center and is ranked nationally in seven pediatric specialties. Dr. Nazer became the impetus for WC SAFE to take on pediatric cases, Hurst says, because she knew they weren't able to treat child sexual abuse cases adequately in their always-hectic ER. While the ER handles non-acute exams, WC SAFE handles what are considered the acute exams, meaning they are performed within the first 120 hours of

a sexual assault, when DNA evidence is still obtainable and has not deterio-
rated beyond the point where a court will accept it as valid.

"Now that we're getting more and more research in DNA and the
science is getting better, I have a feeling that time period will probably
become more like a week in the next year or two," Hurst says.

Moreover, she and a couple of her staff members serve on a statewide pediatric sexual assault work group that is developing and refining
best practices for administering the pediatric sexual assault examinations and treatment for children.

Hurst labels WC SAFE's growth "fast and furious," since they
started with a $20,000 budget from the money Blue Cross Blue Shield
of Michigan donated and their budget for 2017 is up to $1.8 million.
Seeing approximately seven hundred victims annually, the center's volume of patients now ranks among the highest in the US, and Hurst
ensures that they offer a full range of services to anyone of any age
who needs help. The WC SAFE clinics are open 24-7 365 days a year.
Roughly 80 percent of their calls come from hospital ERs, whether the
person presents as a sexual assault victim or it becomes evident during
a medical exam. They enforce a serious commitment to empowerment,
so they never force a victim to have a rape kit done. It is always their
choice, and they can stop the procedure at any time. They also have the
choice whether they want law enforcement involved. If not, WC SAFE
will store the evidence indefinitely, so the victim has the option to press
charges in the future.

Recognizing that, unfortunately, they are one of the most at-risk
populations, WC SAFE added special services for the LGBT community. Hurst is also diligent in forming relationships with different
assistance agencies where the center can safely refer its LGBT clients.
Additionally, over the past year or two, they've formalized their efforts
to assist victims who have been trafficked by adding a human trafficking
specialist and serving on a local trafficking task force. Hurst says they're
definitely seeing more victims in this area, so they have stepped up
their presence; they offer unique services to help those individuals who

frequently develop PTSD after experiencing prolonged drug or alcohol dependency and usually brutal physical, psychological, and emotional trauma during their subjugation.

The energetic Hurst remains assiduous in her active involvement in the prevention of sexual violence and treatment programs for victims. She is the SART (sexual assault response team) coordinator for the community. Many cities have SARTs, multidisciplinary teams that typically meet quarterly to share best practices, keep everyone informed on important cases, pending legislation, or other related activities, and foster networking and communication among professionals dealing with rape and sexual assault. Members include local and national law enforcement agents (i.e., police, FBI, ICE, US Marshals), prosecutors, nurses, advocates, educators, and so on. According to Hurst, Detroit's SART formed in 2008, but it had a poor initial response. She credits the involvement of SANEs and SAFEs—yes, there are a lot of acronyms in this field—with organizing and energizing Detroit's SART into a highly effective community consortium a couple of years ago.

Currently, Hurst serves on Michigan's governor-appointed, legislatively mandated Sexual Assault Evidence Kit Tracking and Reporting Commission. Streamlining SAK tracking and storage is one of the next wave of steps that needs to be taken to keep the SAKI project rolling effectively, but also to ensure that kits cannot be lost, misplaced, or hidden again in the future.

Michigan is developing a statewide database that would track the kits and where they are in the investigative and prosecutorial processes. Since the focus is on tracking, it will not contain detailed information about the cases themselves. She tells me she's very excited about the progress they've made on this effort and, at that time, they were waiting on bids from a couple of potential vendors to provide the tracking and storage services.

"It's still something that a lot of communities are really struggling with," she observes. "So we're hoping that some of the things we develop continue to be a guide or at least a successful example of what other communities could potentially do to ensure that these kits are tracked and stored like they should be."

WC SAFE remains a busy hive of activity within a building designed by the legendary Albert Kahn, affectionately referred to as "the architect of Detroit" (the German native designed many of the city's landmark buildings in the late nineteenth and early twentieth centuries). Kahn's iconic structure was built as the S. S. Kresge World Headquarters in 1927 and occupied by the big box department store titans until the company (now known as Kmart) relocated to suburban Troy in 1972. It was later rechristened the Metropolitan Center for High Technology. Now on the National Register of Historic Places, Kahn's E-shaped edifice with a limestone façade is owned by Wayne State University and serves as a business incubator for start-up enterprises and nonprofit organizations.

During the center's time in the building, the entire midtown neighborhood has burgeoned into a hip, refreshed urban center, all part of Detroit's post-industrial reboot. The building faces a lovely park featuring a statue of Scottish poet Robert Burns, and flanked by an historic Masonic temple, the MotorCity Casino, and Cass Tech, one of Detroit's magnet high schools. On the opposite side of the park from Kahn's structure, abandoned apartment buildings were razed to make way for the new Little Caesars Arena for the beloved Detroit Red Wings hockey team.

"It's nice to see the cleanup and the revitalization, for sure," Hurst comments later. "I wouldn't say people feel safer, but there is definitely more reason to come downtown and be social and spend money. We have better transportation options for our survivors to use, such as Lyft or Uber. So, Detroit has a long way to go overall, but we hope the revitalization leads to lower crime in the end."

When I visited Hurst in April 2017, I was immediately met by a sign saying "Welcome to WC SAFE! Please ring the bell and have a seat, your advocate will be with your shortly." I was a little early, so I did take a seat in the serene waiting area.

Entering WC SAFE's space feels more like you're walking into a coffee shop, with comfortable couches and chairs beneath artfully appointed walls. The giveaway is the racks loaded with flyers ranging from services and organizations pertinent to a victim of sexual assault (Children and Family Services, La Vida, and KIDS-Talk) to flyers containing information for domestic violence victims (how to obtain personal protection orders, handle threat management, or move to safer housing). There was also a pen and paper attached to a poster instructing visitors to "Let Go, Release, Breathe, Peace" and asking them to "Share a poem, a kind word, a picture, or a part of your story. Your words illustrate the light that is 'you.' Other survivors may read your expressions/thoughts; know that together, we inspire, we dance, we become stronger in our sharing."

When the seemingly indefatigable Hurst breaks free, she leads me down to her office at the far end of a corridor. The space has fifteen other offices that counselors use when meeting with clients. The DPD and Wayne County SAKTF also meet victims here as it is a safe, secure, and relaxed place to notify them about testing their backlogged kit or to interview them, if they agree to participate in their reopened case. Street parking around the park is easy, too, and clients can stay afterward if they would like to speak to an advocate or counselor.

Mainly, we catch up on her priorities for the center these days. One of her major roles, Hurst knows, is to serve as the conscience for the other members of the SAKTF initiative. In other words, she feels responsible for ensuring that everyone continues to provide compassionate, victim-centered care when dealing with the backlogged kit survivors and practicing the trauma-centered tenets set forth in Dr. Campbell's research whenever interviewing them or victims of new sexual assaults. She does see it gradually becoming standard operating procedure, but, "the need for it to be ongoing and constant," she avers, "is imperative to the continued success of all of this hard work!"

Ever the advocate, Hurst does regular public speaking engagements, so a second major role is to continue raising awareness around all elements of rape and sexual assault, including the need to change our victim-blaming culture and to comprehend just how damaging those attitudes are. She believes people still don't understand the frequency of sexual violence, either.

"One of the statistics I reference when I'm doing public speaking," she says, "that seems to hit home for people is when you say one in eight women has breast cancer—and think about all of the women you know who have either had or are battling breast cancer—and then think about how one in six women have been sexually assaulted. It really hits home how much it's *not* being talked about. I can guarantee you that there are way more people sitting there going, 'I don't think I know anybody who's been sexually assaulted,' but they do."

She does her best to keep up with salient stories in the news, such as the Bill Cosby trial or the rape victims rallying against concerns about the proposed new health care bill that would consider sexual assault a preexisting condition and therefore not cover it. (At the time of our interview, the Harvey Weinstein story had not been published.)

Ultimately, Hurst knows that they are providing compassionate, respectful care and support for people who have suffered a terrible trauma. Good SANE or SAFE treatment represents the first steps in the healing process for a victim of sexual violence. She also knows that one of the reasons the number of victims they see continues to grow is not because sexual assault incidences are growing that rapidly, but because more people know their services are available. In the past, they might have just gone home and never sought treatment and counseling or evidence collection to prosecute their assailant. Making that difference means everything to this medical professional who will never forget how she struggled to help her first patient all those years ago.

As we're finishing our conversation, I notice a teal silk cape suspended from the coat hanger on the back of her office door. It started with the inside joke that all of the people who worked at WC SAFE were superheroes and should own the appropriate accessory: long-flowing capes. Last fall, Hurst commissioned her mother, a gifted seamstress, to help her craft the capes with the aid of her "fancy-schmancy" sewing machine.

Thus, for Christmas 2016, Hurst presented each of her staff members with teal capes emblazoned with their initials. Throughout the year, they occasionally schedule cape days so everyone wears them together. But they are also there for staffers to wear when they need a lift. The clients and the other SAKTF members think they're perfect, too, and smile or laugh when they see the bright mantles flowing down the hallways of WC SAFE.

"Sometimes you may be having a bad day," Hurst says. "But you put that cape on, and it helps. It lightens the mood a little bit, and it acknowledges the importance of what we're doing and gives people that pat on the pack, that kudos for the hard work that they do every day."

PART 3

Individual Change Makers

Chapter 14

Marathon Woman:
Liz Ferro and Girls with Sole

WITH HER BACK against the wall of a full-sized gymnasium, Liz Ferro sits, legs crossed, smiling and brimming with her usual vibrancy, rocking her colorful fitness gear ensemble of a black T-shirt, black-gray tights, and black running shoes. She is in her element: surrounded by at-risk girls aged fourteen through seventeen, who, for a variety of reasons, are serving short-term sentences in the Multi-County Juvenile Attention System in Canton, Ohio, just below Akron. They are girls who need her brand of exercise and energy to help them heal and deal.

The facility is located in South Canton, considered by many to be the northern border of the Bible Belt. It's south of the Faith Family megachurch and several billboards along I177 that proclaim Real Christians OBEY Jesus's teachings and Real Christians LOVE their enemies. It's also several exits past a different kind of temple, the Pro Football Hall of Fame with its trademark half-football dome, and down the street from Phantom Fireworks.

The drive down from Cleveland is nice on a cool, sunny Groundhog Day in February. A few miles out from the center, a Canton sports talk radio host cracks: "[New York Knicks president] Phil Jackson saw his shadow coming out of his office today. So that means rumors of [small/power forward] Carmelo Anthony being traded to the Cleveland Cavaliers will go on for another six weeks."

While "juvenile attention system" conveys a refreshingly progressive approach to juvenile corrections, it's still a prison with a lot of thick, locked doors and security stations. The girl inmates have to earn their leave privileges to visit family or do special activities such as a 5K run with Ferro. Most of them are in for acting out against parents who are separated, on drugs, neglectful, physically or sexually abusive, in and out of prison themselves, or any combination of the above.

That's where Ferro comes in. Growing up in Rochester, New York, Ferro lived in four different foster homes before she was adopted at age two. Her adoptive parents loved her and treated her well, but without their knowledge, she was repeatedly molested and raped by a neighbor. Unfortunately, she did not receive any support from her mother when she later found out. Her mom feared that her husband would not be able to handle the information in a safe, legal manner.

Nor did Ferro learn of any effective support mechanisms, until she discovered the positive impact of school athletics on her own healing when she joined the swim team in high school. She went on to become an accomplished long-distance runner at Miami University and has been running ever since. In addition to marathons, she has completed two 50K Ultras, four Iron-distance triathlons, and countless road races and triathlons.

After college, as a way to deal with her anger and frustration at having been sexually assaulted as a child, she lived a fairly adventurous and, at times, recklessly wild life. Fortunately, it was running that became a healthy addiction for Ferro. "I was running so much that I took care of myself and started treating myself better, because I didn't want to ruin the one good thing I had going for me," she recalls. "A lot of people don't think that it all goes together, but it does. That's why we teach each girl to train her mind, body, and soul, because you need to address all three to be healthy."

Learning from her experiences, Ferro began to think of a way to help other girls attain the benefits of running and staying fit. She had worked a number of jobs in marketing, recruiting, or HR, and then accepted a job as executive director of a small nonprofit agency, Wigs for Kids, that provided wigs for children who'd lost their hair to cancer treatments.

"I have a passion for helping people, primarily children," she says. "So I loved it, but it still wasn't exactly what I wanted to do, because it didn't incorporate my love for fitness."

She did some research and couldn't find many programs that combined fitness and running to help young girls get on track for a healthier lifestyle. In August 2009, she took a risk, left her job, and launched her organization that makes running available to young women who may not have done much in the way of exercise. The programming includes yoga, dance, and nutrition classes to get the girls more focused on their health and help them appreciate their bodies, no matter how they are built.

It also teaches them to overcome obstacles by applying Girls with Sole's (GWS) POWER Principles: perseverance, optimism, wisdom, energy, and resilience. Ferro has in-kind donations of shoes, sports bras, and water bottles for each girl, generously provided by Second Sole, a store for runners in Lakewood, Ohio, just northwest of Cleveland.

Ferro takes GWS programming to a variety of schools and community centers throughout Northeast Ohio. For the past six years, she's brought her self-contained class to the Juvenile Attention System in Canton once a week from 4 to 5 p.m. on Thursdays. The girls are happy to see Ferro when she enters the locker room/lounge area adjacent to the gym. One says, "What's shakin', bacon?" At about 3:55 p.m., Miss Hightower, supervisor, checks with the girls to see if they have finished their cleaning chores so they can join "Miss Liz" for class. The girls all point to their various cleaning tools and nod or say yes. Except for one: "Lenore."***

*** Because the girls are minors, I am not using their real names for obvious legal concerns. However, I want it noted that it greatly pains me, because each of these incredibly brave young ladies gave me permission to use her real first name.

"Ruh-ro," Ferro frowns.

Five of the girls follow their beloved exercise instructor to the far wall. Lenore will join them later.

Once they're all seated around her, which takes a few minutes, because, understandably, they're bubbling with a lot of pent-up energy, Ferro dumps out a crammed duffle bag at their feet. They marvel at the cornucopia of new running shoes, plastic water bottles, top-of-the-line sports bras, and large, fluorescent green T-shirts from GWS's annual fall LULA race (Lacing Up for a Lifetime of Achievement). Excited by this week's selection of mostly donated but often Ferro-purchased gifts, the girls dig in to see what fits.

"The girls need to get new things," Ferro explains later. "Would you want to give them a sweaty jog bra? Even if someone washed it or only used it for a month? I would never do that. But they really are grateful for anything that I bring them."

Next, they go around the circle and at Ferro's request reveal something good that happened today. Christine was named student of the week. Bianca earned twenty-two hours of home visits. Destiny's mother visited.

"I got to leave today and go on an outing, Miss Liz, and I wasn't even in shackles!" one girl enthuses.

"That's awesome! Where did you go?"

"Court," she replies.

After a short pause, all cheer that it's Girls with Sole time! At 4:11 p.m., Lenore rejoins the group, as does Andrea, who had to explain her tardiness to Miss Hightower, who is sitting at a table just inside the gym door. Ready to roll with the full crew, Ferro has them stand and recite the Girls with Sole creed:

We're Girls with Sole and
we're on the move.

We're strong and proud you
can't stop our groove.

We know who we are and
who we want to be.

We sail through life with
resiliency

At Girls with Sole we set
goals and believe.

If we keep lacing up we will
always achieve.

The girls learn the creed from their Girls with Sole fitness journals that feature a number of inspirational quotes, journaling exercises, and questions to answer. The book comprises part of their introductory package that includes new running shoes, sports bra, and a copy of Ferro's autobiography, *Finish Line Feeling* (Unlimited Publishing, 2012). Reading it helps the girls understand that she shares with them the experience of childhood sexual abuse and trauma. (Ferro estimates that 90 to 100 percent of the girls she works with have been sexually abused.) Yet, she still went on to overcome her abuse, have a happy family life, thrive, and be successful.

She's been waiting anxiously for several minutes to do so, but Haley finally gets the signal from Ferro to hit the music button on the mini sound system. Throughout class the girls—and Ferro—dance and rock out to a number of hip songs, songs so hip that I have to ask Ferro for the titles and artists later. So, if you have teens and want them to think you're cool (at least by 2017 standards), here are some you can program for a party music mix: "Classic," MKTO; "Best Day of My Life," American Authors; "Just Like Fire," Pink; "Wildest Dreams," Taylor Swift; "Slow Motion," Trey Songz; "My House," Flo Rida; and "Glad You Came," The Wanted. You're welcome.

Ferro knows a lot of the best music to move to from her more than twenty years as a group exercise, certified aerobics, step aerobics, and spin instructor at different fitness clubs around greater Cleveland. She stopped teaching after committing herself completely to Girls with Sole.

The girls all pump their fists and bound out to the middle of the gym floor, where they form a circle around Ferro. She leads them in warm-up exercises that include jumping jacks and an activity she designed called partner planks, in which the girls assume a push-up position but do a patty-cake move with their hands between push-ups. It makes it harder to hold the plank, but they're also having more fun and laughing while trying to clap hands. "If I told them just to hold plank, they'd be complaining, not doing it, falling down," Ferro says. "Plus, they have to work with somebody."

Okay, there's a little bit of falling down. But lots of laughter. Ferro cheers, as they all yell and celebrate being able to perform the clapping callisthenic: "Good job! I'm proud of you guys!"

Next up: dragon tails. They split into two teams of four that must work as one. Normally, having kids join hands for a game isn't a concern. But not here. For safety reasons, including fear of fostering a budding lesbian relationship that could result in emotional challenges while in confinement, the rules are no touching, no holding hands. For this game, however, they need to join hands and work as one to become a single dragon.

"I know the rules are that you can't touch each other in here, but this is a game, and the staff understand that we're Girls with Sole, and we're playing a game that entails holding hands, and that's okay," Ferro assures them.

The lead person plays the head and the person at the end plays the tail, with a bandana in her back pocket. The objective? The head of one team chases and tries to pull out the dragon's tail of the other team. The girls in the middle, the body, have to whip around in unison with the head. Let go of each other and you're done. "If you're not working together, you're going to lose!" Ferro yells.

When Miss Hightower calls one girl over to resolve an issue with her and a couple of other staffers, Ferro fills in as the head. In the heated chase, one girl falls down. "Walk it off," Ferro counsels. "Get some water. Then, we'll do one more."

While the girls chase dragons, Jenny Pollard, thirty-one, a licensed professional clinical counselor, talks with me for a few minutes. She provides individual, group, and family counseling for the girls and works closely with Ferro to coordinate activities, especially outside the center, such as last summer's paddle boarding excursion at Portage Lakes. Currently, they're planning for an outdoor run in April. She's been working there for the past five years; her predecessor brought in the Girls with Sole program.

She explains that the girls in Residential Treatment Center No. 1 are from Stark, Tuscarawas, Wayne, Columbiana, and Carroll counties, since the Multi-County Juvenile Attention System provides detention and rehabilitation services to the juvenile courts of those five counties. The teenagers are mild to moderate offenders, which could mean anything from running away to light drug use and stealing. None are felons. Typically, their sentences range from six to nine months. Most come from more impoverished or inner-city settings, but they also occasionally have girls from wealthier areas of Stark County, which includes Canton.

The maximum occupancy of RTC 1 is nine girls, and they all live down the hallway on the other side of the building from the school area, where the Canton Local School District provides classroom instruction during the week. They all have private rooms. When they are halfway through their program, the girls can start to earn outings to go home and back into the community to test whether there will be any issues when they are released.

According to Pollard, there are no official numbers for recidivism. "We do have a lot of kids that do well when they leave," she allows. "We do have some that get in trouble again."

As for what Ferro and Girls with Sole provide the young inmates, Pollard says first, "They love her." They also have regular gym classes and a volleyball team, but the girls always look forward to their GWS sessions every Thursday. "A lot of it has to do with Liz's background and story and just being open with them. A lot of the girls see themselves in her, and they see the possibility if they do get their stuff together that they could do the things that Liz does. All the girls love when she gives them her book, they love the things they do, and they comment on how positive and upbeat [the activities] are. They need that because they don't have a lot here, so she brings something very positive to the RTC."

When I ask if some of the girls have been sexually assaulted, she replies, "Yes. Most of our kids have experienced a lot of trauma. A lot of trauma." And Ferro being experienced and conscious of that helps? "Yes."

Pollard adds that it helps her to see the way Ferro interacts with the girls as a reminder that they're just kids. "Sometimes they can be very irritating, because they can make some really bad decisions," she explains. "Liz always sees the positive and the good in these girls, and that's a good reminder, especially when you work with them every day."

Pollard runs the trauma group at the facility, so she understands the benefits of exercise and running as good tools to burn off anger or frustration from having been abused. "I'm always trying to teach the girls coping skills," she says. "I like to build off what Liz does and use her as an example, because physical activity is a good, positive coping skill, whereas a lot of our kids rely on negative coping skills. So she's a good, concrete example that they see on a weekly basis."

Around 4:30 p.m., once again with all of the girls in play, they try another new game: Star Catcher, kind of an obstacle course–style tag. One girl stands mid-basketball court. The other girls start on one end of the court and try to run past her. If she can tag one of them they have to sit where they were touched, and then they can tag someone when they run past the next time. Before they run, the girl mid-court yells, "How many stars are out tonight?" To which the others respond, "Too many for you to catch!" and then scramble past her and any of her teammates. The game becomes increasingly difficult as the "it" girl's tag team grows. In full marathon-condition, Ferro, of course, sprints back and forth, dodging tag attempts with ease. Until she and one girl are the only runners left.

After they play a couple more rounds, Ferro screams out, "It's good to be hot!" She's in the minority on that opinion. Most of the girls are collapsed on the floor or hunched over, catching their breaths. Liz tells one to get up and walk it off, that it's bad for her to stop moving completely after heavy exercise.

As they gather around Ferro to wrap up the day, she asks if anyone would like to talk with me. One by one, I take those willing to be interviewed a few yards away to the front corner of the gym. I offer them the chance to make up a name to be more anonymous, but they all proudly prefer to use their own first names. (See footnote on page 209.)

Christine, sixteen, is first. This is only her second time in juvenile detention. Both times, she was busted for taking crystal meth. She's been in the RTC for two months and has five or six more to go. "Jail is really hard. It's really, really hard," she tells me. "I had a good family before I got here."

She's thankful for Girls with Sole for a couple reasons: "I really need it because when I come, I get really motivated to do things for the rest of the day, not just mope around," she says. "We eat a lot here, so we have a lot of weight gain, and this is one of the only times we have to exercise."

She feels a personal connection with her fitness instructor because she knows Miss Liz has been through a lot, too. She's one of the nicest people Christine has ever met, and whenever she or her comrades discuss personal situations, Ferro is never "quick to judge."

She pauses for a moment and then finishes by saying, "I know that if I keep doing what I'm doing, I'm going to die. So deep down inside me, I want to get better and stuff, so I'm going to try really hard not to come back here." She hopes to pursue a career in art someday, perhaps painting or drawing. "I'm not really good enough to do it now, but I'll get better. Everyone still needs to learn."

When she first arrived at the RTC three months before, Lenore thought Ferro was just someone hired to teach gym classes. Then she read *Finish Line Feeling*. That gave her a completely different perspective on their bubbly, blonde, indefatigable Thursday afternoon fitness guru. "She's one of the most powerful women in my life, because of what she's endured and how happy she is these days," Lenore says. "Every time I see her, I study her and think if she got through that stuff, then I can, too, and I can change my life and break the cycle in my family."

She's got only three months to go on this sentence, but at fifteen, Lenore's already a seasoned veteran of juvenile corrections. She's been locked up seven times. "I do drugs, and I love to run away," she discloses. "I like to run away from my problems, and that's what I want to change. I also have unhealthy relationships."

She's all too familiar with justice system lingo. "I was supposed to get a Nebraska court placement, but they decided to take me here to be closer to home, since I'm from Canton," she says.

"My family life has been very rough," she adds in explanation of her predilection for hitting the road. "Both my parents were drug addicts, and my dad was really bad on crack, meth, and heroin. He was sober for four years, and then fell off. Now he's sober for a year again, ever since I came to jail, because he was scared for me and wanted to be here for me and take me in and so did my mom, so now it's a happy family that I can go to."

Even inside this low-security, progressive approach facility, she feels there are problems that prevent her from thinking about herself or about the problems she faces on the outside. In here, she can't run away from either, so she's working on facing her problems. Ferro's class helps her blow off steam, but the end-of-class discussion gives her more focus. "The class really gets me thinking about myself, because Miss Liz is a big self-motivator," Lenore concludes, before heading back to the group. "She makes me change my outlook."

Unfortunately, Haley's no stranger to corrections centers, either. The fifteen-year-old arrived at the Canton RTC a couple of weeks ago, but she had been in another placement. A native of Lebanon, near Cincinnati, the court sentenced her to the Buckeye Ranch in Grove City, Ohio, south of Columbus. "I was kind of just chilling there for no reason," she sighs. "So my case worker decided I needed to go to a more strict program, where I'd be required to do some treatment stuff."

Haley's serving time for domestic violence. She and her stepmom don't get along. "She's a pretty degrading person," the troubled teen states. The woman got in her face one too many times, so Haley struck her. The Ohio juvenile corrections system's plan was to send her home, again, but she said, "No," so they had to keep her in a facility. Her new goal is to return to her mother's home. She thinks. "It's a little calmer than the household I was in before," Haley says. "But I guess it's still pretty chaotic in a way."

She doesn't have much of a relationship with her dad. "I don't know. He doesn't want to talk to me at all," she says. "I would have to say my relationship with my mom was much better."

Moved by Ferro's horrific experiences as a child as chronicled in her book, Haley was surprised to meet the radiant, positive presence that Miss Liz is today. "She's gone through plenty of struggles, some equivalent to what people here have gone through, some possibly worse," she says of her new role model. "Then seeing her, I was like, 'Wow!' She just seems like such a positive person, who's like definitely looking forward to the future, kind of making things better for everyone, so I do enjoy her class."

Haley concedes that Ferro always makes it enjoyable, even for someone like her, who's "not really into physical activity at all for real." Never has been. More of a desk person.

"I like the games and stuff like the Dragon and Star thing," she says. "They were fun."

Looking down the road, she wants to attend college and study some combination of art, music, design, and architecture. "I still don't know enough about everything, but I'll figure it out in college, because there will be classes and options I can explore."

As she runs back to the group and Cassandra runs toward me, I think each of the girls has been pretty friendly, expressive, thoughtful, and articulate for teenagers who've seemingly not had the easiest child-hoods or the most understanding and supportive parents.

Cassandra tells me she spent the majority of her fifteenth and part of her sixteenth years in jail. Why? Domestic violence charges. She kicked her mother in the shin, she claims. She's slated to go home in a couple of months. "I think I can handle it, because I've realized that the person I was before wasn't the right person for me," she says. "So I've been able to turn my life around and become a better person for my family's and my good."

"I was abused," she continues. "I took it out on my little brother. When he would get on my nerves, I would smack him upside the head and just be ridiculous."

She's benefited from the opportunity to exercise and play games in Ferro's sessions. "It's helped me realize there's more than fighting and getting on people's nerves," she says. "You can help your body get stronger, rather than decreasing your body's limitations."

In fact, the various programs of the RTC have aided her tremen-dously in dealing with her pent-up anger and frustrations from having been abused. "They've helped me step forward into my life and kind of shine a light on what I need to fix," she says. "I was kind of sitting back in the dark for a long time, so the groups really help me."

That includes Miss Hightower's anger management group. "She helps you with your anger in so many ways, and you don't give her atti-tude for nothing, or she will go off on you, and she's a serious person."

She also loves Miss Pollard. "She's inspired my life so much [know-ing] that there are more things out there," Cassandra reveals. "She's taught me that you can be successful, no matter what, and that life can go on, because I've gotten kicked out of this place, and I've gotten brought back, and I did ten times better than I did the first time around. I promised them that I would do better, and I did."

She has a pretty heady aspiration that keeps her moving forward: "I'm trying to pursue the highest degree I can, so I can be a really amazing doctor and help save lives." When I tell her I think she'd make a great doctor, she gets a huge smile on her face, thanks me, and runs back to the group.

Ferro tells me after the class that Lenore came over to her and said, "I told him from my heart, so I hope he tells you what I said." I know it's good for them and that it seems like a decent place to be, if you have to be a child in detention. Still, seeing these girls in here breaks my heart. They've been deprived of the pleasures and freedom of a carefree childhood. I hope they give themselves the chance to become the architects, artists, and doctors that they want to be, but I know it won't be easy.

At the end of class, as part of their cool down, Ferro sometimes has a guest talk to the class about the advantages of being positive and working toward success, no matter the obstacles you may encounter. If there's no guest, she has the girls do art projects or something related to self-esteem building, such as filling out a form that itemizes "Things that you're thankful for."

During another exercise, "Soul Essentials," Ferro makes sure they know what the word *essentials* means, and then asks them to write down things they are passionate about or that "make their soul sing." "It's very important to know those things and focus on them," she says. "That will help keep them from getting pissed so easily and focusing on the negative things."

As part of self-esteem building, she uses a "blessings for the body" worksheet with the intent of getting them to be grateful for their bodies and not bash the way they look.

"It's easy for young girls to bash their bodies, especially for girls who've experienced abuse like me," Ferro informs. "I hated my body so much, like almost my whole life. It's only been about twenty-five years or so where I've totally felt healthy and love myself, but I used to hate myself."

The exercise sheet isolates each piece of the body and has a line for them to write down why they are thankful for that body part, such as "I want to thank my hand for being able to hold someone else's hand" or for being able to hold a fork or whatever about it makes them grateful. She likes to remind them of Gandhi's insight that your thoughts become your words, your words become your actions, your actions become your values, and so on. She wants them to know that if you have specific values, you can choose what you become.

As Cassandra and I walked back to the group sitting closely around Ferro, once again against the wall, the girls were all chewing tentatively with an "eww" look on their faces that could double as Halloween masks.

One of the gifts she always brings for the end of the class is energy bars. Today's treat, Quest protein bars, apparently, are not just healthy, but "super healthy" and "completely clean," meaning there's an abundance of protein, fiber, and good-for-you nutritional stuff combined with a dearth of sugar. Struggling to swallow, Cassandra spits, "These are disgusting!"

"So, you don't like them?" Ferro deadpans, with a characteristic sparkle in her eye, and then laughs really hard.

Fortunately, to counter the taste-challenged snacks, she's also given them Neutrogena shampoo and face wash, basic needs that the center tries to provide but doesn't always have the funding to purchase for them. The girls are delighted.

"One time, as a reward for achieving the goal of running a certain amount of mileage, I got them all PINK sweatshirts and body wash from Victoria's Secret," Ferro recalls. "They acted like they had won a fifty-million-dollar lottery! It wasn't fancy, but at their age, the girls go crazy for that stuff."

Shortly after 4 p.m., the girls line up in single file by the door with Miss Hightower. Miss Hightower is cool. Earlier, when a green intern displaying his commitment to rules without thought photocopied my driver's license and politely but aggressively questioned me on who I was and why I was there, she pooh-poohed him and said Ferro wouldn't bring in anyone they couldn't trust, then ushered me into the lounge/locker room area outside the gym shaking her head at the rookie.

Sitting in the lobby after class, reviewing the highlights, Ferro says: "You saw when they were worried about holding hands. They were like, 'Are you sure?' Because everything is a problem in their lives. Everything's negative. So to see them positive, that is my purpose. They moved, they got funny, they were out of breath, and they were laughing. They were like actual kids! I'm like, 'I won! I totally won today!'"

"They were running a lot. For them, that was a ton," she continues. "That's my purpose for playing those particular games. They're easy. They're fun and awkward, and they're laughing and goofing around together. But they do complain really quickly about being hot, like it freaks them out, or if their hearts start racing, which is what exercise does. It makes you hot and uncomfortable, but they're not used to it. They're not in awesome shape, and they don't do it all the time, so they get freaked out. So, if I make it fun, and even though the games are almost in a way juvenile, they like them. They laugh. To see them laughing is huge."

Here, as in her classes at other schools and recreation centers, Ferro has her charges play basketball, soccer, fitness stations, and she's had yoga and Zumba instructors as guests so the girls get real experience in each activity. She also brings in non-exercise specialists such as an aesthetician who did makeup facials on the girls, which they loved. Then they quizzed her on how could they follow her career path through aesthetician school and finding a job.

"I like exposing them to as many positive people as possible, and I want them to know that there are options," Ferro says. "They're not used to having people building them up, telling them they're smart and wonderful and that they have a voice. So having many positive people around them is awesome!"

Recently, Ferro's trainer for the grueling Great Wall of China marathon she's preparing for in May did a fitness workout with the girls. Started in 1999, the Great Wall Marathon gives a field of more than 2,500 runners from more than 60 countries a chance to take "5,164 steps into history" on "one of mankind's greatest monuments," the marathon website boasts. Ferro, who doesn't consider herself a professional runner but lives an "avid runner's lifestyle," will do it as a lifelong marathoner's challenge and also as a highly visible way to raise awareness for GWS.

On Facebook shortly before the marathon, Ferro posts pictures of mountains from two previous marathons she ran and writes: "You have been assigned this mountain to show others it can be moved." #tbt to Alaska and Montana. At the time, experiencing childhood sexual abuse made no sense, and seemed to have no purpose. Today I know why I was assigned that particular mountain, and I won't stop until I show every girl in need that mountains can be moved."

In 2015, Ferro completed a three-year-plus endeavor, "50 States for Sole," to run marathons in all fifty states to raise funds and awareness for GWS. She's already collected thirty thousand dollars, spoken at various expos and pre-race dinners, and made hundreds of new friends and supporters of her innovative program to help at-risk, inner city girls heal and Lace Up for a Lifetime of Achievement. Fittingly, in July 2016, she ran her fiftieth marathon in Missoula, Montana, where many female students from the University of Montana have been raped and were the subject of Jon Krakauer's book *Missoula* (Doubleday, 2015).

Ferro is the recipient of a 2011 Classic Woman Award from *Traditional Home* magazine and the American Red Cross of Greater Cleveland Hero Award.

In 2016, Ferro traveled to Charleston, South Carolina, where the first regional office of GWS opened at the Orange Grove Charter

School, thanks to the assiduous planning and work of a retired sexual assault nurse examiner who had been assaulted as a child.

While Ferro's goal is to make GWS national by 2020, right now her main focus, she says, is on building her nonprofit's infrastructure in Cleveland so that she can hire staff and pay herself. Thanks to a generous donation of space, she was able to move into an office building. That not only gives her organization more nonprofit credibility, but she also no longer has to work out of her dining room, where each evening, she had to clear all of her files so that she could enjoy dinner with her husband and two children.

The altruistic athlete promises that nothing will ever stop her on her run to help girls in need.

"These are the things that helped me and literally saved my life," Ferro concludes. "So, if no one else is going to do them for these girls, I am."

Chapter 15

Marathon Man:
Mike Pistorino Shatters the
Silence of Child Sexual Abuse

"**H**ELLO, EVERYBODY," YELLS Mike Pistorino at the front of a group of fifty or more US Army soldiers. The young men and women with faces of all races have gathered in the 108th Air Defense Artillery Brigade's mess hall, now preferably called the DFAC (dining facility) or chow hall by soldiers, at Fort Bragg in Fayetteville, North Carolina. More soldiers drift in throughout his presentation until it's more than one hundred troops. Some are there voluntarily, some as part of their quarterly training requirement.

"Thanks for having me," he continues his greeting. "Thank you, Kathy. This is our third event today. After this, I get to get the hell out of North Carolina. It's hot and you people tawk funny here. All right, you can tell by the way I tawk I'm not originally from Cleveland. I'm from the Bronx. That's why I tawk normal, unlike everybody else."

Kathy is Katheryn Smith, victim advocate, who has invited Pistorino down from Cleveland in April 2017 for Sexual Assault Awareness Month as part of the Army's Sexual Harassment/Assault Response and Prevention (SHARP) activities.

While Pistorino's primary focus is child sexual assault, he also addresses adults who were victims of CSA and male rape. According to the National Sexual Violence Resource Center, one in four girls and one in six boys will be sexually abused before they turn eighteen. In fact, the stats indicate that every eight minutes, an American child is sexually assaulted.

After the majority of his speaking events, many adults and children come forth to divulge that they had been raped or assaulted, as several male soldiers will do today. His contracts stipulate that a professional counselor be present, since he is not one, and he refers them to the counselor. Many of his events, such as his annual 5K run in Cleveland that he started last November, will also have police, FBI agents, and biker groups in attendance. The mission of Bikers Against Child Abuse (BACA), for example, is to protect children who've been assaulted in any way they can; they frequently serve as a menacing wall between a child and his or her assailant in court so the defendant can't threaten or intimidate the child into not testifying. Pistorino joined forces with them a few years ago and goes to court when he can.

Fortunately, the first event of the day at Fort Bragg, a 5K run, started at 7 a.m., when it was a little cooler. Travel sites I consulted say the hot season in Fayetteville does not start until May, and Fort Bragg's campus is distinguished by acres and acres of towering Carolina pine forests. But by 1:30 p.m. when Pistorino's second presentation of the day starts, it's already 83 degrees in the shade, and the direct sun feels like you're standing too close to a heat lamp. An avid marathoner, Pistorino ran pretty well for a forty-three-year-old man versus young, sinewy soldiers. When he asks the room who had a better time than he did, only one soldier raises his hand.

Pistorino is almost as colorful as the Army's SHARP exhibition display boards he's standing next to. About 5'9" tall, he resembles a mixed martial arts fighter, muscular and tattooed from shoulders to ankles. Some of the tattoos are images of his children. Some were inked in prison. One of the most recent, on his thigh, is the image of a suicide note written by an incarcerated child molester who was afraid of him, and it says: Bogey man. This is all your fault. I hope that you are happy.

Smith, who introduced Pistorino, is a veteran who represents everything the troops are here for today. She enlisted at seventeen and served from 1984 to 1990; her home base was Fort Bragg. She is a survivor of child sexual abuse and trauma. In the service she estimates that she was sexually harassed or assaulted every year she served. In her final two years, she was raped while stationed in Germany and then stalked by an officer who she mistook for a friend. Her assailant was finally court martialed for raping and beating her and six other women. Smith was the only victim subpoenaed to testify. Despite her testimony and all the evidence, the trial ended in a hung jury, although the assailant was later chaptered out of the army for mental illness. Smith's still haunted by those violent experiences. "Throughout my army career, I had experiences that weren't pleasant," she allows. "Then I went to therapy for a really long time, so when I listen to clients, it's like, 'yeah, I get it.'"

Several years ago, she was working in Fayetteville as a licensed therapist with the Lighthouse Counseling Center and seeing kids at the Falcon Children's Home and Family Services before the army hired her in 2014 as part of its new SHARP initiative. She's been a professional counselor since 2001, with a master's in mental health counseling. Her specialty areas are counseling children and teens who were victims of sexual trauma and dealing with substance abuse, but now she is an advocate for adults, too. Problems had reached a level of severity and complexity that the army needed to address the widespread problems that range from sexual assault during domestic violence incidences to child abuse within military families or by a child's caretakers when a parent is shipped overseas.

"The biggest issue army-wide," Smith acknowledges, "is when you deploy, how do you deal with where your kids go to know they will be safe? I didn't want my kids being raised by somebody else. I didn't want anybody touching my kids. Knowing what I went through, I just didn't want my kids to ever have to go through that. So, if you were molested at home, there's no way in hell you're going to send your kids to your mom or dad."

Smith, obviously, chose not to send her kids to her parents when she served overseas tours. "I knew my kids would never stay with my family because no one protected me, and there's no way I would ever put them in the same predicament," she says. "A lot of soldiers go through the same thing, but I got out of the army because I was going to get married and have children, so I needed to protect my kids. A lot of soldiers don't have that option."

Fortunately, when it launched SHARP, the army finally realized it needed civilians to manage some of the cases. "The army was right," Smith says. "They needed more civilian control because commanders were not respecting the rights of their victims, and a lot of times were covering things up. So to fix that, slowly but surely, we've been integrated into the process."

The transition has not always been smooth, Smith relates, but she now has a strong sexual assault response team (SART) of civilian and army consultants around her, including several counselors and sexual assault nurse examiners from Fayetteville who are here today. Officers and the rank and file are cooperating more readily.

In 2015, as part of her professional credentialing requirements, Smith attended the National Organization for Victim Assistance annual conference in Dallas in November. There she had "the Pistorino experience," where this bald, tattooed, charismatic sexual abuse and rape prevention speaker had the audience in the palm of his hand for an hour. She knew then she wanted to recruit him to address the troops. "He was amazing," she recalls. "Every time I turned around, I kept hearing about Mike. He's just so dynamic, down-to-earth, point blank, just in your face with it that people need to hear him."

As I scan the rows of dining tables that seat roughly twenty soldiers each, I see that all are "eyes on" Mikey from the Bronx. "I'm going to tell you a story today," Pistorino continues. "This story's going to show you that no matter what you've been through in life, you're going to be okay. It could be as bad as what happened to me or worse, or somewhere in the middle, and it includes trauma you've suffered as a solider and you're going to learn to stick together. Kick ass together. I do this because people that rape little kids piss me off, so I get the honor to travel around the country chasing those dirt bags down, getting them locked up, and having them suffer the consequences when they go to jail."

For the next half hour, as he always does at his numerous speaking engagements, Pistorino regales the rapt audience with his incredible story of childhood rape, resulting in two decades of a downward spiral into drugs and crime followed by borderline miraculous recovery and rehabilitation.

The son of a "drunk mom who owned a bar and a drunk dad who was a corrupt New York cop," Pistorino ran amok on the streets of the Bronx as a child, since no one cared. He ate out of garbage cans or stole food for almost every meal. At the age of five he stumbled into a sordid world at a neighbor's house, where young adults convened to "drink, smoke, do drugs, and play 'grab ass.'"

Soon, one of the men began to fondle him. Pistorino didn't know if that was okay. The man told him he loved him. No one else did. He gave him food. He let him watch cartoons. He gave him hugs.

"He knew that nobody loved me," says Pistorino, who unconsciously shifts his shoulders or adjusts his hips like a baseball batter while pacing in front of the room or standing and delivering. "He knew I had no place to go. So, one day he shoved his hand down my pants. I was six years old, and I didn't know if it was right. I didn't know it was wrong. I knew I didn't like it, but who am I going to tell? If I tell somebody, he won't let me come over anymore. Where am I going to go on weekends or after school?"

"You see, the people that hurt little kids, the people that rape people, they spend all of their time grooming society and grooming you and grooming me and grooming children for that. We will deliver our children to them. They take positions as priests, as Boy Scout leaders, as coaches, as teachers. They put themselves in the spot where you're going to drop the kid off and say, 'You go in there and you be good and you listen to Coach Harry. Coach Harry's going to tell you what to do."

So, if Coach Harry tells them to do something inappropriate, you just told them to listen to him."

Finally, Pistorino reveals, after about a year, when the boy accidentally broke a planter and got cactus needles in his leg, the man told him he would be in serious trouble with his mom when he got home, but that he would help him, so Pistorino should undress and get into the bathtub. The man joined him. That marked the first of between six hundred and seven hundred times, Pistorino estimates, that he was raped. He doesn't hold anything back about his experiences that involved "a lot of blood and shit." Because his underwear got stained with both, he would throw them out in a field near his school. His father would then smack him around for losing his underwear. He candidly recounts the most savage details of his ordeal so the terrors that victims of child molesters endure are clear, as are the unhappy consequences.

When he was twelve, three important things happened to Pistorino: First, the angry boy discovered he could hit kids as hard as he wanted while playing organized football. Second, after a police presentation at his school, he learned that for $10, he could score a substance—cocaine—that made him feel "different," which sounded like a good thing. He found a coke dealer in the Bronx who told him not to do coke; it was bad for him. He held up $10, and the dealer led him to the basement of an abandoned building, where he put his money in a hole and someone behind the wall pulled out a brick and placed the coke there. Third, his rapist was stabbed to death in a drug deal gone bad.

Although the rapes stopped, the damage was done. His parents, teachers, neighbors, even his rapist told him he was a bad kid. So the bad boy grew into a bad man. Since no adult stepped forward to save him and let him know it wasn't his fault and he wasn't bad, he fell into sixteen years of violent crime and addiction, stealing anything that wasn't locked down, selling drugs, and constantly getting in fights, all while living in one of two places: Rikers Island or the street.

He's not afraid to tell the soldiers about his less-than-distinguished career as a soldier, highlighted by the gut-tearing tale of his time imprisoned in the US Disciplinary Barracks at Fort Leavenworth. There, at twenty-two, he was sentenced to seven years for assault. Every day was a battle for survival.

In reception, some of the Aryan Brotherhood guys warned him that because he was young and white, the black prisoners would try to rape him. They also instructed him on how to pull off the cone-shaped hardware around the button to turn the shower on to use as a weapon. On his second day, a significantly larger inmate told Pistorino he was going to make him his girlfriend.

"I know how bad rape is," he tells me later about his initial survival reaction. "It was not going to happen again. I was going to die, or he was going to die. He could rape my dead body, but he was not going to rape me."

When the guy grabbed him, he yanked the metal hardware off the wall and, with a charge of adrenaline, started cracking the guy in the head and face, sending his attacker's blood and brains everywhere, he recalls, until he dropped lifeless to the ground. There were only three guards for a wing housing three hundred inmates. People were scrambling everywhere, but a guard finally ran up, stood there looking at the bloody mess, and just said, "Fuck." Then he grabbed Pistorino, shoved him to the ground, hogtied him, and threw him in the hole, a dank, dark, tiny isolation cell.

Pistorino turned down an offer of an additional fifteen years on his sentence, because it was clearly a case of self-defense. So they left him in the hole for a month. When he came out, the Aryan Brotherhood told him he was now a member. He had killed one of their enemies. That meant they would protect him. He joined to survive an environment where racial boundaries were clearly defined and enforced.

Prison only sharpened his beliefs about child molesters, commonly referred to as "chomos," as you may have heard on an episode or two of *Law and Order: SVU*. Chester, Pistorino remembers, is also a popular nickname taken from the *Hustler* magazine "Chester the Molester" cartoons. And yes, it's true they're the lowest of the low, often the targets of hits, he explains, especially by prisoners serving life sentences who don't mind adding another count of murder to their file. Anyway, one day, the prisoner in the cell next to Pistorino confided that he hoped they never released him, because he hated himself and knew he could never stop raping children.

According to FBI statistics, Pistorino educates his audience, child predators or pederasts commit an average of 181 assaults before they are caught or die. So, the sooner we catch them, the fewer children they assault.

Two years into his sentence, he was sitting around watching television one night with a friend, Kevin. All of a sudden, several members of the Heavy Blacks ran around the corner, chasing a guard they had set on fire. A prison riot was underway. They immediately surrounded Pistorino and screamed, "You're dead!"

Relying on his quick wit, he replied, "It's not a black/white thing! It's a guard/inmate thing!"

They all roared "Yeaaahhh!" and ran off.

"Shit, I can't believe it worked," he said to Kevin.

Nearly two days of rioting, window breaking, TV smashing, gang fighting, and other chaos exploded all around Pistorino. "It was the most exciting day of my life," he confides. "It was the only time I had absolutely no rules. It was survival of the fittest. If you're a badass, you'll live. If you're not, you might die."

But his innate goodness that had been corroded by all that happened to him as a raped child won out. He and several other inmates circled the corrections officer who had been severely beaten and burned by boiling water, found a prisoner with medical experience to treat him, and stood around them as a shield.

"He was a nineteen-year-old kid just going to work and didn't deserve that," Pistorino explains, adding to clarify the hell that is prison: "If he was a jerk-off, maybe we wouldn't have helped him."

When it appeared that the riot had run its course and they were about to be overrun by "bulls," police and national guardsmen, a bunch of the prisoners wanted to kill the commanding officer. Pistorino grabbed him, dragged him into his cell, wrapped him in a blanket, and shoved him under his bed. When the riot ended, he informed the terrified and enervated guards that he had put the CO under his bed. They misinterpreted it as a boast. They beat Pistorino senseless. He regained consciousness in the hole.

When the young CO awoke in the hospital, he let the guards know that Pistorino had actually saved his life. On the basis of that action, the captain of the guards moved Pistorino into a private cell and notified him he would be released about a month later, after two years served. He returned to New York, but his predilection for drugs and crime persisted.

"One day when I was twenty-nine, after all these years of suffering, shame, and guilt and believing that I'm a piece of crap, because everyone always told me I'm a piece of crap," he says, "I woke up on the 6 subway train, where I'd spent so many nights that the conductor would wake me when we turned around in the Bronx. I was freezing, my socks were wet, I was miserable and crying, didn't have no more drugs. The conductor suggested that I go into a rehab where his wife worked, so I moved into a rehab on 125th Street in New York called Daytop Village."

He tells the soldiers how he struggled with the underlying treatment philosophy. "People were like, 'Hey, Mike, you're doing a great job. Hey, Mike, we love you.' I'm like, 'Oh, what do you mean, you love me? Get the hell away from me, you freaking weirdo.' They would try to hug me. 'No, I'm from the Bronx. There's no hugging. Don't touch me.' It was so hard to accept that people loved me and I might be a good person that I had to split. I would do a score. I would get high. I would go back to jail. I'd go back to rehab. I'd get fifty days clean. I would split. I would do a score. I would get high. I'd go to jail."

Typical of his more than one hundred speaking engagements over the past few years, the room remains silent during these revelations. However, his effectiveness as a public speaker lies in the cathartic balance he provides. Just when his recollections of epic battles to get clean and sober—like the third time he overdosed and had an out-of-body experience watching the paramedics fight to resuscitate him, screaming in his head "I'm a piece of garbage. Just let me die!"—and bouncing in and out of Rikers grow almost unbearable, he says, holding his hands together in front of him: "I finally figured out that I was allergic to drugs, because every time I did drugs, I broke out in hand-cuffs." The soldiers laugh.

One day, he tells them, he met his new counselor, Krishell Benjamin, the manager of the drug clinic. "Hello. I'm a badass black bitch from Brooklyn," she informed him. "And I'm going to love you until you love yourself." Again, he wondered why this woman loved him. She didn't even know him. He was an ex-con. He did drugs. He didn't like black people. In fact, he didn't love anyone. Even when he would screw up, leave, get high, get arrested, she would still love him. Pistorino had finally met his match.

The last time he got high, he called Krishell. She responded with her beautiful, twisted form of draconian love, "Here's a quarter. Next time you get high, call someone who gives a shit, but stop calling me. I'm done." She was forty-four; she was dying of bone cancer. He was rattled, but then she said, "There's something so evil in your belly, Mike. Until you share it, you're never going to get clean. And you'd better get clean, or you're going to have the ghost of a badass black bitch from Brooklyn haunting you."

Briefly, he had a mother in Krishell. She remains with him in spirit to this day, as do the permanent changes she wrought in him. Now, maybe he could be happy. Maybe he could be successful. Maybe he could love. Anyone, any color. As long as they don't hurt or rape children or adults. "She loved all the hate out of me, and she showed me that good people are good people and bad people are bad people," he remembers. "That night, I wrote down on a piece of paper that I was raped as a little boy, and I threw it into a bonfire. I felt a little better. Like, 'Oh my God. Look at this. It's not mine no more.'"

He started following the rules of treatment. Then he met a young woman named Cynthia on the subway. She was crying, so he asked her if she was okay. She said she was from Cleveland, was there to buy purses, but was lost and didn't know what to do. "Give me your wallet," he responded. Not really, but that's what he tells the trainees and gets a good laugh. Instead, he told her he was going to marry her. He took her phone, called his phone so he would have her number, and then speed-dialed her mother and broke the news to her. She screamed and hung up.

Shortly after, he took a bus from New Yawk to Cleveland, called Cynthia, who, after a brief hesitation, picked him up, and they were later wed. He got a sales job at Concrete Fastening Systems, where he is now, fittingly, vice president and in the process of taking over from the founder. Pistorino felt good physically, but still wasn't comfortable in his skin.

"When my daughter started to get to the age that I was when I was first raped, I would freak out," he says. "I'd be at the mall with her, and a guy would be standing around. I'd grab the guy. 'You! You're out of here!' I'd throw the guy out of the mall. People were looking at me, and my wife was like, 'Whoa! What are you doing?' 'He was going after the baby!' 'No, he's cleaning up the frickin' French fries.' 'Oh, shit. Sorry.' So, I dusted the guy off and brought him back inside."

Cynthia suggested he get some help. The turning point was finding a pleasant, compassionate advocate on the Cleveland Rape Crisis Center hotline. The volunteer he spoke to listened patiently the first two times that he called then quickly hung up, believing that they wouldn't help a man who had been raped as a child. The third time, she addressed his concerns and said, "Whatever you got, we'll try to help you. Are you going to come in and get help?" He finally agreed to visit for treatment and participated in twelve weeks of private and twelve weeks of group counseling.

In 2014, he became a member of the CRCC's speaker's bureau and began speaking to small groups at churches and community centers. He quickly made a name for himself, however, when he offered to fill in as a last-minute keynote speaker at the organization's biennial fund-raiser because they had had to fire political commentator (and adopted son of former President Reagan and his first wife Jane Wyman) Michael Reagan after his anti-homosexual comments on a radio program. "I'm from New Yawk. I love to tawk. How hard can it be?" Pistorino famously responded when told he wasn't a professional speaker. His harrowing tale of rape, recidivism, recovery, and redemption inspired the audience to blast the record for donations on a single evening.

He did the speech and raised the money, but he was still in deep conflict, he tells his army audience. "I was hating God. I hated people who just got along and were nice. Until I was doing a speech one day in a small town in Southern Ohio and telling my story, and a little girl ran on stage and says, 'Mr. Mike, Grandpa puts his fingers in me.' I said, 'Baby girl, I love you. I believe you, and I'm going to make it stop.' I went to the cops and I said, 'She just told me this,' and the cops said, 'Oh, well, we've got to look into it.' I said, 'You're going to get this guy or I'm going to get this guy,' and based on my criminal past, they went really fast to get the guy."

The soldiers love it. But he continues to reveal how helping that little blonde eight-year-old girl was a life-changing epiphany for him. "I was like, 'Oh my God. That's why,'" he says. "That's why I went through all the addiction, the army, the homelessness, part dead, prison, fighting for my life, and pain and suffering, so that I could do this! I had to know her pain to be able to help her."

When I ask him for more details later, he tells me it happened at a 5K event three years ago in Springfield, Ohio, and the guy did go to jail. It was only his fifteenth or twentieth speech, he estimates, but it was an important one, because the organization actually paid him $500 for travel expenses, his first paid gig.

"As soon as she came up to me—it was my first rescue ever—I was like, 'Oh my God. I'm going to adopt her, bring her home, and I'm going to kill all of these people. She has to be okay!' I got messed up behind it. So, I went to CRCC. I couldn't talk about it without hysterically crying. I went back to see my therapist at the center, did a little bit more screwy eye stuff, had to learn to trust in the environment, trust in the other counselors and everybody to take care of her."

The "screwy eye stuff" is his endearingly Bronxish way of saying eye movement desensitization and reprocessing (EMDR), a fairly new, nontraditional psychotherapeutic treatment for people suffering from PTSD. Helping the little girl who was being abused had "triggered" his own experiences as a child. It also taught him he couldn't afford to get personally involved in each child he rescued, each adult who disclosed to him.

Next, he tells the soldiers about his coloring book, *Listen While I Color*, which he published last fall and has already distributed more than twenty thousand copies at schools, hospitals, and other organizations around the US and in the UK. (One state, which has asked not to be named at this time, has mandated his coloring book be distributed to every third- and fourth-grader in 2019 and has ordered 54,000 copies.) After he earned his initial investment of three thousand dollars back, any money made from the book he reinvests into printing more copies. The book features a number of images of children's bodies the kids can color in, including some with their penis or vagina, and they are instructed to color where an adult has touched them. The pages say that is not appropriate, that no one should touch them in the areas their bathing suit covers, and if someone has, they should talk to a trusted adult—a teacher, a firefighter, a police officer—and let them know. In the short time it's been available, Pistorino can't even estimate how many busts he's been informed of, as children reveal who has been touching and abusing them. His goal is to get it into as many children's hands as possible, especially in schools.

"Whatever you've gone through in your life that's dragging you down, you just have to figure out why because you can't change it," he counsels the soldiers. "I can't change the fact that I was brutalized for six years, but I can use it as fuel to be awesome. To be powerful. To rescue little kids from monsters. Or I could use it to be a sad, cut-up-in-chunks piece of garbage."

"So, what's it going to take? What do you got that's been dragging you down? That's been hurting you? That makes you sad and makes you inadequate, makes you feel just not happy?" he continues. "You have to let it out. There's counselors here. Tell everyone you can. Tell one of your peers. Tell your command. Tell your first sergeant. These people are all here to help you. Everybody's here to help you, and I absolutely promise you that once you get it out, it's not yours no more. Get rid of that garbage, and you're going to be a freakin' ball of sunshine like me!"

After they laugh, he continues: "I told my daughters if anybody ever shows you a penis, you call Daddy. Pretty simple but no one ever told me that. I didn't know. So my daughter went to her first day of first grade. She gets to the bus. 'Hi, bus driver. I'm Allie.' Bus driver goes, 'Hi. I'm Bill.' She goes, 'If you're tempted to show me a penis, don't do it because my daddy told me that if you do, he's going to give you a set of choices, and they're not going to be very nice ones.' The bus driver's freaked out like, 'I have no intention of showing you my penis!' But you know what? She knows now. Because somebody some day is going to try."

Later, he tells me he really appreciated when First Sergeant Todd Fields, who runs the SHARP program for this battalion, reminded the soldiers that they swore an oath to protect the US from all enemies, foreign and domestic. That means if someone in your platoon is a rapist or sexually harassing a fellow soldier, you have to say something, because they are domestic terrorists.

"Guys, I invite you to join my fight," Pistorino concludes around 2:30 p.m. "I invite you to help each other. Somebody in this room needs your help. Which of your peers is suffering? Which of your peers never leaves their room? Which of your peers are always crying? Help them. Stand up. Be that voice. Lead the way. Be the one who says I'm not going to stand for this shit no more, no matter what. If somebody's drunk, you scoop them up. You drive them home. You don't let people touch them. You don't let people hurt them. You hold them accountable. You hold them to the same standards that you hold yourself. Guys, thank you so much for letting me share."

He receives a sizeable cheer and round of applause. The soldiers linger for a while in the air-conditioned hall, and from what I could overhear, chat about what they've just heard or what they're doing next. Several approach Pistorino and lean in close to him to talk privately for a few minutes.

Gradually, before marching out into the unrelenting midday sun, soldiers who have not already signed a sheet to prove their attendance for training credit queue up to do so. Smith's commanding officers are there, too, to see how the event went and to check up on her. They are fully conscious of what she endured while serving and want to make sure Pistorino's candid oration did not trigger her memories. Their awareness and sensitivity to her suffering is a good thing. Commanders are now held accountable for their subordinates who are raped or assaulted. That, too, is a good thing. There is much more work to be done to adjust the requisite macho culture of the military, but a tiny evolution has transpired.

"We have to make sure that they sign because we get inspected, and they want to know that we're actually doing our job, that we're not just here for the victims, but also to prevent," Smith observes. "Prevention is becoming more and more a huge part of what we do. It didn't used to be. It used to be all about reaction, which was so annoying, because we really needed to address more than just after it happens. Let's talk about what we can do before."

One of the things she's already planning to do is bring Pistorino back for several other events.

———————————

During the past couple of years, Pistorino's become increasingly popular on the national speaker's circuit as an advocate and beacon of hope for all who have suffered as he did or want to end child sexual abuse. In just a few years, he has already presented in numerous states from Alaska to Florida. In April 2016 alone, Pistorino gave nineteen talks in nine states, rescuing eleven children who came forward to reveal they were being abused. Many adults are now in treatment and counseling after disclosing their past molestation or assault. His talk is especially effective at the youth detention and correctional facilities where he speaks. Currently, he has a contract with the Ohio Department of Youth Services to talk to inmates at the state's facilities throughout the year. Additionally, he consults with the police and FBI about how sexual predators behave or helps them track down offenders.

Though he's extremely jealous of this time with his "minions," as he calls his three young girls, and he's busy running his company, Pistorino always makes time to tell his story at events to end child sexual abuse. I traveled with him to the same NOVA conference in Dallas in 2015 where Smith first saw his dynamic presentation, "Fit to Thrive: Utilizing Exercise to Help Survivors of Sexual Abuse Recover," which was ranked one of the most popular presentations at the convention. After his talk, about fifteen people who either wanted to learn more about his program to use running and exercise therapeutically for recovering victims or to disclose their own past assault formed into a line snaking through the room.

Becky Perkins, communications coordinator for the Ohio Alliance to End Sexual Violence, which oversees all rape crisis centers in the state, works closely with Pistorino on a variety of projects and believes his presentations vary from other survivor accounts in the way he leaves his audience feeling. "Mike's so happy and joyful to be alive and doing well that it's just infectious. He makes you want to take on the world and kick some ass."

"You look at him, and he's this tough guy, but really he's a big marshmallow down deep," adds his friend Cathy DuBois, founder of

Reinventing the Cycle. "He's one of the most passionate people I know, and I don't know how he [has time to sleep] with everything he does to help people." Pistorino often accompanies DuBois at PTA meetings throughout the state to convince them to adopt her prevention program, which she hopes to have in all eighty-eight Ohio counties soon. He's happy to inform them that they and their principal are fostering child molestation by ignoring this program.

"He has no fear," says Sondra Miller, president and CEO of the CRCC. "He can say things that even we can't say to push the envelope and get the community to think about how sexual assault impacts people, families, and society."

Ultimately, Pistorino knows the children and organizations he speaks for need him on their side. "Sondra, Cathy, and Becky are such caring, loving, welcoming people, sometimes they need a little muscle," says the engaging enforcer. "We're fighting a really mean, deceptive, horrible enemy, so sometimes I gotta be a bully for the good guys."

The first weekend of June 2016, we rode the Greyhound bus overnight to New York. I noticed he was a little freaked out walking through Penn Station. He points out a couple spots on the ground where he used to sleep when he was living the junkie life. "Anytime I walk into a building that I haven't been in clean, it's weird," he says. "Anytime I go to New Yawk, it's like, 'Oh my God! I robbed this place!' or 'I slept in this corner.'"

He's returned to be the kickoff speaker Sunday morning at a march of two hundred people across the Brooklyn Bridge to City Hall in lower Manhattan to promote passage of the New York Child Victims Act. The legislation would eliminate the twenty-year statute of limitations, since children usually aren't in a position mentally, physically, or emotionally to pursue prosecution of their rapist for many years.

This bill—which has been blocked for more than a decade by a small but powerful cadre of state legislators in Albany—would open the door to the prosecution of many priests, for example, so the Catholic Church is lobbying against it. Shortly after the first march—he was the opening speaker for the 2017 march, too—Pistorino answered a call at his office from the Archdiocese of New York asking for someone in human relations. Suspicious, he pretended to be the director of human relations. The caller then demanded that he fire their employee Mike Pistorino for participating in the protest march. When Pistorino stopped laughing, he hung up.

When I call Tommy Kienle, a guy Pistorino grew up with in the Bronx, he laughs when he recalls EZ7, the street crew they were in together. "We was a bunch of outcasts," he says of the seven friends. "I guess we didn't fit in." But then he becomes pretty serious.

"Mike was a crazy kid. I never knew what happened to him. He never told anybody," recalls Kienle, who survived his own rough years but now lives in Virginia and works as a cook and caterer. "Mike was a good dude. He was quiet. He was fuckin' fearless. There was nothing that kid was scared of. Anytime you needed him, he would drop everything and come full steam for you. He wasn't violent, but if someone tried to bully us, he wouldn't stand for it. He'd put his hands up and, you know, defend himself."

Kienle tells me he only learned of the appalling abuse his friend suffered when he reached out to him on Facebook a couple years ago and Pistorino reached back. All of a sudden, those times when Pistorino would disappear made more sense. "It's hard to think about one of your closest friends going through that, and you didn't have a clue. For all them years, you couldn't help him. That shit is real tough to deal with, man, because that dude helped everybody. He would be there for you, man. He would be there in an instant." Like the night Kienle was cold, so Pistorino gave him his Mount Saint Michael football letterman jacket to keep warm. He thinks he still has it somewhere.

All things considered, Pistorino's pretty happy these days, living the life of a suburban dad in Cleveland, light-years from his Bronx upbringing. "At one point in my life, my biggest fear was: if I am not drinking and I'm not fighting, what am I going to do with all my time?" he says.

"Now, my time is spent dancing in my yard, wearing princess crowns, singing 'Skinny Marinky Dinky Dink' with my girls."

The list of his accomplishments to help victims is long, impressive, and ever-growing. He still gets children's clothing donations from Sears for Liz Booth's closet at Metro and the other SANE centers, and now he's asking them to donate furniture for Metro's new SANE unit under construction. He still runs marathons and has raised tens of thousands of dollars for the CRCC and other favored organizations. He has little trouble finding sponsors.

"I've realized that I'm a gifted communicator who can make people do what I want them to do," he smirks.

In spring 2017, he learned how to ride a motorcycle and got his license. He then purchased a sleek, all-black Dyna Wide Glide Cruising Motorcycle with a flame-streaked gas tank at the Harley-Davidson store in Mentor, not far from his family's new home on eight wooded acres (he wants his kids to have the wonderland he never did). Before he signed the deal, he convinced the store to place bins he had from his recent move by the counter for children's underwear donations to add to the SANE closets. Harley-Davidson now displays these blue bins at most of its stores in Northeast Ohio. If they don't, he will visit the store and tell them, "You're the only store that doesn't help kids who've been raped." Whatever it takes.

He hates wearing a helmet, which he thinks looks stupid, but he knows he has several important reasons to wear one.

"I feel like my public speaking is putting the final nail in the coffin of my addition," he says, now more than fourteen years sober. "I'm not going to shoot dope. Just not. I've got this mission now. The main mission is protecting my three girls. I've gotta change the world. I can't have them have guys at school grab their boobs and it's okay. I can't have them get drunk and get raped and everybody says it's okay. I can't have a job they can't get because they're girls. They have to be able to do whatever they want to do."

One of his missions is to get all of the biker groups nationally who are interested in working to protect children—for example, BACA, Kindred Breed, and Bikers Against Abused and Neglected Children (BAANC) in Northeast Ohio—to work together locally and nationally. Because of the territorial nature of biker groups, he knows it will be a tough task, but the expanded protection network for the children would be priceless.

A core strategy moving forward is to increase his audience sizes, whether it's conferences with ten thousand people in attendance or Congress or *The Ellen DeGeneres Show*. Man, he really wants to be on *Ellen* so he can goofy dance with the popular TV host like he does with his girls.

"It's a simple formula: the more people I reach, the more kids we're going to save," he says. "I want this thing to grow so big that it just becomes normal for kids to tell on molesters immediately. People are always going to touch them, but they're going to touch them less if it's not going to be secret, and they're going to go to jail or they're going to kill themselves, whatever."

It's easy to see that when it comes to the offenders, the ones who hurt innocent children, Pistorino has no sympathy. That's not his job. He remains ever-focused on helping the kids. To do so, he has two other obstacles that need to change: One, parents' self-serving prudish approaches to sexuality that prevent them from instructing children to not let anyone touch their penis or their vagina or in any intimate way and two, the silence when no one wants to address or confront a potential child molester in their family or in a community.

Of the former, Pistorino says, "Don't be worried about your stupid feelings. The kids need to know no one should touch their genitals. Otherwise, you're making them more vulnerable to a molester."

Of the latter, he concludes, "For years, child molesters raped kids counting on that silence. They know it exists. They know it's never shattered because people are afraid to talk about sex or they don't want to admit that Uncle Frank could do that or a coach at their kids' school.

"Now, through my speeches and everybody else in this field's hard work, the silence is shattered, and it's going to send the child molesters running like cockroaches because they can't hide behind it no more. Now that I'm clean and I've got all this to live for, and my enemy is so weak, there's not even a battle. It's like playing basketball with midgets. They're not tough enough to protect themselves or their actions. They have to hide behind everybody else not saying nothing."

After a slight pause, he looks straight into my eyes, smiles, and confirms, "There's nobody on this planet who can make me not say nothing. Nobody's built like that."

PART 4

Learning from Mistakes

Chapter 16

Triumphs and Tribulations in
Memphis and Other Cities

ON THE EVENING of December 21, 2016, *CBS Evening News* ran a story about untested rape kits in the United States, with a lead-in about Memphis, Tennessee. The producer, Laura Strickler, bookended the story with a Memphis resident who asked to be identified as Jane. With her face and voice left undistorted, the courageous woman told correspondent Jericka Duncan of the brutal beating and rape she endured at gunpoint in 1990 outside her apartment building. Although she agreed to the through and invasive rape kit examination afterward, nothing came of her evidence—for twenty-five years. Police records indicate the last time a detective worked on her case was two weeks after her rape.

"You have fingerprints and DNA available to catch someone and you don't test the kit? I would say they didn't try to catch him," she said to Duncan. Her kit was finally tested in 2015, but by then, the statute of limitations for the case had expired.

"Whatever road that I was on that night was taken away," she continued. "It's made me scared of the dark."

Jane's hope, she disclosed in the interview, is that his DNA profile will match another assault in the CODIS database. "He might be dead, which I hope; he might be behind bars," she said. "I might not be able to find out, but I need to know."

Amy Weirich, district attorney general for Shelby County, Tennessee, had the public relations misfortune to follow Jane's story. Duncan pressed her on what happened in Memphis. "How do you get to twelve thousand? I mean, why wasn't there an alarm I guess that went off at two thousand, three thousand, five thousand?"

"I don't know how it actually built up and how that number got to be what it was, but it did, and we immediately said, 'here's what we are going to do,'" replied Weirich, who joined the DA's office in 1991 and became the first woman to head the office in January 2011. In addition to her accomplishments thus far, she has had to defend herself against allegations of prosecutorial misconduct and ethical complaints lodged against her by the Tennessee Board of Professional Responsibility, an oversight arm of the state's supreme court that supervises the conduct of attorneys.

Part of an ongoing *CBS News* investigative series about the status and successes or failures of rape kit testing and investigating in the US, this story focused on the fact that, even with all of the jurisdictions finally processing backlogged kits collected from police property room shelves, the conviction rate for most was astonishingly low. Of the 28,600 back-logged kits tested to that point, the segment reported, only 1 percent resulted in convictions.

Comparatively, at that time Cuyahoga County and Cleveland had tested—and investigated—5,000 kits that led to 239 convictions, more than the other three cities they looked at for the report combined. They dropped in a colorful bar graph, showing 69 convictions for Detroit (10,000 kits tested), 28 for Houston (6,600 kits tested), and 10 for Memphis. Of the 7,000 rape kits that Memphis had submitted for testing at the time, 3,742 contained some form of DNA evidence. Still, only ten people convicted of rape.

The difference, they cited? Resources. The state of Ohio paid for the testing, which enabled the SAKTF to deploy the county and federal funding it had acquired specifically for the SAKI project to hire twenty-five additional investigators and six prosecutors.

Then they dropped in a comment from Rachel Lovell, a senior research associate from Case Western Reserve University, who serves as Cuyahoga County's embedded researcher. "They could proceed almost like to second base, where they could focus on investigating and prosecuting," she said. "The savings doesn't come with the testing. The savings comes with what you do with that test."

Lovell ended up catching a little flak from her SAKTF colleagues in Memphis for even commenting. But if you get to know the sincere, professional, and completely dedicated researcher as I have over the past couple of years, her mission is purely to discover, analyze, and educate. She was just trying to help by pointing out the realities of this recent phenomenon of testing massive amounts of long-backlogged sexual assault evidence. The one truth everyone seems to have learned is that testing is only the first step. Successful prosecutions and convictions are the reward for thorough investigation and follow-up.

As for Jane, the *CBS News* segment reveals that she joined a class-action lawsuit suing the city for failing to test her rape kit. (As of April 2017, that suit numbered forty plaintiffs, but in July 2017, in a legal victory for the City of Memphis, the judge limited the case to the original three plaintiffs.) "This is as much about resources as prosecutions," Duncan concluded the segment. "In Memphis, they've added an additional investigator and a prosecutor."

———————————

As this national movement to test and investigate sexual assault kits continues to grow roots and spread, there are still non-SAKI project cities and jurisdictions that have ignored the initiative or reluctantly implemented some components of the new approaches. Frankly, the movement is only a few years old, so there are still some growing pains and a Mount Everest–sized learning curve to overtake millennia of incorrect and ineffective procedures. Even the cities, counties, and states that have proactively jumped onboard as SAKI sites and are making great progress face challenges, such as limited resources or lack of effective leadership in certain disciplines.

Memphis is a good example of the latter situation. When the news hit in 2013 that the city had more than twelve thousand untested kits, the mayor at the time, A. C. Wharton Jr., issued an aggressive executive order that led to the formation of the multidisciplinary Memphis SAKTF in 2014. Significant changes have come from those efforts, improvements that should be permanent. Memphis, however, has encountered some big bumps along the way. My intention with this chapter is to look at both as the realities of what jurisdictions may encounter when trying to do the right thing.

In fact, originally, I was planning to write an entire section about Memphis. Before the September 2016 SAKTF summit in Detroit, I had several productive conversations with some of the Memphis SAKTF people and met a few others at the conference. Then, in January 2017, a reporting trip to Memphis collapsed when several people I was planning to shadow and interview changed their minds and decided not to talk to me. It appeared that, after being burned by the *CBS News* report, everyone had circled the wagons. I was disappointed, because I'd had great introductory interviews with several people, including General Weirich, as she is called in Tennessee, who was very forthcoming and helpful. However, I understand their reticence, even though their tribulations weren't my intended central focus.

Memphis has had its share of difficulties to deal with, as have many major cities as they wrestle with post-industrial challenges arising from impoverished, unemployed, underemployed, and often uneducated or disenfranchised urban citizens. In fact, the police departments of Cleveland, Detroit, and Memphis, the triumvirate of partnered SAKTFs, have each recently had consent decrees imposed upon them by the Department of Justice because of excessive force or civil rights violations, discriminatory policing, or a glaring need to rebuild community trust.

In talking to a Memphis source who asked not to be named, the person went on for ten minutes, rattling off a litany of challenges facing the city beyond federal oversight of the police, including a convoluted governmental structure with separate mayors of Memphis and Shelby County, each with thirteen-member elected legislative bodies and a Forbes ranking of number four in the "Ten Most Dangerous US Cities" list, primarily because of a violent crime rate of 1,583 per 100,000 residents with a total population of 652,725. In 2016, the city experienced its worst murder rate in two decades since the crack epidemic of the 1990s, with 228 homicides or 29.7 deaths per 100,000 residents. This person and a couple of other Memphians I spoke to believe the current uptick in homicides interferes with other priorities such as rape and sexual assault for police and law enforcement agents.

Comparing the two other cities' crime statistics is quite revelatory. Detroit, a city of 677,116 people, recorded 302 homicides in 2016, which works out to 44.6 per 100,000 residents. During the 1970s, the Motor City became known as the Murder City, because its annual homicide numbers often topped six hundred, a total that remains one of the highest murder rates in the nation's history. Cleveland is about half that size, with 385,809 residents, and 2016 was its deadliest year in a decade with 136 homicides, up from seventy-two in 2010. The Cleveland region, unfortunately, recorded one of the highest figures in the United States for opioid overdose deaths, with more than five hundred. So it's easy to see how urban police departments, typically understaffed and under-resourced, experience difficulties in fighting sexual violence offenses on top of other violent crimes.

Additionally, Memphis's efforts to address rape and sexual assault have been impaired or at times overshadowed by lawsuits against the City of Memphis filed by survivors whose rape kits remained untested for years (as previously mentioned), and in some cases their rapist was an offender who wasn't caught because other kits were not tested. In an April 2017 story in Memphis daily newspaper the *Commercial Appeal*, attorney Daniel Lofton said that "forty plaintiffs are involved in a lawsuit that alleges authorities mishandled and failed to prioritize the testing of rape kits that date back several years." The story also reported that of the total accumulation of 12,375 kits announced by Memphis in

2013, roughly 62 percent had been tested and of those, 306 cases were past the statute of limitations.

———————

In May 2016, I had a good telephone conversation with Weirich and Carrie Shelton Bush, an assistant district attorney who was then-chief of the Special Victims Unit in Weirich's office. They had attended the first SAK summit in Cleveland, hosted the second summit in Memphis, and were looking forward to the third summit in Detroit. The sexual assault kit team includes the SVU, which works closely with the Memphis Police Department Sex Crimes Unit and the Tennessee Bureau of Investigation, meeting on a weekly basis.

Every other week, those meetings include victim advocates. "We make sure that the victim's rights support groups have been at the table with us from the beginning to enhance what we do in reaching out to victims," Weirich said. "That's what this is all about, getting justice for those victims after far too long. So, everything that we do from the beginning to the conclusion has got to be victim-centered."

At that time, Memphis had 164 prosecutions pending and had closed fourteen cases, including six convictions with sentences averaging fourteen years. The rest of those cases had either been dismissed or the victim declined prosecution. They also filed about thirty-three John Doe indictments or warrants to hold the statute of limitations until that assailant was indentified at some point on CODIS. Tennessee's legislation has also enacted a law that removes the statute of limitations from cases in which victims of aggravated rape report within three years of the time the crime was committed.

Grants her office had received from the Memphis City Council, Cyrus Vance and the District Attorney of New York (DANY), and SAKI helped pay for the testing of the entire backlog of 12,374 kits. Weirich was pleased with the fact that they had made such progress and, as of March 2016, had only 1,974 kits left to be tested. (By June

2017, Memphis's untested and unprocessed kits were down to 506.) One of the biggest challenges for Memphis in processing the kits has been the capacity of the forensics laboratories they use to do the testing, since private labs that meet the stringent qualifications necessary for handling criminal evidence are testing kits from many other jurisdictions, not just Memphis. Still, they expect to have all of the backlog kits tested by 2018 or 2019.

Consisting of seven prosecutors, an investigator, and a victim witness staff, the SVU is a vertical unit that handles all child abuse and adult rape cases. "The MPD Sex Crimes Unit works side by side with Carrie and her team every day not only on working the backlog cases, but the new cases that come through the door, too, because we don't want another backlog," she said.

During summer 2013, the police director Toney Armstrong announced the city's lode of untested kits dating back to 1980. According to Weirich, Armstrong also immediately issued an executive order mandating that any forensic rape kit collected by police must go to a lab for testing, removing any question or decision of whether or not to test a kit.

Previously, the SVU had handled only child physical and sexual abuse, but Weirich had folded adult rape and sexual assault cases, backlogged or new, into the SVU's jurisdiction. "That is our way of saying to victims that we've realigned things here to make sure that your experience in the criminal justice system after an indictment is as victim-centered as it possibly can be," she explained. "Our office has one hundred six prosecutors, so when a victim has to come down here to tell their story several times to several different faces, it gets unnecessarily daunting. Having the same prosecutor on their team from day one helps eliminate some of that angst."

Weirich and Bush boasted about Shelby County's Rape Crisis Center, founded in 1975, as a shining beacon for victims.

"Within the past couple of years, they have really focused on the advocacy services," Bush said. "So they have more advocates assigned to be with the victim when they come in. They've increased counseling and their ability to counsel victims, whether or not they are participating in the criminal justice process. They're working more closely with law enforcement so they can take statements from victims at the rape crisis center, not the police station."

If victims do decide to participate in the prosecution of their assailant, Bush adds, the center monitors the status of the case and helps them keep up with court appearances or other trial milestones. "We have a very significant group of professionals over there who are determined to make this work," she says. Unfortunately, when I emailed her in January 2017, my source at the Shelby Rape Crisis Center, after our initial contact at the Detroit summit, apologized but said she wouldn't be able to talk with me.

Unlike Cleveland and Detroit, 95 percent of victims who report an assault have their sexual assault nurse examiner rape kit exam at the rape crisis center, unless they need to be hospitalized. For that 5 percent of victims, Shelton says, the SANE from the center will be called by a police dispatcher to perform the exam at the hospital. Moreover, Memphis's rape crisis center is located in the same building as the Crime Victims Center and Family Safety Center, a one-stop resource for domestic violence victims.

"There's a lot of overlap in the worlds of domestic violence and sexual assaults," Weirich says. "So having all of those resources and experts in those fields all under one roof has been a benefit to these victims. It's only a couple of blocks away from our office, too."

On the investigation side, Memphis gained a bit of a reputation for creative options when the DNA evidence doesn't pan out. "I think [Cuyahoga County Prosecutor] Tim McGinty and [Wayne County Prosecutor] Kym Worthy would tell you that they've learned from our offices and our law enforcement how to employ the good, old-fashioned gumshoe detective techniques if the science doesn't get you a suspect," Weirich said of the benefits of the SAKTF triumvirate. "We've all learned from each other, and we all reach out to one another for support and guidance."

Rick Bell from the Cuyahoga County Prosecutor's Office confirmed this and said working with Detroit and Memphis, especially having the summits, enabled them to devise all of their best practices regarding testing, swabbing, victim notification, investigation, and so on. "The areas where we saw we had come up with the same answer and had determined to handle in the same way, we realized that these were best practices," he told me.

When I ask whether they've learned anything from the trainings of the omnipresent Rebecca Campbell, their fulsome responses are not unexpected. Campbell has done a couple of training sessions in Memphis and was scheduled to return in fall 2017. She helped them completely "rethink the way we as law enforcement have investigated sexual assault for years," according to Bush.

"We have twenty-year veterans who, after listening to her, all of a sudden, their investigations looked different," Bush said. "Their victims were cooperative, and everybody was slightly stunned at just how successful that initial training had been." The Rape Crisis Center and Victims Center have both been sponsoring similar training for law enforcement, she adds.

———————

He's moved on to a new life, having retired from the Memphis Police Department after twenty-six years and now commercially rated as a multi-engine pilot with his own plane, and training with and on call to fly for a man in Huntsville, Alabama, who owns two private jets.

"I've really tried to close the door on my past," says Cody Wilkerson. "I really got way too emotionally involved." A cardinal sin for a sex crimes investigator. He even held a transition ritual using his files from every case where he had indicted the suspect. "I had a little ceremony in my backyard with my wife and son. As I drank a beer and smoked a cigar, I burned all of my case files in a little fire pit."

Wilkerson tells me he spent the last three years of his MPD career as the highest-ranking officer working on the untested rape kits in the DNA unit full time, before getting "run off." "They weren't doing the things I thought needed to be done and they just want to protect themselves while civilly liable," he claims. In 2015, he hurt his back moving furniture and took five months off to recuperate. When he returned, he was told he had been sent back to uniformed patrol, so he retired in January 2016.

Reluctantly, he spoke to me by phone in June 2017, and emphasized that everything he said was his opinion and in no way represented the MPD. I felt like he might be making this the last time he would speak about what deeply troubled him about how rape kit testing and victims were handled. For example, he didn't like seeing victims tossed in the back of a cruiser. "They're the victim of a violent crime," says the former lawman, who believes every police officer should be required to take Rebecca Campbell's training to learn how to work with victims of trauma. "If you're going to put them in the car, they should be sitting in the front seat with you."

He admits he was guilty of a lot of that victim blaming twenty-five or thirty years ago, when he was a young police officer. Ignoring a rape case of a woman who had an arrest for prostitution on her record was common, too, unless she was brutally beaten, but it's not as frequent now. "We've slowly, slowly changed, but [there's] still a long way to go," he says.

Wilkerson actually spoke very highly of many of the people involved, including the district attorney general. "If you thought a suspect was guilty and you had a decent amount of evidence, they pursued the case," he states. "They pursued some cases we just knew we were going to lose and didn't. So, I love Amy Weirich and [the deputy district attorney general] Jennifer Nichols and [the assistant district attorney in the SVU] Abby Wallace. They all put their heart and soul into this project."

Working with Nichols, Suzanna Parkinson, then a victim advocate and now a sexual assault response coordinator for the US Navy, and his supervisor, they devised a protocol to handle the backlog rape kit cases modeled on Detroit's and Cleveland's SAKTF protocols. "We were very successful with that," he remembers. He was responsible for getting the kits inventoried and shipped to the DNA labs and returned and put back into police department inventory. He assigned all cases to the detectives, trained detectives, and supervised the investigations. "I read every case the police department investigated," he says.

The thing that disturbed Wilkerson most was the way the MPD handled cases. "Absolutely, in my opinion, 75 percent of the blame should go on the police department, if not more," he says. The biggest problem, according to Wilkerson, was the lack of accountability for detectives. "There was absolutely no oversight to our investigators in Memphis, and I suspect it is the same in all of your major jurisdictions," he says. "There was no oversight, so a detective, for whatever reason, could close a case and ship it off into cyberspace. Unless the victim came to the police department and complained about it, nobody ever knew about that."

He started to press for more accountability, hounding his superior officers to look into cases that he believed were closed for no reason. In one case he found, there was even a CODIS hit that wasn't investigated. Eventually, he was ordered by a chief to leave those cases alone. The response was: no, you can't charge that officer, and stop using words like "criminally negligent behavior by police." All of which enhanced his growing reputation as a disgruntled detective.

"We had way too many cases like that," Wilkerson concludes. "And guess what? To this very day, there's zero oversight, zero accountability."

Members of some victim advocacy groups continue to question the transparency of MPD's rape case investigations. In a June 2017 *USA Today* article about the backlogged hits, Meaghan Ybos, an outspoken advocate for her fellow survivors of rape and executive director of People for the Enforcement of Rape Laws, said, "The public should be skeptical of any claims of progress from the MPD." Ybos happens to be one of the forty plaintiffs in the lawsuit against Memphis. She also pointed out that the number of kits tested is not proof that police are then properly investigating the cases tied to the kits.

The article also included some of the latest monthly statistics from the detailed monthly SAKTF report submitted to city council members that tracks the status of the kits tested and other activities: two investigations were closed, three indictments were completed; 618 to 620 investigations remain active; and thirty investigations were initiated.

———————————

Deborah Clubb, executive director of the Memphis Area Women's Council, introduced herself to me at the Detroit summit, but we didn't talk until June 2017 via phone. We speak a little about her perspective on the police. "MPD's commitment is there, but it's a massive institution with our many challenges," she says, citing—similar to the Detroit Police Department—a high amount of turnover in leadership, a focus on addressing the city's resurgence in homicides and narcotics cases, and even the controversial situation with a respected officer, Lieutenant Ouita Knowlton, one of the founders of the cold case DNA Unit, who had been mysteriously relieved of duty on April 4, 2017, due to an ongoing investigation. (It was later determined that Knowlton leaked case files for a rape investigation to a suspect's relative; as a result, she was reassigned and demoted to sergeant.)

"My next worry," she says, "is the state of funding and how many attorneys are going to be devoted to the backlog cases and how our juries are going to see these cases. So, we have to see if the DA's office will show the same kind of commitment to investigation and prosecution."

Clubb toiled as a reporter and editor for the *Commercial Appeal* in Memphis for twenty-five years. She covered a variety of topics, but focused mainly on women's issues. But as newspapers evolved in the era or electronic communications, she wasn't comfortable with having to shoot and post videos. "I was more of the crunch through data and be a long-form journalist," she says with a laugh.

She learned of a new nonprofit organization with a focus on women's advocacy and reported on one of their early meetings that launched the Women's Council. In May 2004, the organizers invited her to apply to be their staff person, and she did.

"The Women's Council has had gender violence as a primary focus and mission since it began, along with health issues and equal wages and so on," she explains. "But this decade has really brought the violence issues to the front, so we wanted to be part of the response to all of the fallout from the backlog rape kit testing, investigations, and prosecutions, and figure out what to do for the community whose trust was shattered."

After Mayor Wharton formed Memphis's task force in 2014, Clubb was named to the group to focus on the community outreach components. She has since organized numerous feedback events where they could communicate what the task force was working on and listen to the community's concerns.

"We've been proud and sometimes a little cocky at Memphis's capacity to have that task force," she says. "We just had a moment when the city mayor had the capacity to start it this way, with people around him advising the multi-agency team would be the way to do it for a community that was going to be outraged and feel unserved."

Another landmark achievement of Memphis, she says, was building a state-of-the-art evidence storage facility. Completed in May 2015, the climate-controlled, secure building features rolling, hand-crank, compact, high-density storage units with computer-inventoried shelving space. From what I'm told, this structure is coveted by every other jurisdiction involved in the SAKI project. The facility should certainly help prevent rape kits from falling into the chaotic state of disarray they once did in Memphis.

Clubb agrees that Memphis has benefited greatly from the partnership with Cleveland and Detroit, and they have worked closely with Ilse

Knecht, director of policy and advocacy, and others at the Joyful Heart Foundation in New York. "They were the voice that helped us explore and implement this idea of a multi-agency task force," she informs me. "They always were [certain] that you have to have a community voice, you must have community advocates, and you must have people in there talking about the victim's needs."

Modeling Joyful Heart's "No More" campaign, the Women's Council launched its own "Memphis Says No More" campaign in June 2015 as an umbrella entity for community outreach and prevention awareness activities.

"Just having the conversations, even saying the word 'rape' in your community as a way to raise awareness and build in some prevention and changing behaviors, that's a real important part of what we've done," says Clubb, who coordinates the campaign. "I would like to see more communities pick it up and copy it everywhere because it does seem to be moving people's thinking."

Among other things, Clubb enlisted the participation of several community leaders and later four stars of the Memphis Grizzlies NBA basketball team to support the campaign. Their images, along with the slogan "Memphis Says NO MORE—Together We Can End Domestic Violence and Sexual Assault," hang on banners in FedExForum, where the team plays, on posters in the baggage claim area at Memphis International Airport, on buses, and at churches, gyms, coffee shops, and so on throughout the city. They're visible on www.MemphisSaysNoMore. com, and the organization also paid for airtime on the local NBC affiliate to run PSAs when they first rolled out the ad campaign in June 2016.

"We did pre- and post-ad focus groups and surveys, and we saw a change in people's attitudes," Clubb declares.

One of my key advisors throughout this project has been Jim Markey, thirty-year veteran police officer and sex crimes detective in Phoenix and now independent consultant and member of the SAKI Training and Technical Assistance Team. When I asked him about Memphis, he said he feels they've done a great job pushing to get the kits tested, but they're struggling a bit on the investigative follow-up side for both cold and new cases.

"Their effort has been phenomenal to try to get a handle on it all," he commented. "But they're still falling a little bit short on delivery. There are some things that, because that's the way they've investigated and done things in Memphis for so long, that approach has become pretty engrained. They need to freshen and update their investigative strategies, because there are better ways than what they have in place."

One national expert I interviewed, who asked not to be identified, said Memphis has problems but has reached a point that's comparable to a lot of jurisdictions. "We'll see great things in Memphis in the coming months and years," the person opined. "They're just finding their feet right with how to proceed to the next stage, from 'Okay, we've tested all the kits. Now what?'"

I will leave the final words about Memphis SAKI efforts to Weirich, from our May 2016 interview:

"I can't see any downside to what we've done. The worst part is standing up in front of the community and saying, 'We've got twelve thousand untested kits,' and getting past that. But we can follow that sentence with, 'Look at all of these people that are standing here, side by side, committed to righting this wrong. This isn't something that happened overnight. We're not going to fix it overnight, but we're going to do everything we can to make it right.' And every day, everybody comes to work committed to do that. It's amazing, really."

PART 5

***

What's Next?

Chapter 17

The Pillars of Rape Kit Reform: Ilse Knecht and the Joyful Heart Foundation

IN THE SAME way a great rock guitarist makes her instrument an extension of her body, Ilse Knecht coaxes masterpieces from her cell phone as if it were a Gibson Les Paul. As director of policy and advocacy for the Joyful Heart Foundation, Knecht frequently has her phone fused to her hand or ear, making calls to state and national legislators all over the United States to discuss refinements to rape kit reform bills they are drafting or strategizing with advocates managing community rape awareness and prevention activities.

In the time I spent with her at Joyful Heart's offices in the Chelsea neighborhood of New York; in Harrisburg, Pennsylvania, to meet with Brandon Neuman, Pennsylvania state representative (D, Forty-Eighth District, Washington County); or on the Amtrak train for the two-and-a-half-hour ride in between, she spends a significant amount of her time emailing, texting, or talking. Nevertheless, she makes plenty of time to discuss the organization famously founded by *Law & Order: Special Victims Unit* star Mariska Hargitay in Kona, Hawaii, in 2004.

Although the content of her television show opened her eyes to the prevalence and barbarism of sexual violence in our country, Hargitay was particularly moved by the fan letters informing her that the writer had been raped or assaulted many years ago and had never told anyone. Since then, Joyful Heart has raised more than $33 million, received

$147.7 million in donated and in-kind services, directly served more than 18,500 individuals through healing programs, and connected to nearly four million individuals through website and social media efforts.

Implemented through healing, education, and advocacy programs, Joyful Heart's "mission" is to transform society's response to sexual assault, domestic violence, and child abuse, support survivors' healing, and end this violence forever," according to their website.

Knecht and her staff have two specific objectives: First, monitor the progress of the hundreds of thousands of backlogged rape kits being tested and investigated as well as the attached assailants prosecuted and convicted across the country. Second, actively advocate for and participate in the development of legislation that enacts JHF's six pillars of comprehensive rape kit reform:

1. Annual statewide audit: Inventory all untested rape kits periodically to understand the scope of the problem and monitor progress.
2. Mandatory testing of all backlogged kits: Eliminate the existing backlog by requiring law enforcement agencies to submit all previously untested kits to the lab, and requiring that these kits be tested.
3. Mandatory testing of new kits: Prevent future backlogs by requiring law enforcement agencies to promptly submit all newly collected kits to the lab, and mandating the lab test these kits within a specific timeframe.
4. Tracking system: Ensure that hospitals, law enforcement, and labs are using the same system to track rape kits. Build in a way for survivors to check the status of their kits throughout the process, from collection to analysis.
5. Victims' right to notice: Grant victims the right to receive information about the status and location of their rape kits.
6. Funding for reform: Appropriate state funding to address these issues.

On June 7, 2017, after much encouragement and advice from Knecht and her staff, Texas became the first state to institute all six pillars with the passage of HB 281, which requires the Texas Department of Public Safety to establish statewide tracking to monitor rape kits from collection to analysis. In a JHF media release issued that day, Knecht stated: "Joyful Heart is proud to stand with State Representative Donna Howard, former State Senator Wendy Davis, and our tireless advocacy partners, including the Texas Association Against Sexual Assault, who have fought for years for comprehensive rape kit reform. With this passage, Texas has demonstrated its commitment to bringing justice to survivors, holding violent perpetrators accountable for their crimes, and promoting public safety for all residents."

If you'd like to see how your state fares in these efforts, you can visit JHF's online monitoring and reporting initiative www.EndTheBacklog. org. On the backlog status map, Cleveland, Detroit, and Memphis get stars as spotlight cities because of their SAKI accomplishments, but their three states are light blue, meaning they have enacted only limited statewide reform.

Updating current legislation is the reason why Knecht is train-bound for the state capitol of Pennsylvania to confer with Brandon Neuman on Wednesday, April 5, 2017. After a staff meeting at Joyful Heart's offices on Tuesday, we board the train at Penn Station and speed through fields and farms, stop at some small towns and the large city of Philadelphia almost midway, then more meadows, forests, and farmland flash past the windows until we pull into the beautiful nineteenth-century train station with an old-fashioned waiting room, now promoted to the Harrisburg Transportation Center.

Located at Fourth and Chestnut streets, the station is only about half a mile from the capitol building, but because of the length of the train ride, we stay overnight in a motel across the river for the morning meeting. Knecht has dinner with Kristen Houser, a friend, while I watch a basketball game and prep for the morning. When she returns to the hotel after midnight, she continues reviewing the language of a bill they worked on in the JHF office on Tuesday and sends her revisions to Liliana Rocha, JHF's policy and advocacy manager, in the morning. (I had met Lily the day before, along with Bianca Rey, JHF's policy and advocacy coordinator whom I had met in Detroit, when they had their staff meeting with Knecht that included a phone conference with Natasha Alexenko, who collaborates with JHF as an advocate, speaker, and activist. The office is staffed primarily with hardworking, compassionate young women who are driven to execute JHF's mission and don't mind living in New York on nonprofit salaries.) We reconvene in the lobby to take a taxi into town and inhale coffee and croissants at Little Amps Coffee Roasters down State Street from the Capitol.

There, we bump into two other participants from Pennsylvania who will actually lead the meeting, with Knecht chiming in where needed. Her dinner companion, Houser, is the chief public affairs officer of the Pennsylvania Coalition Against Rape (PCAR) and the National Sexual Violence Resource Center (NSVRC), and Barbara "Babs" Sheaffer is the medical advocacy coordinator for PCAR. A long-established national expert on sexual violence, Houser serves as lead spokesperson for the two organizations. Recently, she's appeared as part of the coverage mix on the Jerry Sandusky and Bill Cosby cases. Sheaffer provides technical assistance and training to advocates and other professionals across the state and nation on how to better serve victims of sexual assault in the health care setting.

We walk down to the state capitol building, which truly is an immense and magnificent example of public architecture. In fact, at its dedication in 1906, President Theodore Roosevelt enthused that the beaux arts beauty was "the handsomest building I've ever seen." Modeled after St. Peter's Basilica in Rome, the capitol dome rises 272 feet and, according to the online brochure, weighs 52 million tons. Of course, even more tons of marble reside in the grand staircase inspired by the Paris opera house, the description goes on to say. Climbing said staircase with heavy briefcases and bags on a hot day like this contributes either to weight loss or improved endurance.

We maneuver our way through the hundreds of people in the rotunda lobby for the Pennsylvania Blue Ribbon Champions Award Ceremony and Rally for Kids to raise awareness about protecting children from child abuse, where actors sporting Spider-Man, Wonder Woman, and other superhero costumes circulate. We wind our way through the warren of hallways, offices, and elevator banks to get to Rep. Neuman's office.

The first thing you notice about Neuman is his handsome, golden boy presence. A close second is his broad shoulders accented by his well-fitting navy blue jacket, white shirt, and light blue tie. In fact, the centerpiece of his expansive corporate desk is a memento of his days as fullback and captain of the University of Richmond football team: a helmet with a leggy red spider crawling up the side of a midnight blue field. Richmond is, my cursory research tells me, the only collegiate team that appointed an arachnid as its mascot.

What really matters today, though, is the fact that Neuman has been an aggressive ally in the crusade to put the most effective legislation in place to ensure rape kits are monitored, tested, and investigated and victims are treated with dignity and compassion. In addition to the three women, a representative from the Pennsylvania auditor general's office is filling in for Eugene DePasquale, who had to cancel at the last minute. In league with Neuman, the progressive DePasquale has been highly supportive of rape kit processing efforts, and in September 2016 issued a thorough report on the status of untested rape kits in the state. Knecht tells me later that in addition to legislators, she and her team often enlist the aid of state auditors, since they control the purse strings.

Neuman believes DePasquale's special report on untested rape kits pinpointed where Pennsylvania can improve its Sexual Assault Testing and Evidence Collection Act, which his Act 27 strengthened. The new legislation he's working on would implement recommendations from that report and "give them the force of law."

Neuman's House Bill 272 (Act 27) received unanimous support throughout the Pennsylvania House and Senate before it was signed into law by Governor Tom Wolf on July 10, 2015. The act uncovered nearly two thousand rape kits that had remained untested for more than a year. Neuman feels his follow-up legislation to improve the process of the established state police standards and data collection procedures is receiving similar support. He wants it to address serious shortfalls in staffing, equipment, and funding at the state's public crime laboratories to ensure that Pennsylvania has the necessary resources to get offenders off the streets and better protect potential future victims.

"Although Act 27 requires improved testing and reporting of evidence, I am not willing to say the job is done until every rape kit is tested in a timely fashion and every rape victim is able to seek justice," he said in a December 2016 media release.

Sitting around a conference table in the state representative's office, the group starts the meeting around 10:35 a.m. Neuman, who was sworn into his fourth two-year term in January 2017, is focusing on ways to tighten and clarify the language in Act 27, which helps ensure that sexual assault victims and their families receive timely attention and justice. His proposed legislation would create a commission of local and state agencies to review funding needs and enhance communications, by, for example, establishing a hotline for hospitals to call if a rape kit is not picked up by law enforcement for testing within seventy-two hours.

One of the early topics in the meeting is pending legislation in several states, including California and Texas. '   .d a one-dollar donation box citizens can check on their taxes or driver's license forms to support the processing of rape kits. Some states are considering charging a strip club tax for that purpose, but Neuman feels that's too controversial.

The conversation is focused, but cordial and relaxed. "We have an opportunity to get our proposed changes fast-tracked," he says. "So, I'm open to suggestions from you guys, because you're the experts, to make the bill everything we want it to be."

At 10:45 a.m., as Neuman stands to get a legal pad from his desk, Houser raises the need to consider adding a specific timetable for kit testing to replace the vague phrase "as soon as possible but no later than."

Jotting notes in her small spiral binder, Knecht inquires about the concerns of various jurisdictions. She suggests that perhaps the attorney general's office could oversee the kit transfers from hospitals to law enforcement, because they have the power of state police to ensure kits get picked up. A discussion of the need to define exactly what the process should be to destroy rape kits ensues. Sheaffer explains that there are a variety of laws pertaining to the number of years required to hold the kits ranging from five years to until the statute of limitations expires. Knecht raises the issue of whether there should be victim consent involved, and suggests victims should also have the right to obtain notice of their kits' destruction, which is in line with federal best practices.

Neuman says Mike Schlossberg, Pennsylvania state representative, recently introduced a bill that would give prosecutors and police control of the kits. The women all vehemently argue that must never be the case. Neuman quiets the conversation quickly by saying, "Not happening." The discussion moves to possibly incorporating additional mandatory training for police officers, but Neuman says he has to be careful about not asking for too many mandates for training because of the additional expenses police departments would incur.

A few minutes later, around 11:30 a.m., Neuman rises and moves toward the door of his office. "I have to go to the floor now, but you can stay and continue the conversation, if you like," he says. "I'm going to get this done by June."

Back on the train after a delicious but rapid lunch at a vegan restaurant—Knecht has gradually transitioned from vegetarian to vegan—we chat about the meeting and Neuman's obvious commitment to this issue.

"It's amazing to have a member just sit down and take his time and get into the weeds with you," says the seasoned shaper of legislation.

Our conversation is broken by several scheduled phone calls, but we find a block of time to talk about growing up in Champaign-Urbana, Illinois. Her interest in social justice and helping people has just "been a thing" her whole life. She laughs when she thinks back to how she and some junior high school friends formed an organization called Students for World Improvement (SWI) and in high school she raised money to send school supplies to El Salvador. For a while during and after college, she volunteered for a pro-choice group, protested the first Gulf War, and served as the volunteer coordinator for a Green Party candidate for city council and mayor. She was also a leader with the Student Environmental Action Coalition. She worked in an urban garden for a while; at lunch she told me she's thinking of starting one in her community in Brooklyn.

Her need to "feel like I have a purpose" and "make myself useful" all came from her mother. "My mom was one of those people who pointed out horrible things and had extreme compassion for people," Knecht fondly recalls. "I remember thinking, 'Well, that's fine, but how do you fix it?' So, that's why we founded SWI."

For the past twenty-five years, she's been completely committed to ending violence, starting with her previous job at the National Center for Victims of Crime, where she created the DNA Resource Center and led the center's efforts to reform policies and practices related to testing rape kits. She befriended several members of the Joyful Heart Foundation because of mutual work on backlog kit issues, and ended up joining JHF in June 2014. There, her staff bio says, she is honored to "lead the Joyful Heart's policy and advocacy work to eliminate the backlog of untested rape kits and bring reform to the way survivors— men, women, and children—are treated in our society and criminal justice system."

Due to the nature of her work, people she knows or meets often like to challenge her on issues such as the campus sexual assault problem or the prevalence of sexual assaults in Rikers Island, New York City's main jail complex. "It's horrible, and it's right here in my backyard," she says. "But I'm very laser focused on our strategic plan and carrying that out, and I know there are other people working on those issues, so I have to trust that they are doing a good job. I know there are lots of campus organizations, and RAINN does a lot related to campus assaults, so it's not a place where Joyful Hearts needs to join in."

She prefers to remain "laser focused" on helping create meaningful change through legislation and education. (During this year alone, she tells me by text in early August 2017, JHF has had its hands in the development of seventy-six bills in thirty-four states, with fourteen passed and a couple of key states, California and New Jersey, still in session.)

As we approach Philadelphia on the train, after several voice and text conversations and a little tweeting thrown in, our conversation turns to where things are today and what still needs to happen. Knecht feels there are still too many jurisdictions where they don't employ the new approaches or understand the simple truth that testing and investigating rape kits provides a win-win that can help victims heal and send bad guys who hurt people and property behind bars.

There are several questions she often finds her brain going to when pondering jurisdictions that still don't get it. Why are we doing the SANE exams if we never use the kits? Whey do we put the victims through that? Should we be rethinking that process?

"It's a broken system that you would collect that stuff and then just do nothing with it," she says. "It goes back to what we know as far as the prejudices, the not understanding trauma, that everybody is lying or thinking that it doesn't matter in acquaintance cases. That's the cultural bias."

I ask if she's optimistic or pessimistic. "I think it's changing," she allows. "We're seeing it in these communities when they get the hits and see the cases that are being solved. 'Oh my gosh!' The light bulb goes off."

She is concerned about the low conviction rate for rape and sexual assault cases. She knows that prosecutors often cherry pick the cases they know they can definitely win to keep their conviction rate high—and voters happy—while neglecting cases that they could possibly win but would require more investigation. She tells me about AEquitas, an organization funded by the Office on Violence Against Women (OVW), that is working to change that perspective. "They got money from OVW to implement a project called the Sexual Assault Justice Initiative that analyzes how to change the goal of prosecutors and not to think about numbers or winning cases but pursuing justice," Knecht says.

The flip side of that is, sometimes just making the case in court, even if you lose, can help victims by showing them that law enforcement and prosecutors care. "A lot of survivors will tell you that it's okay to lose to show survivors that the process is just as important as the outcome," she explains. "The way they are treated along the way matters as much or maybe even more than the outcome of their case. Ultimately, that brings the survivors a sense of justice, that they matter and deserve to be taken seriously, that somebody believes them, even if the jury doesn't say 'You're guilty.'"

Even testing rape kits beyond the statute of limitations for use as 404(b) character evidence in other cases or parole hearings is important, too, she adds, as proof that the criminal justice system values these survivors and their cases.

Our conversation turns briefly to *I Am Evidence*, the documentary directed by Trish Adlesic and Geeta Gandbhir and produced for HBO by Mariska Hargitay and JHF about the effectiveness of the backlog rape kit testing, with Cleveland and Ohio featured prominently. She's very excited about the potential the film has as a vehicle to raise awareness exponentially, and after its premiere at the 2017 Tribeca Film Festival, Joyful Heart has been inundated with requests to show the film throughout the US. Part of Knecht's "To-Do List" portion of her staff meeting the day before dealt with identifying ways to leverage the film as a marketing and awareness tool for the End the Backlog campaign.

Before the meeting, Knecht introduced me to Vaughan Bagley, special projects manager for JHF, who was greatly anticipating the first showing later in April.

"We will be leading the charge from the premiere forward on making sure that when people see the film they know exactly what they can do to join the movement," Bagley explains as we sit in her cubicle office. "We want to focus on the reform cities that Ilse is working with that need a little extra encouragement, where we want to educate and empower grassroots participants, show them the film, and bring people together. We're working with the coalitions and all our partners who are already championing this cause so they can use it as a tool. We're trying to figure out in the next legislative season where those key reform areas are and where we can bring the film."

One of the obvious choices should be Baltimore. In January 2017, after two years of violent riots sparked by the death of Freddie Gray, a twenty-five-year-old African American man who died from a spinal cord injury after being transported in a police van, the Department of Justice and city officials announced the consent decree now in place in Baltimore. Buried within the DOJ's 164-page report detailing widespread systemic issues within the BPD pertaining to excessive force and racism were several pages that revealed how police mistreated and neglected victims of rape and sexual assault, especially if they were urban residents of color.

Officers openly expressed to prosecutors, for example, their "contempt of and disregard for a woman who had reported a sexual assault." A prosecutor's response is equally appalling. "This case is crazy. . . . I am not excited about charging it. This victim seems like a conniving little whore (pardon my language)." The officer's reply read: "Lmao! I feel the same."

Incidents of victim blaming were typical. According to the Justice Department, police would "discredit the reports of victims who delayed in reporting the assault to the police," which the DOJ says "suggests gender bias by the detectives." Additionally, the report says that sex crimes detectives asked questions like, "Why are you messing that guy's life up?" All of these police behaviors represent the abhorrent, and now, thanks to research by Rebecca Campbell and others, antiquated approach to treating victims of sexual assault.

As we hurl along the tracks, getting closer to New York, I ask Knecht about cities emerging as leaders in the movement to reform rape kit laws and implement the newer victim-centered best practices. She rattles off a short list of areas who have become leaders, such as the state of Kentucky, or cities starting to acknowledge their need to change and adopt the newer approaches, such as Fayetteville, North Carolina.

At Knecht's recommendation, when I get back to Cleveland I look into two locations she and Joyful Heart have worked closely with over the past few years: Washington State and Portland, Oregon. I had met Tina Orwall, Washington state representative, at the Detroit summit in September 2016, where she was conversing with and ravenously absorbing as much as possible from the experts there. Orwall has definitely positioned herself as a leader in the movement to reform permanently the clearance of backlogged kits and the way rape and sexual assault cases are processed and prosecuted.

Primarily, she has aggressively introduced and pushed through several key bills in her state legislature. Orwall has sponsored a handful of bills that enhance kit testing laws and improve the way victims are treated. In 2015, after learning that Washington had approximately six thousand untested sexual assault examination kits, she got Washington HB 1068 passed. The bill requires law enforcement agencies to submit all SAKs to the Washington State Patrol Crime Laboratory for testing. It also creates a workgroup to study the issue of untested kits and review best practices for how to respond to victims of sexual assault.

In April 2016, thanks to Orwall's efforts, HB 2530 was signed into law, requiring the Washington State Patrol to create and operate a statewide sexual assault kit tracking system that will come online in January 2018, making Washington the first state to track rape kits. It also requires law enforcement to train in sexual assault trauma so they can work more effectively with victims and survivors. Concurrently, Gina McCabe, Washington state representative, sponsored HB 2711 that commissioned a study to determine the availability of SANEs in Washington and recommend improvements.

"We have two survivors on our statewide committee, and they, along with Joyful Heart, have helped us steer all of the steps we've been taking," Orwall says. "The system is really broken, and my goal is not only to test the older kits, but to fix the system." One of the steps has been to expand the capacity of the Washington State Patrol by adding seven new staff members who are dedicated to testing kits.

Washington's attorney general obtained a SAKI grant in 2016, and Orwall was waiting to hear about the pending grant for 2017 when we spoke. The plan is to apply for additional support to fund a cold case team, and for another grant in 2018 and for as long as they are available. She's currently working with Sue Rahr, executive director of the Washington State Criminal Justice Training Commission, to ensure that Campbell's teachings about the neurobiology of trauma are incorporated into police academy training. Orwall has attended the summits in Memphis and Detroit, and she's traveled to New York to meet with Knecht and Joyful Heart. She's met with numerous survivor advocates working on a national level.

"As a legislator, I have been trying to think, how do you apologize? How do you just say, 'I'm sorry?'" Orwall asks rhetorically, who believes we're fast approaching a tipping point of cultural change regarding rape and sexual assault. "I just feel like we let so many survivors down. I do feel like this work has been really healing to all the survivors. I am just hoping we are creating a system where this doesn't happen again."

We chat briefly about the next national summit, which will move out of the Midwest and travel to Portland, Oregon, in early October 2017. Thus, I talk to a couple of key members of the multi-disciplinary task force in the City of Roses. Susan Lehman, victim services coordinator and advocate for the Portland Police Bureau, quickly dispels my thought that Portland was new to this endeavor.

The jurisdiction's backlog of SAKs were first brought to the police bureau's attention by then Sergeant Peter Mahuna in late 2013, after he had read several articles about untested rape kits and had been contacted by JHF about auditing the bureau's kits. Mahuna then enlisted Lehman, who transferred to the unit on March 17, 2011 (she had worked as program coordinator in the records division for the prior seventeen years). The two developed an auditing system and determined who would handle it and how they would document the process.

However, Portland has had advocates embedded in its Sex Crimes Unit since 2008, after the City of Portland audited the unit in 2007 for its investigators' techniques. They declared that the unit's efforts fell short of a victim-centered approach. The unit implemented all the recommendations of the auditor's office. Under Sgt. Mahuna, the unit even created two "soft interview rooms" for victims by remodeling two offices to resemble living rooms, with a sofa, soft chairs, curtains on the windows, and a Keurig single-serve coffeemaker for privacy and "a comfortable, homey atmosphere," says Lehman.

"We did better on our 2014 audit," Lehman says. "But it's a moving target, so there's always ways we can improve."

At that time, Portland had 1,797 kits waiting to be tested. In 2015, Lehman explains, the guidelines for mandatory submission to the Oregon crime lab were if the suspect was unknown, if the suspect was known but there was an allegation of violence in the initial report, or the known suspect had a history of violence. In addition to deciding if a case met the guidelines, detectives would also determine whether it was beyond the statute of limitations, had been adjudicated, or the suspect was deceased.

To relieve detectives of some of the workload, the bureau used clerical staff to complete the special reports for cases already submitted to the lab. They created a spreadsheet to track the progress of each case, which they submitted to the Bureau of Justice Assistance as part of their application materials and as a result received a SAKI grant. The bureau has continued to work with Knecht and JHF ever since the organization contacted Sgt. Mahuna in 2013.

Lehman says the victim-centered approach instituted in 2008 continues to grow, and they have learned from Campbell's teachings, although the professor has not been involved in Portland directly, as well as the research of David Lisak, a forensic consultant who studies the behavior of predatory sex offenders. "To this day, however, you read a police report and go, 'Hmmm. That's not what I expected,'" she says. "Then one of the sergeants simply contacts that officer and lets them know why it wasn't a good idea to ask that question or do whatever they did in the report that made us say that's not the model we want to project."

Lehman also takes a few moments to boast about Portland's groundbreaking Sexual Assault Management System (SAMS). The comprehensive database is the envy of every other jurisdiction and SAKI site. According to Lehman, George Burke, who was the commander in charge of the Detective Division when SAMS was developed, said if they used $100,000 of forfeiture funds to build it, they would give the program blueprints away, too. And they did. To date, they have donated SAMS to five other jurisdictions, she says, and she was part of the team that presented it in a session at the Detroit SAKTF summit. The bureau later applied for a supplemental grant of $825,000 to improve the database to add barcode tracking, and electronic SANE nurse reporting, and email test notification for victims.

As a preview, she reports the summit in Portland will feature forty-five breakout sessions that will accommodate the interests and needs of both professionals who are well-heeled in the new approaches and those who are brand new to it all. The National Crime Victim Law Institute at Lewis and Clark College in Portland will present a special segment for advocates and police on victim's rights sexual violence cases.

I also spoke on the phone to one of her colleagues, Molly Daul, detective supervisor and SAKI site coordinator for Portland, who was kind enough to give me a small chunk of her vacation at a mountain resort in Idaho. She's been with the Portland Police Bureau for twenty-three years, passed the detective test in 2004, and served in Sex Crimes when there was one sergeant and five detectives.

"It wasn't really a sought-after unit back then, in part because of the scope and amount of cases," Daul admits. "So it didn't garnish the attention that it deserved."

What has she seen since returning to the unit in 2015 as a supervisor, after nine years in homicide? "There's been an evolution of resources now directed at sex crimes, and that really is the key to giving us the appropriate capabilities to investigate survivors' reports," she says. "It's not just a reflection on the police bureau, either. Society is catching up and starting to see sexual assault for what it is instead of all of the outdated old norms and stereotypes." At full strength, the unit now counts two supervisors, twelve detectives, and Lehman as its victim advocate program coordinator, with four embedded advocates working side by side with detectives. Daul considers it a progressive model of a victim-centered, trauma-informed unit. The unit handles cases of sexual assault victims ranging in age from fourteen through sixty-four.

Before we sign off, Daul tells me a little bit about Portland Police Bureau's Rose Project. The innovative community outreach initiative is for those individuals who have reported a sexual assault and completed the sexual assault kit examination. Victims can call a phone number or email the PPB at any time to check on the status of their kits. Portland's oldest backlogged kit is from 1985. Thus far, fewer than a dozen people have contacted the bureau via the Rose Project, but Daul sees it as an important resource for those survivors. "It's always there," she says. "If a victim feels they're not ready to talk to an investigator or an advocate, it gives them the power to know that we have the information, if they want it."

Daul is encouraged by the fact that the community, law enforcement, prosecutors, and the judicial system have changed because everyone has become more knowledgeable about sexual assault. Ultimately, sex crimes detectives now have the resources to investigate a case fully and are better suited to investigate every case.

"We start by believing," Daul says. "You go into that case not doubt-ing or victim blaming. You investigate it until you have brought it to fruition or your investigation comes to a natural end. So the biggest change I've seen is law enforcement has become better educated and trained on how to approach the initial investigation of these cases as a detective."

———————

As our train makes its approach into Penn Station in New York, Knecht tells me one of the things she made sure of before accepting the posi-tion at Joyful Heart was to make sure everyone had a sense of humor. Humor, she knew, arms them with a crucial buffer against the dark and difficult subject they deal with on a daily basis.

"We kid about not getting overly serious and being too 'Joyful Hearty' sometimes," she says. JHF actually is quite conscious of the health and wellness of its employees, providing "wellness days," where everyone is given the day off and forty dollars to do as they like, including getting their nails done, going to the gym, seeing a movie, or just relaxing at home. As expected, the ever-assiduous Knecht struggles with it, often answering emails anyway, but she tries to take off another day once in a while. If she can. Still, she loves the fact that she gets to work in her ideal social justice job *and* get paid for it.

"I thought about being a therapist at one point in my life," she reveals. "Then I thought, 'I want to make a bigger change,' and by changing laws and policies you have the ability to affect a really large population of people at the federal—national—level, and at the state level, where you see it so clearly."

The Amtrak train slows as it pulls into the station.

"Seeing that all the work we're doing is actually changing hearts and minds, but also changing the law and making it so this is the way you have to do it from now on is very satisfying to me," Knecht continues. "If you live in this state, just this little microcosm, this little world that we have that they're to have their rape kits tested or they're going to have certain rights no matter where they live. So, it's just like checking it off the list. Next state down, and keep going."

We walk into the lower level of the station that is continually under construction while refurbishing the old floor and walls, with people shopping or hustling in all directions. I've thoroughly enjoyed my time hanging with Knecht. I worry a little about her health, but I am thankful she—and Joyful Heart—are out there as vigilant guardians. We say goodbye, and I head upstairs to grab a cab on Eighth Avenue to LaGuardia Airport. She's off to catch the subway home to Brooklyn.

After a few strides, I reflexively look over my shoulder. Knecht has her cell phone to her ear and is animatedly talking as she turns and descends the stairway to her train platform.

Epilogue

The Sexual Assault
Paradigm Shift of 2017

Since I finished writing *Shattering Silences* in August 2017, much has happened in the realm of rape and sexual assault. I see it as an inevitable synergy that was boiling—or festering—for decades, if not centuries, underneath all of the great work emerging with the new movement and solutions detailed herein.

In October, almost eight years to the day that I began reporting on the topic of sexual violence, multiple allegations of sexual harassment and assault against Hollywood producer Harvey Weinstein that dated back several decades unleashed a flood of similar accusations of sexual misconduct against more than fifty other Hollywood celebrities. The bombshell revelations were the result of in-depth investigative reporting by the *New York Times* and the *New Yorker*. The list of accusers of Weinstein and other celebrities began closing in on one hundred, and the list of accused continues to grow.

That these egregious offenses occurred wasn't necessarily new or a surprise. Our current president had unintentionally confirmed this for us when his recorded comments about how he had freely molested women from a 2005 interview with TV personality Billy Bush for *Access Hollywood* were released during the 2016 presidential campaign.

What was different this time was the vehemence of the response of the women and some men who had been abused. The #MeToo phenomenon emerged as a highly public response by not only celebrities, but everyday individuals who had been sexually harassed or assaulted at some point in their lives. People posted on Facebook or tweeted the comment "Me, too," and in some cases gave specific comments or detailed accounts of who their assailant was and how they had been assaulted. Thus, public perceptions of sexual harassment and assault have shifted immensely. The high-profile #MeToo movement affected a sea change in our culture, empowering men and women to stand up to their abusers.

In December, the *TIME* "Person of the Year 2017: The Silence Breakers" magazine cover grabbed a lot of attention. The cover story recognized the brave people who stepped forward to reveal their personal tribulations, revealing the prevalence and enormity of the problem, however you choose to label it: rape, nonconsensual sex, sexual assault, sexual harassment, sexual misconduct—sexual violence.

That was soon followed by a second wave reaction, the #TimesUp counterattack on these predators who had abused the skewed power dynamic of Hollywood. Of course, we know the power dynamic is always abused, no matter the field: business, entertainment, education, politics, religion, restaurants, sports, tech firms. Fittingly, to start the New Year, on January 1, 2018, three hundred prominent actresses—led by Brie Larson, Ashley Judd, Rose McGowan, Gwyneth Paltrow, Natalie Portman, Mira Sorvino, and Reese Witherspoon—and other female Hollywood and entertainment professionals joined forces to launch their initiative to fight sexual harassment.

They announced they had collected $13 million in donations to establish a legal defense fund intended to help less privileged women—janitors, nurses, and workers at farms, factories, restaurants, and hotels—protect themselves from sexual misconduct and the fallout from reporting it. (Concurrently, an article in *Reveal* by Bernice Yeung and a team of investigative reporters raised awareness of sexual abuse of women in low-profile jobs and led to a new law in California that mandates sexual harassment training for all janitorial companies and a law in Oregon to protect janitors.)

The long-range objectives of the #TimesUp movement include lobbying for legislation to penalize companies that tolerate persistent harassment, and to discourage the use of nondisclosure agreements to silence victims. They also plan to sponsor a drive to reach gender parity at studios and talent agencies that has already begun making headway.

Moreover, the revelation in 2017 that a physician had been molesting Olympic gymnasts for twenty years was difficult to imagine, let alone accept. In January 2018, Michigan State University sports doctor Larry Nassar pled guilty to seven counts of first-degree criminal sexual misconduct and was sentenced to 175 years for assailing 156 known victims on top of 60 years he was already serving for child pornography charges. Judge Rosemarie Aquilina aroused some ire through her controversial decision to condemn the heinous nature of his actions by saying "I just signed your death warrant."

During the sentencing phase of the trial, she allowed the victims to step up to the podium and give impact statements. I didn't have a problem with it. Let them confront their despicable assailant. Let the 156 women tell their stories of courage and resilience to millions of people worldwide. The coward will die in prison, but somehow even that doesn't seem like punishment enough. The case is definitely not over, either, because the other burning question we're left with is, How could anyone knowingly let child athletes be sexually assaulted for two decades?

So, in addition to the MSU Athletic Director and USA Olympics Board members who deservedly lost their jobs, Michigan's attorney general assigned a special prosecutor to pursue an "open and ongoing" investigation of MSU to identify any other guilty parties. Anyone who turns a blind eye to sexual violence deserves to be penalized far beyond loss of employment. As *The Daily Show* television host Trevor Noah half-jokingly suggested, they should serve 10 percent of the offender's total sentence as their "commission." That wouldn't be a bad start. People need to know being an accomplice in any way is unconscionable and unacceptable.

So what happens next? We find ourselves in a bit of a gray area, as we attempt to determine the best way to process and resolve these mass disclosures. In the fall, I heard several interviews with distinguished editor Tina Brown, who was supporting her new book, *The Vanity Fair Diaries*. Amid all the indignant censure and condemnation, I found her commentary most lucid, rational, and profound. In one interview on NPR, she labeled all of the disclosures "a watershed moment for women," but she also expressed concern that it shouldn't devolve into a wave of frivolous law-suits with accusers claiming, "He touched my knee in 1985."

In an early December interview with CBC News program *The National*, Brown called this "a purifying moment," where women are saying "enough is enough." She found it a natural progression from the downfall of Fox News CEO Roger Ailes and Fox News personality Bill O'Reilly and comedian Bill Cosby, as well as the national march in January, where millions of women and men rallied against the "tsunami of sleaze" embodied by Donald Trump who had outed himself as a serial sexual harasser.

Brown expressed great admiration for Ashley Judd and the other early whistleblowers for fomenting a revolution that had to happen. "What determines if the #MeToo movement endures? Where's the risk for this movement?" asked CBC host Adrienne Arsenault.

"All revolutions come with risk, and we are seeing a revolution, and revolutions get bloody, and revolutions often get off the rails," Brown cautioned. "So you're going to see corollary damage. You're going to see some decent men who are falsely accused. You're going to see unfair reprisals. But I think that the larger picture is going to be a healthy one."

Fortunately, in this historical cultural moment, she said, "There are tons of men who are just as appalled by this as women, and many of them asking themselves *How can we make sure that can never happen to a woman again?*"

I have had the great fortune to meet many such men and profile them in the book. They are doing what they know is right, and everyone knows one of the most significant paradigm shifts will occur when men stand up, speak out, and act against sexual violence.

Closer to home, the Cleveland Rape Crisis Center notified me they had seen what they consider an "unprecedented" increase in new clients from throughout Northeast Ohio who had built up the courage to call and request appointments. In fact, the average number of calls per day to the CRCC's twenty-four-hour crisis and support hotline has nearly doubled when comparing 2016 data to recent months following the headlines and the #MeToo movement. Through the end of October 2017, the CRCC answered 5,259 calls, texts, and chats to its crisis and support hotline, or 8 percent more than in all of 2016.

On an average day, the main office in downtown Cleveland receives seven to ten calls. In 2016, the daily average was thirteen. Five years ago, it was eight. But on November 29, forty-three new clients called, the most the CRCC has ever received in a single day. On November 30, another thirty-seven new clients called. They believe the spike was triggered by NBC's firing of longtime *Today Show* host Matt Lauer on November 29.

Near the end of the year, I spoke to Sondra Miller, executive director of the CRCC. I asked her what she thought the result of this current phenomenon might be. She told me some of the survivors calling in were reporting that this national attention normalizes their experiences and helps them feel more comfortable disclosing their assault, seeking treatment, and accessing help. Other survivors, however, share that this type of news coverage is triggering and exacerbates pre-existing trauma symptoms.

Survivors stepping forward to reveal their abuse can be doubly beneficial, first by putting away more offenders and predators, and second, by serving as their first step toward healing. Yet it can also hurt survivors all over again, if they are not careful. That is the danger we must be fully conscious of and vigilant in monitoring. I believe we are fortunate to have the systems, best practices, and most importantly, the people in place who lead these efforts to provide victim-centered, trauma-informed care, as we continue to find ways to prevent, reduce, and eliminate sexual violence.

Ultimately, the foundation of *Shattering Silences* is courage: The courage of the survivors, whether they choose to report to law enforcement or disclose what happened to them or not. The courage of the professionals and volunteers making this absolutely needed change in culture and practices.

"While we are reminded that, even today, many survivors are still suffering in silence, we are hopeful that the national conversation is propelling the anti–sexual violence movement to a new level where it gets the attention and resources it deserves," Miller stated. "We see signs that we are moving away from a culture that ignores and even enables sexual victimization, toward a culture in which perpetrators are held accountable for their actions, and survivors are believed and supported."

Selected Bibliography

Adichie, Chimamanda Ngozi. *We Should All Be Feminists*. New York: Vintage, 2014.

Allen, Beverly. *Rape Warfare: The Hidden Genocide in Bosnia-Herzegovina and Croatia*. Minneapolis: University of Minnesota, 1996.

Anderson, Irina, and Kathy Doherty. *Accounting for Rape: Psychology, Feminism and Discourse Analysis in the Study of Sexual Violence*. Oxford: Routledge, 2007.

Ashworth, Georgina. *Of Violence and Violation: Women and Human Rights*. London: Change, 1986.

Atkinson, Matt. *Resurrection After Rape: A guide to transforming from victim to survivor*. Vancouver: R.A.R. Publishing, 2008.

Bancroft, Lundy. *Why Does He Do That?: Inside the Minds of Angry and Controlling Men*, New York: Berkeley, 2003.

Bevacqua, Maria. *Rape on the Public Agenda: Feminism and the Politics of Sexual Assault*. Boston: Northeastern University Press, 2000.

Brownmiller, Susan. *Against Our Will: Men, Women, and Rape*. New York: Ballentine, 1993.

Buchwald, Emilie, Pamela R. Fletcher and Martha Roth, eds. *Transforming a Rape Culture, Revised Edition*. Minneapolis: Milkweed Editions, 2005.

Clark, Annie E., and Andrea L. Pino. *We Believe You: Survivors of Campus Sexual Assault Speak Out*. New York: Holt Paperbacks, 2016.

Connors, Joanna. *I Will Find You: A Reporter Investigates the Life of the Man Who Raped Her*. New York: Atlantic Monthly Press, 2016.

Conte, Jon R. *Critical Issues in Child Sexual Abuse: Historical, Legal, and Psychological Perspectives*. Thousand Oaks, CA: Sage Publications, 2001.

Deer, Sarah. *The Beginning and End of Rape: Confronting Sexual Violence in Native America*. Minneapolis: University or Minnesota Press, 2015.

Ehrlich, Susan. *Representing Rape: Language and Sexual Consent*. Oxford: Routledge, 2003.

Factora-Borchers, Lisa, and Aishah Shahidah Simmons. *Dear Sister: Letters from Survivors of Sexual Violence*. Oakland: AK, 2014.

Fairstein, Linda A. *Sexual Violence: Our War Against Rape*. New York: Berkley Books, 1995.

Fergusson, David M., and Paul E. Fergusson. *Childhood Sexual Abuse: An Evidence-Based Perspective*. Thousand Oaks, CA: Sage Publications, 1999.

Ferro, Liz. *Finish Line Feeling*. Nashville: Unlimited Publishing LLC, 2012.

Freedman, Estelle B. *Redefining Rape: Sexual Violence in the Era of Suffrage and Segregation*. Cambridge, MA: Harvard University Press, 2013.

Friedman, Jaclyn, and Jessica Valenti. *Yes Means Yes: Visions of Female Sexual Power & A World Without Rape*. Berkeley: Seal Press, 2008.

Girschik, Lori B. *Woman-to-Woman Sexual Violence: Does She Call It Rape?* Boston: Northeastern University Press, 2002.

Grigoriadis, Vanessa. *Blurred Lines: Rethinking Sex, Power, & Consent on Campus*. Boston: Houghton Mifflin Harcourt, 2017.

Harding, Kate. *Asking For It: The Alarming Rise of Rape Culture – and What We Can Do About It*. Philadelphia: Da Capo Press, 2015.

Herman, MD, Judith: *Trauma and Recovery: The Aftermath of Violence – From Domestic Abuse to Political Terror*. New York: Basic Books, 2015.

Holcomb, Justin S., and Lindsey A. Holcomb. *Rid of My Disgrace: Hope and Healing for Victims of Sexual Assault*. Wheaton: Crossway, 2011.

Katz, Jackson. *The Macho Paradox: Why Some Men Hurt Women and How All Men Can Help*. Naperville: Sourcebooks, 2006.

Kellemen, Robert W. *Sexual Abuse: Beauty for Ashes*. Phillipsburg: P&R Publishing Company, 2013.

Kimmel, Michael. *Guyland: The Perilous World Where Boys Become Men*. New York: Harper Perennial, Reprint Edition, 2009.

Kirby, Dick, and Amy Ziering. *The Hunting Ground: The Inside Story of Sexual Assault on American College Campuses*. New York: Hot Books, Skyhorse Publishing, 2016.

Krakauer, Jon. *Missoula: Rape and the Justice System in a College Town*. New York: Doubleday, 2015.

Leo, Jana. *Rape New York*. New York: The Feminist Press, 2011.

Maltz, Wendy. *The Sexual Healing Journey: A Guide for Survivors of Sexual Abuse, 2nd Edition*. New York: William Morrow Paperbacks, Revised, Updated edition, 2012.

McClelland, Mac. *Irritable Hearts: A PTSD Love Story*. New York: Flatiron Books, 2015.

McGuire, Danielle L. *At the Dark End of the Street: Black Women, Rape, and Resistance – A New History of the Civil Rights Movement from Rosa Parks to the Rise of Black Power*. New York: Vintage, 2010.

Mulla, Sameena. *The Violence of Care: Rape Victims, Forensic Nurses, and Sexual Assault Intervention*. New York: New York University Press, 2014.

Nelson, Maggie. *The Red Parts: Autobiography of a Trial*. Minneapolis: Graywolf Press, 2016.

Pfadt, Jacqueline M. *PTSD Raw and Real: A Reason for Hope and Motivation to Fight On*. Meadville: Christian Faith Publishing, Inc., 2016.

Oliver, Kelly. *Hunting Girls: Sexual Violence from The Hunger Games to Campus Rape*. New York: Columbia University Press, 2016.

Raphael, Jody. *Rape is Rape: How Denial, Distortion, and Victim Blaming Are Fueling A Hidden Acquaintance Rape Crisis*. Chicago: Lawrence Hill Books, 2013.

Rush, Joanna. *Kick: It's Not How High. It's How Strong!*. Lowell: Yonanda Productions, 2016.

Sachs, Carly, ed. *The Why and Later: An Anthology of Poems about Rape and Sexual Assault*. Cleveland: Deep Cleveland Press, 2007.

Scarce, Michael. *Male on Male Rape: The Hidden Toll of Stigma and Shame.* New York: Basic Books, 2001.

Seccuro, Liz. *Crash Into Me: A Survivor's Search for Justice.* New York: Bloomsbury, 2011.

Smith, Andrea. *Conquest: Sexual Violence and American Indian Genocide.* Durham, NC: Duke University Press, 2015.

Warshaw, Robin. *I Never Called It Rape: The Ms. Report on Recognizing, Fighting, and Surviving Date and Acquaintance Rape.* New York: Harper Perennial, 1994.

Winslow, Emily. *Jane Doe January: My Twenty-Year Search for Truth and Justice.* New York: William Morrow, 2016.

Index